Islam in Education in E

Religious Diversity and Education in Europe

edited by

Cok Bakker, Hans-Günter Heimbrock,
Robert Jackson, Geir Skeie, Wolfram Weisse

Volume 18

Globalisation and plurality are influencing all areas of education, including religious education. The inter-cultural and multi-religious situation in Europe demands a re-evaluation of the existing educational systems in particular countries as well as new thinking at the broader European level. This new book series is committed to the investigation and reflection on the changing role of religion and education in Europe. Contributions will evaluate the situation, reflect on fundamental issues and develop perspectives for better policy making and pedagogy, especially in relation to practice in the classroom.

The publishing policy of the series is to focus on the importance of strengthening pluralist democracies through stimulating the development of active citizenship and fostering greater mutual understanding through intercultural education. It pays special attentions to the educational challenges of religious diversity and conflicting value systems in schools and in society in general.

Religious Diversity and Education in Europe is produced by two European research groups, in which scholars are engaged in empirical and theoretical research on aspects of religion and education in relation to intercultural issues:
* **ENRECA: The European Network for Religious Education in Europe through Contextual Approaches**
* **REDCo: Religion in Education. A contribution to Dialogue or a factor of Conflict in transforming societies of European Countries**

The series is aimed at teachers, researchers and policy makers. The series is committed to involving practitioners in the research process and includes books by teachers and teacher educators who are engaged in research as well as academics from various relevant fields, professional researchers and PhD students. It is open to authors committed to these issues, and it includes English and German speaking monographs as well as edited collections of papers.

Book proposals should be directed to one of the editors or to the publisher.

Aurora Alvarez Veinguer, Gunther Dietz,
Dan-Paul Jozsa, Thorsten Knauth (Eds.)

Islam in Education in European Countries

Pedagogical Concepts and Empirical Findings

Waxmann 2009
Münster / New York / München / Berlin

Bibliographic information published by the Deutsche Nationalbibliothek
The Deutsche Nationalbibliothek lists this publication in the
Deutsche Nationalbibliografie; detailed bibliographic data
are available in the Internet at http://dnb.d-nb.de

Religious Diversity and Education in Europe, volume 18

ISSN 1862-9547
ISBN 978-3-8309-2282-7

© Waxmann Verlag GmbH, 2009
Postfach 8603, 48046 Münster, Germany

www.waxmann.com
info@waxmann.com

Book cover: Pleßmann Design, Ascheberg
Typesetting: Stoddart Satz- und Layoutservice, Münster
Print: Hubert & Co., Göttingen
Printed on age-resistant paper,
acid-free according to ISO 9706

All rights reserved
Printed in Germany

Content

Wolfram Weisse
Foreword 7

Aurora Alvarez Veinguer, Gunther Dietz,
Dan-Paul Jozsa & Thorsten Knauth
Introduction 11

Javier Rosón, Sol Tarrés & Jordi Moreras
Islam and Education in Spain 15

Anna van den Kerchove
Islam within the Framework of "Laïcité".
Islam and Education in France 51

Marjoke Rietveld-van Wingerden, Wim Westerman & Ina ter Avest
Islam in Education in the Netherlands 69

Damian Breen
A Qualitative Narrative of the Transition from Independent
to Voluntary Aided Status. A problem for the Concept of
the 'Muslim School' 95

Inga Niehaus
Emancipation or Disengagement? Islamic Schools in
Britain and the Netherlands 113

Dan-Paul Jozsa
Muslim Students Views on Religion and Education.
Perspectives from Western European Countries 131

List of Authors 159

Wolfram Weisse
Foreword

Islam is on the rise in Europe and throughout the world. The religious and public expressions it takes are as manifold as the opinions others hold of it and its adherents. Recently, one dominant feature in the public perception of Muslims has been the belief that they are at least strictly devout, if not militants or even terrorists. However, we can also observe a growing understanding of and respect for both their religion and the role they play in society. Still, much work remains to be done in academia, research and the public arena in order to reduce resentment and allow an open and equal interaction of the various groups in the population.

As an example of an early voice calling for mutual understanding, I would like to quote Paul Ricoeur. Roughly 15 years ago, he made an impassioned public statement in a radio broadcast that touched on three major points: In terms of the societal role of Muslims, he proposed a necessary perspective shift. Instead of admonishing them to integrate into the majority French society, he emphasised the potential of Muslims to contribute 'communitarian' values to that society. These values, strongly represented in Muslim communities, mainly in families, could serve as a resource for societal cohesion in France as a whole, where growing disintegration at the family and group level is observable, (Ricoeur, 1993, 202). Further, he argued against seeing the "*grid of secularisation*" ("*grille de secularisation*") in France as the only standard to judge Islam in the political sphere. On the contrary, he viewed the public expression of religion by Muslims as a contribution towards questioning the deteriorating monoperspectively laïcal system and its dominant position in France. Third, he specifically criticised the mainstream position opposing the wearing of headscarves – which in France is even forbidden to pupils at school – by formulating the provocative statement: "*I cannot help but feel that there is something silly in the fact that a Christian girl may expose her buttocks in school while a Muslim does not have the right to cover her head*".[1]

Another philosopher, Jürgen Habermas from Germany, has recently referred to the new role of religions in Europe and the need to acknowledge the presence religious minorities, including Islam, in the public arena of contemporary democratic societies. Habermas' high opinion of religious tolerance as the "*pacemaker for multiculturalism*", (Habermas, 2005, 263), ties into his conviction that real tolerance can only begin beyond discrimination, (Habermas, 2005, 264). With reference to different contexts – including the French – he stresses the political relevance of including minority groups like the Muslims in a democratic society as the central question.[2] He views their inclusion as a necessary step towards a fully

---

1 « *Je ne peux pas m'empêcher de penser qu'il y a quelque chose de bouffon dans le fait qu'une fille chrétienne puisse à l'école montrer ses fesses tandis qu'une fille musulmane n'a pas le droit de cacher sa tête.* » (Ricoeur, 1993, 204)
2 "*Integrating religious minorities into the commonwealth serves to increase our sensibilities for the legitimate claims of other minority groups. The recognition of religious groups is well placed to take on this exemplary function because it can tangibly demonstrate and create broader awareness of the claim that minorities have to inclusion.*" ("*Die Einbeziehung religiöser Minderheiten ins politische Gemeinwesen*

multicultural citizenship rather than as an act of integration into the majority system: "*A multiculturalism that understands its nature fully is more than a one-way road towards a defensive cultural identity of groups coexisting in parallel. An equal coexistence must not mean a separate existence. It depends on the integration of all citizens – fully cognizant of their subcultural affiliation – into a shared political culture.*"[3]

The points Paul Ricoeur, Habermas and others have emphasised form the necessary basis for an argument that sees the role of religions and interreligious dialogue not only as an issue for theology or interreligious learning, but as a vital question for the core values our society needs in order to ensure peaceful coexistence of people with different cultural and religious backgrounds, (Council of Europe, 2008).

This makes it more necessary than ever to analyse current developments in our societies. Research in this field forms a daunting task for academics, who must empirically address the question whether and how the aims expressed by these philosophers can be realised. One of the international research projects looking into the possibilities and limits of interreligious dialogue is the REDCo project. The results presented in this book have been produced in the context of this Europe-wide study. Thus, a brief introduction of this research project is in order.

The research project REDCo: 'Religion in Education. A Contribution to Dialogue or a Factor of Conflict in Transforming Societies of European Countries?' was funded by the European Commission between 2006 and 2009. It included universities from Estonia, Russia, Norway, Germany, the Netherlands, France, England and Spain. Its purpose is to establish how religions and values can contribute to dialogue or tension in Europe (Weisse, 2007). Researchers from both the humanities and social sciences co-operated in it to develop a thematic and methodological approach designed to gain better insight into how European citizens of different religious, cultural and political backgrounds can live together in peace and enter into a dialogue of mutual respect and understanding. Its focus lay on education, especially schools. From a historical perspective, (Jackson, Miedema, Weisse & Willaime, 2007), it studied the emergence of religions and religious values. Differences between countries were looked into, showing their impact on modern Europe and the lives of its citizens. The main aspect of the project, though, was to empirically establish how the religious differences existing within European societies today can be addressed in education without creating conflict or exclusion. Qualitative, (Knauth, Jozsa, Bertram-Troost & Ipgrave, 2008), and quantitative studies, (Valk, Bertram-Troost, Friederici & Béraud, 2009), targeting students in the 14-16-year age group and, looked into students' percep-

---

weckt und fördert die Sensibilität für die Ansprüche anderer diskriminierter Gruppen. Die Anerkennung des religiösen Pluralismus kann diese Vorbildfunktion übernehmen, weil sie auf exemplarische Weise den Anspruch von Minderheiten auf Inklusion zu Bewußtein bringt.") (Habermas, 2005, 274)

3 „*Denn Multikulturalismus, der sich nicht missversteht, bildet keine Einbahnstraße zur kulturellen Selbstbehauptung von Gruppen mit je eigener Identität. Die gleichberechtigte Koexistenz verschiedener Lebensformen darf nicht zu einer Segmentierung führen. Sie erfordert die Integration der Staatsbürger – und die gegenseitige Anerkennung ihrer subkulturellen Mitgliedschaften – im Rahmen einer geteilten politischen Kultur.*" (Habermas, 2005, 278)

tions of dialogue or conflict within their different national educational systems. These studies were complemented by studies of observed teaching practice in situations of both dialogue and conflict. In addition, a qualitative study of classroom interaction was undertaken, (Avest et al., 2009), together with an analysis of the responses of teachers to religious and cultural diversity in the different countries represented in the project, (van der Want et al., 2009).

Though initially not regarded as a focal point, the question of Europe's Muslims had been an inherent part of the REDCo project from the start. In the process of data collection and analysis, Islam as a religion and the position of Muslim teenagers in all countries studied took on greater and greater importance. One of the researchers even spoke of an *"Islamisation of the representation of religion"*, (Mathieu 2009, 87). Viewed from the perspective of the project's results, this book represents an outcome of great social relevance. It analyses the question what teenagers in Europe think about to the possibility of entering into or continuing dialogue with others. Analyses of the educational and political contexts of a number of individual countries such as Spain, the Netherlands and England are combined with comparative analyses of the beliefs and opinions of Muslim teenagers throughout Europe. The data were generated by both qualitative and quantitative methods. In addition to the views of the teenagers themselves, some of the contributors direct our attention to the priorities of Muslim confessional schools by highlighting case studies showing the perspectives of teachers and headmasters of such institutions.

I would like to thank all contributors to this book, especially the editors Aurora Alvarez Veinguer, Gunther Dietz, Dan-Paul Jozsa and Thorsten Knauth. For translations and language editing, thanks go to Volker Bach and Francis Ipgrave. Thanks are also due to our publishing house, the Waxmann Verlag, especially to Beate Plugge for her professional support. And we thank the officials of the European Commission that made our research project and the publication of this book possible.

This publication offers a mosaic of new research results on European Muslim teenagers' thinking and Muslim education. It is not the intention of this book to offer final results – how would this even be possible in a field characterised by such forceful and complex dynamics as Islam in Europe? But I view the contributions collected in it as relevant cornerstones for ongoing research in the field that can contribute to a more reliable and differentiated understanding of the position of Muslim teenagers in Europe and of Muslim education. It also presents a productive basis to triangulate its findings with the results of other research projects (see eg. Niehaus, Tayob & Weisse, forthcoming 2010) and of future research.

More empirical evidence from research such as that presented here is direly needed. We also hope our findings will add to the foundations of a more informed and balanced discussions in the academic as well as in the public sphere, in order to support the aims that we share with Paul Ricoeur and Jürgen Habermas.

Wolfram Weisse
Coordinator of REDCo

References

Avest, I. ter, Jozsa, D.-P., Knauth, T., Rosón, J. & Skeie, G. (Eds.) (2009) *Dialogue and Conflict on Religion. Studies of classroom interaction in European countries* (Münster, Waxmann).

Béraud, C. & Willaime J.-P. (Eds.) (2009) *Les jeunes, l'école et la religion* (Montrouge Cedex, Bayard).

Council of Europe (2008): *White Paper on Intercultural Dialogue "Living Together as Equals in Dignity"*, launched by the Council of Europe Ministers of Foreign Affairs a their 118th Ministerial Session, Strasbourg, 7 May 2008. Strasbourg: Council of Europe.

Habermas, J. (2005) *Zwischen Naturalismus und Religion. Philosophische Aufsätze* (Frankfurt am Main, Suhrkamp).

Jackson, R., Miedema, S., Weisse, W., Willlaime, J.-P. (Eds.) (2007) *Religion and Education in Europe: Developments, Contexts and Debates* (Münster, Waxmann).

Jozsa, D.-P., Knauth, T. & W. Weisse (Eds.) (2009) *Religionsunterricht, Dialog und Konflikt. Analysen im Kontext Europas (*Münster, Waxmann).

Knauth, T., Jozsa, D.-P., Bertram-Troost, G. & Ipgrave, J. (Eds.) (2008), *Encountering Religious Pluralism in School and Society – A Qualitative Study of Teenage Perspectives in Europe* (Münster, Waxmann).

Mathieu, S. (2009) Les adolescents et la religion, in: C. Béraud & J.-P. Willaime (Eds.) *Les jeunes, l'école et la religion* (Montrouge Cedex, Bayard), 85-102.

Niehaus, I., Tayob, A. & Weisse, W. (forthcoming 2010) *Muslim schools and education in Europe and South Africa* (Münster, Waxmann).

Ricoeur, P. (1995) *La critique et la conviction. Entretien avec Francois Azouvi et Marc de Launay* (Paris, Hachette).

Valk, P., Bertram-Troost, G., Friederici, M. & Béraud, C. (Eds.) (2009) *Teenagers' perspectives on the Role of Religion in their lives, Schools and Societies. A European Quantitative Study* (Münster, Waxmann).

Want, A. van der, Bakker, C., Avest, I. ter, Everington, J. (Eds.) (2009) *Teachers Responding to Religious Diversity in Europe* (Münster, Waxmann).

Weisse, W. (2007) The European Research Project on Religion and Education 'REDCo'. An Introduction, in: Jackson, R., Miedema, S., Weisse, W. & Willlaime, J.-P. (Eds.) *Religion and Education in Europe: Developments, Contexts and Debates* (Münster, Waxmann), 9-25.

Aurora Alvarez Veinguer, Gunther Dietz,
Dan-Paul Jozsa & Thorsten Knauth

Introduction

Religious education and the place of religion in public education is a 'hot topic' in different European countries; and it is particularly 'hot' when it comes to Islam in Education. Relations between Muslims and the public education systems of Europe are often characterised by tensions. There is often still a perceived incommensurability between the claims of individual Muslims or Muslim communities on the one hand and the aims of public education in Europe on the other. This is not only the case in secularized and strongly laïcist countries such as France. Even those countries who accept the right of Christian denominations to teach their beliefs inside their schools tend to exclude Muslim pupils from the very same right. The relatively recent presence of Islam in much of Europe, the internal diversity of Muslim communities, the lack of a centralized, hierarchical church-like structure – different arguments are used to justify such a discriminatory treatment of one of the largest faith communities in Europe.

Nevertheless, as this book aims to illustrate, there are already rich and diverse experiences throughout Europe of how to integrate Islam into the national and regional school systems, particularly in primary, but also in secondary education. Accordingly, this book provides some analyses of the ways in which Islam is integrated in education in certain regions of Spain, the Netherlands, France and England. These analyses are paralleled by empirical findings concerning the role of religion in the life of young Muslims, their views concerning religion in school, and the impact of religion in education and society in Spain, the Netherlands, Norway, Germany, France and England.

This book is published within the framework of the REDCO project (*Religion in Education. A Contribution to Dialogue or a Factor of Conflict in Transforming Societies of European Countries*). The project was funded by the European Commission within the framework of the FP6 Specific Programme 'Integrating and Strengthening the European Research Area'. The REDCO project's main purpose was to establish the potentials for and limitations of religion in the educational fields in eight different European countries (Germany, Norway, the Netherlands, England, France, Spain Russian and Estonia).[1] Although the place of Islam in education did not form a direct research question in this project, it was consistently addressed throughout the research process. Consequently, interesting data on this issue emerged from our quantitative and qualitative research.

In many ways this book presents a multidisciplinary analysis of concrete and contextual experiences in the respective countries, and each paper is written from a different disciplinary background (sociological, anthropological, pedagogical, historical or theological). However, they all offer a mirror that can contribute to

---

1   For more details on the REDCO project findings, cf. the REDCO collection: Jackson, Miedema, Weisse & Willaime (2007), Knauth, Jozsa, Bertram-Troost & Ipgrave (2008), Valk, Bertram-Troost, Friederici, Béraud (2009), and Ter Avest, Jozsa, Knauth, Rosón & Skeie (2009).

understanding, and consequently, contextualization of the current dynamics and tendencies that Islam in education is facing in different European countries.

Currently, at the European level, it is possible to detect a serious lack of academic production concerning the situation of Islam in education. In most countries the academic production in this area is growing substantially, and atomized analyses from each country are already emerging, since religious diversity is undeniably a hot topic in most European contexts. In this publication, we try to focus our attention on experiences that have incorporated the diverse pedagogical approaches in different countries. It is true that this book does not aim to produce a comparative comprehensive analysis on the European level. Rather, the main purpose is to present the empirical findings from different countries, each with their own significantly different traditions and histories in the way in which Islam is (re)presented, thought of, and managed in each national pedagogical context.

This book underlines the fact that Islamic schools in European countries fluctuate considerably in terms of management, structure, size, teachers' training, academic results and pedagogical positions. Most of them are new phenomena in the educational landscape, often with little support at the national and supranational level, and they are strongly dependent on the structure of the educational system, the relationship between religious communities and the state, integration policies, and the political opportunity structure in each country.

Rosón, Tarrés and Moreras' chapter "Islam and Education in Spain", offers an interesting overview of the history of Islam and Muslims in Spain, as well as presenting some results from case studies carried out within the REDCO project in the regions of Andalusia and Murcia and the Autonomous City of Melilla. According to the authors, the debate on religion in Spain between the perception of the loss of the Catholic Church's monopoly and the verification of the plural religious presence has been resolved. However, there is no specific training or diploma to become a teacher for Islamic religious education in Spain and the introduction of Islamic religious education was delayed for years. The majority of students taking Islamic religious education courses are at the primary level, with a minority at the secondary level. Ignorance, lack of interest, discussions relating to the suitability of the teaching staff in relation to their religious or non-religious affiliation, the suitability of their academic and pedagogical training, low levels of interest and a lethargy in responding to or implementing changes on the part of the administration, which reflects a lack of enthusiasm affecting both parents and communities. These are only some of the problems when it comes to teaching Islamic religious education in Spain. They illustrate the contextual factors in Spain, where the religion traditionally taught in school has been Catholicism and where, until recently, Islamic religious education did not exist, regardless of whether or not there were Muslim students in the schools.

Wingerden, Westerman and Avest's analysis of the situation in the Netherlands illustrates that Islamic religious education has only recently become part of the public debate there. The Dutch example, like the Spanish one, indicates the extent to which an analysis of Islamic religious education can be related to an analysis of migration policy. In both of these cases we can observe different concrete examples of diversity management, where Islamic religious education becomes an additional 'tool' for coping with and responding to the problems caused by migration processes.

Paradoxically, the Netherlands already had a significant Muslim population during the second half of the twentieth century, but no claims about Islamic religious education had been made. Only after family reunions in the 1980s did Muslim parents decide to enter the Dutch pillarized system by opening Islamic Schools of their own.

Van den Kerchove's chapter, "Islam within the Framework of "Laïcité". Islam and Education in France" analyzes Muslim teenagers' points of view about religion and the difficulties faced by teachers in teaching about Islam inside classrooms, trying to accommodate the principle of "laïcité" inside the schools with the role that Islam has for the identity of most Muslim students. 84% of Muslim teenagers in the French sample consider religion to be important and almost the same figure (83%) agree with the statement that students should be able to wear discrete religious symbols at school. For 84%, family is the most important domain of religious socialization and the first place where religion is discussed, whereas friends are the second most important domain of religious socialization.

Breen's chapter, "A Qualitative Narrative of the Transition from Independent to Voluntary Aided Status. A Problem for the Concept of the 'Muslim School'", analyzes life-history interviews with the headteacher of a confessionally-defined school in England which receives state funding. It analyses all the structural changes that accompanied the transition process from 'independent' to 'voluntary aided status'. The author claims that it would be a mistake to use the term " Muslim school" as a homogenised concept since the conditions and circumstances differ considerably between independent (privately funded) and voluntary aided status schools (voluntary aided schools with a religious character are funded up to 85% by the Local Education Authorities). Consequently in-depth analysis should be conducted and the generic term "Muslim school" should be avoided in the English context.

Niehaus's comparative chapter, "Emancipation or Disengagement? Islamic Schools in Britain and the Netherlands" presents the institutionalisation, functioning and self-understanding of Islam schools in Britain and the Netherlands. The chapter analyzes whether Islamic schools promote processes of identity formation within a democratic society or whether they rather lead to disengagement from the wider society. Analyzing the idea of "Islamising the curriculum" and on the requirements to follow "national secular" curricula, Niehaus concludes that the focus has changed in the last decades from an "Islamisation project" to a new emphasis on providing good academic results and preparing active citizens, seeking to offer a "secular" education within an Islamic environment.

Jozsa's final chapter, "Muslim Students' Views on Religion and Education. Perspectives from Western European Countries", traces some general trends with regard to Muslim students, in comparison to Christian students and those with no religion, from a comparative analysis of the REDCo quantitative studies in six countries: England, France, Germany, the Netherlands, Norway and Spain. The chapter shows substantial communalities between the Muslim students in the subsamples which were analysed, and significant differences between Muslim students on the one hand, and Christian students and those with no religion on the other.

The six contextual factors mentioned above demonstrate the evident need to reopen an active debate on the European level about different models of religious education and their practical dimensions, since, as this book shows, they have become powerful and clear indicators of national diversity management policies. Furthermore, the cases analyzed illustrate the types of intercultural relations that operate in each of the geographic arenas chosen, as well as the relations with the "others" that predominate inside each given school system.These factors are therefore relevant not only for future comparative discussions on Islamic religious education in particular, but also for identifying more general "quality indicators" and "good practices" for inter-religious and intercultural diversity treatment inside European schools.

References

Avest, I. ter, Jozsa, D.-P., Knauth, T., Rosón, J. & Skeie, G. (Eds.) (2009) *Dialogue and Conflict on Religion. Studies of classroom interaction in European countries* (Münster, Waxmann).

Jackson, R., Miedema, S., Weisse, W., Willlaime, J.-P. (Eds.) (2007) *Religion and Education in Europe: Developments, Contexts and Debates* (Münster, Waxmann).

Knauth, T., Jozsa, D.-P., Bertram-Troost, G. & Ipgrave, J. (Eds.) (2008), *Encountering Religious Pluralism in School and Society – A Qualitative Study of Teenage Perspectives in Europe* (Münster, Waxmann).

Valk, P., Bertram-Troost, G., Friederici, M. & Béraud, C. (Eds.) (2009) *Teenagers' perspectives on the Role of Religion in their lives, Schools and Societies. A European Quantitative Study* (Münster, Waxmann).

Javier Rosón, Sol Tarrés & Jordi Moreras
Islam and Education in Spain[1]

1. Introduction

This article provides an in-depth analysis of the general context surrounding the ways in which Islamic religion is taught in Spain. Particular attention is given to case studies carried out under the auspices of the REDCo project in the regions of Andalusia and Murcia and the Autonomous City of Melilla, and then extended to the rest of Spain. Operating in the background is the historical framework of Islam and Muslim communities in Spain (part 2), as well as the regulatory – political and legislative – framework (part 2.1 and 2.2) which guarantees the right of parents to ensure that their children receive religious and moral instruction in accordance with their own convictions in public schools. However, the implementation of the rights of these groups, on both a national and regional/local level (part 2.3) has been insignificant and/or inoperative, and has only managed, if such a thing is possible, to make the concept of 'minority' increasingly more negative in the setting of a Spain that is, at the same time, increasingly more plural and multi-religious. In order to fully analyse this context, we will thoroughly explore both the empirical findings (part 3) and pedagogical reflections (part 4) on Islamic Religious Education (IRE) which were developed over two years within the framework of the REDCo European project.

2. A brief overview of the history of Islam and Muslims in Spain

For many centuries, Spain was a country of migrants. Throughout the 20th century and until the end of the 1980s, people emigrated to Europe, Latin America and even Australia, while, at the same time, it became a country of destination for a certain group of retired Europeans and North Americans who discovered Spain and its shorelines a pleasant place to spend the final stage of their lives. However, from the middle of the 1980s onwards, a change in direction has occurred: from being a country of emigrants, Spain has become a country of immigration for people from the lands south of the Mediterranean, Latin America and, at the end of the 1990s, from Eastern Europe as well.

Spain is now a country of immigrants, much like most other countries in the European Union. Although the proportion of immigrants is low in comparison with neighbouring countries, and indeed in comparison with the classic countries for immigration, the increase in migratory flow in recent years has been notable. This has led to concern amongst some people, who have gone as far as to suggest that such immigration has become a problem, acquiring the dimensions of a 'national

---

1 We gratefully acknowledge the crucial collaboration of the other Granada and Melilla REDCo team members Francisca Ruiz, Iman Katarzyna Kluza and Latifa Abdelmalki.

problem', despite the fact that the proportion of foreigners in Spain (including EU citizens) represents approximately 12 per cent of the total population.[2] Moving away from the well-worn mono-directional perspective of migratory processes and analysing the data qualitatively, it is clear see that Spain is witnessing a very heterogeneous model of migration, with at least four different strands, which at times interweave, and with different source and target destinations: Europeans, Latin Americans, East Europeans and Africans (basically Moroccans). Less than 20 per cent of the people in these migratory processes are Muslim or Arab in origin.

However, to all intents and purposes, the perception and visibility of the Muslims who are settling in various regions of Spain is, for a large part of the local population, far superior to the perception and visibility of any other immigrant group, for example the aforementioned Latin American influx. A large part of the immigrant population which comes to Spain (López García, 1996; García Castaño, 2001; Martín Muñoz, 2003; López García-Berriane, 2006), is made up of Muslims, most of whom are Arabs. They form part of a heterogeneous process of migratory flows, generated directly by the demand for labour (Gil, 2004) in sectors characterised by high seasonality and a lack of regulation. Therefore, it is important to distinguish, on the one hand, between Arab Muslims who have residence permits or are in the process of arranging their papers and, on the other hand, the unknown number who are, at present, illegal immigrants in Spain. To this total must also be added the Moroccan and Palestinian students who decide to study in Spain rather than in their traditional alma mater, France. This number is increasing, with almost sixty thousand qualified students/immigrants living temporarily in Granada, and they have, in turn, begun to generate their own transnational migratory process (González, 2007). Furthermore, there is also the Muslim population that resides permanently in Ceuta and Melilla, the Spanish enclaves in the North of Morocco.

Parallel to this, and especially in Andalusia, political and social movements have arisen which are characterised by a special religious feeling, of proximity to Islam. These groups of Muslim and neo-Muslim converts began to refer to a population process which was a thing of the past, considering that Islamic Andalusia transcended the values of mythical al-Andalus, and offered an alternative which was more cultural than political. It was at this point, in 1989, that the Spanish Federation of Islamic Religious Entities (FEERI) appeared, in order to offer cohesion for most of the neo-Muslin communities. During the 1990s, this type of movement began to grow, thanks to the international impact of migration. It was at this time that the Union of Islamic Communities of Spain (UCIDE) appeared, on 10 April 1990.[3] Both the UCIDE and the FEERI fought to control the representation of Muslim communities in Spain, but not before embarking upon a process of criticism and self-evaluation which is still ongoing (Rosón, 2008).

These hesitant beginnings found their voice in the appearance of a new Law on Religious Freedom (Organic Law 7/1980, 5 July, on religious freedom). This law gave the Spanish state the chance to define the process of cooperation with religious communities that have what is known in Spanish as '*notorio arraigo*', or well-known, deeply-rooted beliefs, in Spain. Accordingly, and by the unanimous

---

2 See the data of the Instituto Nacional de Estadística (National Statistics Institute), 2007, available online at: http://www.ine.es, last accessed August 19, 2009.
3 Although it originated in Andalusia at the end of the 1970s.

decision of the Ministry of Justice's Advisory Commission on Religious Freedom, Islam was declared to have '*notorio arraigo*' in Spain as of 14 July 1989.

On 19 February 1992, the Islamic Commission of Spain (CIE) was officially formed by the two existing federations which contained most of the Islamic groups inscribed in Ministry of Justice's Registry of Religious Entities. This body, designed to be the sole interlocutor for Muslims in Spain[4] when its legal representatives signed the Cooperation Agreement on 28 April 1992 (Tatary, 1995:169), was formed out of the need to establish some common guidelines for negotiating, signing and monitoring the agreements adopted between the Commission and the state. These federations initially brought together 300,000 to 450,000 Muslims from different communities and associations, and organised a representative body made up of six members with five representatives. These numbers have increased over time, but it is important to note that not all Muslims or Muslim communities take part in this process of institutionalisation.

The Cooperation Agreement meant the articulation, structuring and classification of the legal references needed for group action (Escudero, 2006). In other words, it serves as a legal framework that had not existed until that time in the organisation of Muslim communities on a state level.[5]

As of that moment, mosques, schools of the Koran, organisations etc., began to appear, creating the first meeting places between Spanish converts to Islam and immigrant Moroccan workers. The search for an identity evident in this process was closely linked to the social construction of a common shared space, forging characteristics and hallmarks of identity which brought similar groups together and, at the same time, marked their external differences.

At this time, it is possible to speak of a 'first-second' generation of Muslim children attending Spanish public schools, especially at the primary level (between 6 and 12 years old). This is an important challenge for Spanish civil society, which is facing a growing cultural and religious diversity and demands for educational and social rights. These rights, as will be seen below, are protected by regulations and laws, although their practical application has been very slow and, in some cases, discriminatory and non-existent. Additionally, this study will show how an IRE teacher is found, the type of profile the teaching staff has, and how the classes

---

4   The body representing Islam and Muslims to the citizens, the administration and, in short, the Spanish state.

5   The main points stipulated in the Cooperation Agreement are: (1) A statute certifying Imams and other Islamic religious leaders which establishes the specific rights deriving from the exercise of their religious activities. (2) Islamic right to worship in the army, penal facilities, hospitals and public establishments. (3) Legal protection for mosques and places of worship. (4) The conferring of civil status to marriages held according to Islamic religious rites. (5) Islamic religious education in public and semi-public schools. (6) Tax exemptions for certain Autonomous Community goods and activities belonging to the Islamic Commission of Spain. (7) The commemoration of Islamic religious holidays. (8) The regulation of Islamic cemeteries and burials. (9) The registration of the seal guaranteeing Halal food products and their availability in public centres. (10) And, finally, the participation of the Islamic Commission of Spain in the conservation and promotion of Islamic artistic and historical heritage. For more details, see: Cooperation Agreement between the Spanish State and the Islamic Commission of Spain http://religlaw.org/interdocs/docs/coagrspstislamiccom1992.htm (English version) (accessed 25 November 2008). For a legal study of the contents of the Agreement, see Jiménez-Aybar, 2004.

are given in Spain. Finally, the current map of IRE will be defined for the different regions.

2.1 Regulatory framework of religious education in general, and IRE in particular

Article 27.3 of the Spanish Constitution guarantees the right of parents to ensure that their children receive religious and moral instruction in accordance with their own convictions.[6] It is important to bear in mind that the Constitution is an open legal regulation which permits for different interpretations, and that it must be developed according to different regulations. The right to religious education that is guaranteed by the state means that parents have the right to choose the type of education that their children receive. This does not necessarily mean that a system of denominational education or a specific subject must exist, but rather that it is the parents who determine the denominationalism or lack thereof in a school, as well as how the denominational religious information is given. That said, the state must guarantee these options.

Regardless of the debate that sprang up around the interpretation of the regulation,[7] the Spanish state opted, beginning with the concordat with the Vatican in 1953,[8] to guarantee the inclusion of Catholicism and other religions in non-university education, following the constitutional principles of non-discrimination, equality and the non-denominationalism of the state. Thus, in the 1980 Organic Law on Religious Freedom,[9] Article 2.3 directly states that the state must adopt the measures needed to provide religious education in public teaching centres.

The different organic laws on education that have followed since 1978 include the provision for the denominational teaching of religion, from the 1990 LOGSE (Law on the General Organisation of the Educational System) which, in its second additional provision, admitted the educational proposals only from those denomi-

---

6 Spanish Constitution, Art. 27.3: "The public authorities guarantee the right of parents to ensure that their children receive religious and moral instruction in accordance with their own religious convictions".
7 For the past several years, a debate has been taking place over the presence of denominational education in schools, based both on different interpretations of the Constitution and different interpretations of the laicism of the state. This debate goes beyond religious education and relates to both the model of the state that should be derived from the Constitution and the Spanish and/or autonomous community education model.
8 The 1953 Concordat was ratified on 3 January 1979 and consists of four Agreements: 1) the Agreement between the Spanish State and the Holy See concerning Legal Affairs of 3 January 1979; 2) the Agreement between the Spanish State and the Holy See concerning Education and Cultural Affairs; 3) the Agreement between the Spanish State and the Holy See concerning Economic Affairs; and 4) the Agreement between the Spanish State and the Holy See concerning religious affiliation in the Armed Forces and military service for clergy and religious figures.
9 LOLR, Art. 2.1c: Every person is guaranteed the right to "receive and give instruction and religious information of any nature, whether spoken, in writing or by any other procedure; to choose both for oneself and for minors or disabled individuals under one's custody a religious and moral education which is consistent with one's own beliefs, both inside and outside of the educational setting".

nations that had agreed to sign a Cooperative Agreement with the State, to the 2006 LOE (Organic Law on Education), which is currently in force and which follows the same guidelines,[10] with the difference being that denominational religious teaching is now established as compulsory for schools but voluntary for students, and it does not affect the final marks as far as obtaining scholarships or university access.

The Cooperation Agreement referred to in the LOE, in addition to the Concordat with the Holy See, decrees that the signatories representing the three religions in 1992 – the Federation of Evangelical Religious Entities of Spain (FEREDE), the Federation of Hebrew Communities in Spain (FCJE) and the CIE – have '*notorio arriago*'. These three Cooperation Agreements in Article 10 refer to the educational setting, which in the case of Islam establishes the following:

> "*Muslim pupils, their parents and any school governing bodies who so request are guaranteed the right of the first mentioned to receive Islamic religious teaching in public and private subsidised schools at the infant, primary and secondary education levels, providing, in the case of private institutions, that the exercise of such right does not conflict with the nature of the school itself*".[11]

The importance that the debate concerning the presence of religion in schools has acquired in Spain in the last few years is an indicator of the recent transformation in Spanish society's perception of the social relevance of religion. Two closely related processes have been generated. Despite the facts that, in Spain, references to religion are still commonly made in the singular, and that matters relating to religion are identified as a private (and exclusive) matter belonging to the main religious tradition (the Catholic Church), important indicators of public opinion reveal a diversification of religious expression and a plurality of new forms of worship flourishing in Spanish society. The first process shows that the religious panorama in Spain has diversified, with several alternatives to Catholicism, which is losing its monopoly in the religious sphere. However, at the same time that these alternatives are becoming present, social perceptions and constructions that define new religious alternatives are also being formed. The first process of demonopolisation has been accompanied by another one, favouring the generation of religious alternatives, the definitions of which incorporate references with a cultural and historical content as a means of establishing a gradation of this otherness.

---

10 The LOE, in its second additional provision, establishes that "the teaching of other religions will be adjusted as established in the Cooperation Agreement signed by the Spanish State and the Federation of Evangelical Religious Entities of Spain, the Federation of Jewish Communities of Spain, the Islamic Commission of Spain and, when appropriate, any religious denominations that may sign in the future".

11 The legal counterpart of this article from the Cooperation Agreement is found in Royal Decree 2438/1994 of 16 December, which regulates religious education, the Order of 11 January 1996 (BOE 18.1.96), which approves the curriculum for Islamic religious education in compulsory nursery, primary and secondary school, and in the Resolution of 23 April 1996, which authorises the signature of the Agreement on the Economic Contracts and Appointments for people responsible for Islamic religious education in primary and secondary public schools. Finally, Royal Decree 696/2007 of 1 June regulates the employment relationships of religion teachers who are not already civil servants in education.

Therefore, the debate on religion in Spain has been resolved between the perception of the loss of the Catholic Church's monopoly (a monopoly that, it is thought, was favoured by successive democratic governments which maintained their privileged status thanks to the Concordat signed in 1979) and the verification of a plural religious presence, which is in part a result of the settlement of different immigrant groups in Spain. If there is a single religious denomination that is identified with the phenomenon of migration in Spain, it is, without a doubt, Islam. Muslim communities are perceived as transplanted communities of immigrants, with very few social roots and a little desire to integrate with society. Islam, then, is perceived as the most obvious expression of this religious otherness, from which Spanish society seems to differentiate itself objectively. Certainly, the construction of this *religious opposite* is fed by stereotypes with a long history, but it is also based in socio-political contexts that are close at hand: since the attacks of 11 March in Madrid, the perception of the nature of Muslims as essentially contrary to the principles, values, desires and will of Spanish society has increased exponentially. And these new perceptions have also actively contributed to a reorientation of the debate on religion in Spain, especially in reference to questions related to financing recognised religious denominations and religious education.

2.2 Legislation relating to IRE

2.2.1 Teaching staff assignments and requests

With regards to IRE teaching staff assignments and requests, it is the parents who must request IRE classes for their children in schools. Today, the enrolment sheets for public and private publicly subsidised schools in the autonomous communities which offer this course[12] give parents the option of deciding whether their children will take religion classes and in which religion, or of deciding whether they wish to choose extracurricular activities. For there to be an IRE teacher in a school, it must have a group of at least 10 students, if possible from the same year and, if not, students from different levels will be grouped together to meet this minimum.

Once the requests have been made, the Autonomous Communities must communicate the list of schools where there is a demand for these classes to the Ministry of Education. The Ministry, in turn, informs the CIE, which is responsible for proposing to the relevant education administrations people suitable to teach Islamic religion at the different educational levels. In the case of the Union of Islamic Communities of Spain, the selection of candidates for IRE teacher posts is done after these candidates have taken a class on Islam and teaching, given in each of the districts where they are present. The central and Autonomous Community administrations are responsible for deciding the destination and start date for IRE teaching staff.

---

12 The Spanish constitution establishes the right to the autonomy of the nationalities and regions that make up Spain. An Autonomous Community is a territorial entity granted legislative autonomy and executive powers, as well as the power of self-administration through its own representatives. At this time, Spain is made up of 17 Autonomous Communities and two Autonomous Cities (Ceuta and Melilla).

2.2.2 IRE teaching staff

The IRE teaching staff, like that of other religions, is regulated by Royal Decree 696/2007, which establishes the requirements that must be met, as well as the employment situation for teachers who are not yet administration civil servants. Candidates must meet the academic requirements demanded of other teachers (have the diploma of *Magisterio* for primary school or *Licenciatura* for secondary school) and have a declaration of eligibility or equivalent certification from the CIE. The teaching staff chosen by the UCIDE must also "speak perfect Spanish". The autonomous communities, in turn, can add further requirements, such as the command of any co-official languages. At this time, the question of whether continuing training of teaching staff should include a course on the Spanish legal code and constitutional values is being considered.

There is no specific training or diploma for IRE teachers, which means that training in this field is uneven and, given the CIE's ineffectiveness in unifying the criteria, depends on the federation that has proposed the teacher. Those attached to the FEERI have usually taken the class "Professional Expert in Islamic Religion, Civilisation and Culture" (initially given by the National University of Distance Learning and currently by the Carlos III University)[13]. With the UCIDE, the teaching staff is selected from among those who have passed a prior course and an examination organised by the federation. The course is a week-long class in which three instructors teach materials relating to Islamic theology, Arabic and IRE pedagogy, and didactics, at the end of which the candidates are examined on these materials. Subsequently, continuing training is offered to the students through conferences on Islam and periodic encounters. However, some Muslim communities believe that the IRE teaching staff training should be controlled, in some way, by the Moroccan Ministry for Religious Affairs.

Religion teachers are generally hired as employees with an indefinite contract, in accordance with the Workers' Statute. In communities which do not have power over religious education, the central administration is responsible for salaries, while in the opposite case, the autonomous administration has the responsibility.

---

13 Inter-university distance learning course in "Professional expert in Islamic religion, civilisation and culture", which is already in its fourth edition and has been completed to date by around 500 students (taking 500 class hours between December and June). Designed, coordinated and implemented by the Didactic Engineering Laboratory of the UNED (Mr. Germán Ruipérez) and the Islamic Council (Mr. Mansur Escudero), it seeks to offer a multidisciplinary vision of Islam and train experts in this area, therefore meeting an objective demand for trained personal in this field (NGOs, directors, judges and public prosecutors, journalists, human resources directors, lawyers, teachers at all education levels and disciplines – also for Catholicism – intercultural mediators, security forces, religious leaders, etc.) who will receive the university title, "Professional expert in Islamic religion, civilisation and culture". This post-graduate course is based on the methodology of blended learning, the combination of multiple approaches to learning. Blended learning can be accomplished through the use of 'blended' virtual and physical resources. In this case, the classes are given over the Internet, using the UNED learning management platform, WebCT, and some voluntary face-to-face meetings.

2.2.3 The IRE course

Finally, considering the course itself, as with other religion subjects, it must have a minimum load of 315 hours in primary and nursery school and 175 hours in compulsory secondary school. The programme for this course must follow the curriculum approved in 1996, which stipulates the contents of each subject at the different levels of nursery, primary and compulsory secondary school. For the most part, the approved curriculum follows traditional guidelines for teaching Islam, both in the appropriate content for the different age groups, and in the level of intensity, which is also age-appropriate.

The different teaching materials available to IRE students, since 2006 and at the initiative of the UCIDE, included a specific manual, *Discovering Islam*. This is a manual geared towards first year primary students, the goal of which, in addition to teaching Islam, is to standardise this subject in educational institutions. It is a pioneer initiative written in Spanish, with a format similar to a support manual used for the subject of Catholic religion in schools. A second manual is being prepared, entitled *Getting to Know Islam*, geared at third and fourth year primary students.

However, and despite the fact that the regulatory framework is complete, putting the course on Islamic religion into practice was delayed for years, until the 2001-2002 school year in Ceuta and Melilla and the 2005-2006 school year on the peninsula. Currently, very few autonomous communities have established this course due to difficulties in "negotiating with education authorities ... who have transferred religious education and payment of the teaching staff [to the communities]" (Planet 2008, 46). In fact, IRE is only taught in those communities which directly depend on the Central Administration for religious education.

Here it is important to note that, due to the quantity of Muslim – and more specifically, Moroccan – foreign students in some autonomous communities, the so-called ELCO-Arabic Plan (Teaching the Language and Culture of Origin) was developed.[14] This began to operate in Spain in 1994 as a result of the Hispano-Moroccan Cultural Cooperation Agreement, according to which Morocco, through the Hassan II Foundation, is responsible for the coordination and payment of Moroccan teachers who belong to it, while Spain is responsible for authorising this program in the Autonomous Communities and schools that request it (Mijares, 2006). The Autonomous Communities that offer this programme are: Andalusia, Catalonia, the Canary Islands, Extremadura, La Rioja, Madrid, the Basque Country and Aragon. Some of these classes are given during school hours, as an alternative to Catholic religion, which could lead to some confusion between the ELCO Programme and IRE; even when ELCO is given in the afternoon after school (which is

---

14 There is also an ELCO-Portuguese Plan. This programme is supported by the "European Community Council Directive of 25 July 1977 on the education of children of migrant workers (77/486/CEE), the third article of which establishes that, in accordance with their national situations and legal systems, and in cooperation with the States of origin, the member States will adopt the pertinent measures in order to promote, in coordination with regular education, education in the mother tongue and about the culture of the country of origin for the children of workers from Council member states who are of the age of compulsory education. This Directive does not bind union member countries to a specific type of education, but at least establishes a relative guarantee for the mobility of workers" (Trujillo, 2008:4).

common in Andalusia, for example), learning Arabic is often confused with religion classes[15]:

> 'ELCO is a completely different thing. With IRE we depend on the Ministry and they depend on the Moroccan Consulate. In any case, it is very common that people confuse us, even the classmates confuse one thing with the other, that I'm not teaching Arabic but rather Islamic religion and that it's not the same thing ... I don't teach Arabic and if I did it would be at a very basic level; I teach Islam" (IRE teaching staff coordinator in Andalusia)[16].

2.2.4 Autonomous communities where IRE is taught

The autonomous communities where IRE has been established are those that have not had powers relating to religious education transferred to them. These are: Andalusia, Aragon, the Canary Islands and the Autonomous Cities of Ceuta and Melilla.[17] Since the 2008-09 school year, this group has also included the Basque Country.

Different federations have complained about the fact that IRE has not been established in public schools, even though it is a right recognised in the Cooperation Agreement and in the LOLR. They have also claimed that some autonomous communities, like Madrid, Valencia and Murcia, do not even want to listen to their demands. In general, the most common justifications from the autonomous communities where IRE has not been implemented are: lack of requests, the lack of a single and valid interlocutor for all of the Muslim communities, and the lack of suitable instructors to teach the subject.

The case of Catalonia is unique, since it is dedicated to having inclusive, non-segregated schools and has found that voluntary, denominational religious education can produce situations of discrimination. This community is considering the option of teaching a course on 'Religious Culture', which would be a non-denominational subject, and which would study religion as a cultural and constitutive element of history. This class would eventually replace all denominational religious education in public schools and would not contradict the constitutional guarantee that parents can ensure that their children receive religious and moral education in the school. However, this option means revising the Concordat with the Holy See and the Agreements with minority denominations and the Constitutional Court is presently debating the competency of the Generalitat of Catalonia in this matter.

---

15 Concerning Arabic, it is important to note that some Muslim groups in Andalusia have requested making Spanish and Arabic co-official languages based on the existence of al-Andalus in the past. Ceuta and Melilla have also made this request, although on different bases, and since the 2008-09 school year, have had permission from the Ministry of Education to give IRE classes in Arabic. Furthermore, some Andalusian secondary schools began the 2008-09 school year with a pilot experiment to teach Arabic as an optional second foreign language although, to date, there is no data on the number of students who have requested this class to date.
16 Interviewed by authors 29/09/2008.
17 Cantabria does not have these powers either, but it does not teach IRE because the minimum number of requests has not been received.

In Ceuta and Melilla, where nearly half of all pupils are Muslims – the majority ethnically Arab in the case of Ceuta and Amazigh in the case of Melilla – the polar opposite is true. In this demographically and socially polarised context, the local school authorities had to concede equal treatment for the Muslim religious communities much earlier. Islamic instruction was accordingly introduced for the first time in 1996. The first pilot project failed, however, as the local Muslim communities in Melilla did not agree on the list of selected IRE teachers (Moreras, 2005). In Ceuta, the first IRE classes were introduced in January 1999, but – contrary to the Catholic religion classes – were relegated to an extra-curricular afternoon timetable, where they were attended by few pupils and soon cancelled by the school authorities. Finally, more regular IRE classes started in both cities in 2002.

Given the diversity of justifications from the Autonomous Community administrations for not teaching IRE, the UCIDE, on behalf of all of the religious bodies federated in it, has proposed an action plan that unifies the criteria and arguments for the administrations:

> *"Since 1996, we have been asking for the Agreement to be applied. Sometimes we are told that the situation is that classes in Islam are undesirable because of Islamic terrorism, but I tell them that when Islam is taught at home, we don't know what the mothers and fathers are teaching and it's not controlled. If we teach it in the mosques, the community controls it, but if Islam is taught in schools, then it is controlled by the whole world and by the Ministry, and that is much better and more controlled"* (UCIDE General Secretary)[18].

The current situation is that IRE classes began in the 2005-06 school year with 32 teachers across Spain. In the 2008-09 school year, according to the data provided by the UCIDE, there are 41 teachers teaching this subject and around 120,000 requests for it throughout the country, although no official figures have been provided on the number of students taking the class.

The current distribution of the IRE teaching staff is as follows: 17 teachers in Andalusia, 2 in Aragon, 10 in Ceuta, 11 in Melilla, 1 in the Canary Islands and 1 in the Basque Country[19]. All of these teachers, without exception, give IRE classes in several schools and, at times, in different cities. This creates an important problem with schedules and the possibilities for teaching this subject, since the school schedules at different schools must be matched and administrators must work with the real possibilities available to them, meaning that the classes are not always taught in an appropriate way.

The majority of students taking IRE are at the primary level, with a minority at the secondary level (only in Ceuta) and they are practically non-existent in nursery school. The profile for IRE students is similar in the different Autonomous Communities: mainly Moroccan and with a growing number of children from mixed

---

18 Interviewed by authors 29/09/2008.
19 Five Basque schools will provide classes in Islamic religion in the next few weeks at the primary school level (6 to 12 years old). They will be the first schools in Basque history to do this experiment. The Education Ministry has authorised schools at Miribilla (in Bilbao), Maiztegi-San Miguel (Iurreta), Legarda (Mungia), Learreta-Markina (Berriz) and Landako (Durango) to teach classes in Islamic religion and at this time is completing the hiring process for the teachers. *El País*, 08/11/2008.

marriages (one partner Moroccan and the other from a different nationality); sub-Saharan students are in the minority, both because there are fewer of them than Moroccans and because their parents do not know that the possibility of IRE exists in some Autonomous Communities. Therefore, from this point onward, this study will concentrate on the case of primary education.

3. Empirical findings for IRE

The research for the fieldwork in the REDCo project was conducted from 2006 to mid-2008 in primary and secondary schools and their surrounding communities in cities in Granada, Melilla and Murcia (Purias). The research incorporated a range of methodologies including 58 ethnographic interviews in Andalusia (36 interviews), Murcia (6 interviews) and Melilla (16 interviews). The sampling procedure adopted consisted of snowball and judgement sampling. The snowball approach involved using a small group of informants who were asked to put the researchers in touch with a person (teachers, pupils, headmasters, etc.) who was then subsequently interviewed. Informants for the IRE study were selected on the basis of their IRE, neighbourhood and school context, as well as on their personal experiences which had provided them with special knowledge. In this respect, we carried out 19 interviews with pupils, 20 with parents, 14 with teachers and 5 with headmasters. Four additional interviews were also conducted in order to learn more about the context in Huelva and Madrid. Quantitative and qualitative questionnaires were given to secondary school pupils and participant observation was carried out in the classrooms, schools[20], NGOs, religious centres and neighbourhoods.[21]

3.1 IRE in primary education

Primary education consists of six school years for pupils aged from six to twelve and is organised into three cycles of two years each. At this stage of education, classes in Islamic religion are only given to a minimum percentage of the total of the 120,000 students that have requested it.[22] In Catalonia, where, as noted above, there are no plans to implement IRE, there has been a curious decline in the number of requests for this type of education in primary school in relation to the number of students with Moroccan origins. For instance, for the 2006-07 school year, a total of 1,341 requests were tabulated, which represents 16% of the Moroccan pupils. Here, the different positions reflect the current status of IRE in Spain, i.e., the

---

20 We would particularly like to thank the inestimable help offered by the Santa Juliana public nursery and primary school (Granada) and IRE teacher Mr. Anwar González.
21 For more details about how we organised the structure of the interviews, cf. Rosón & Álvarez, 2009; Dietz et. al., 2008 and Álvarez & Rosón, 2009.
22 A total of 105 hours during the school year, or 3 hours a week. The percentage of students taking Islamic religion out of a total of enrolled students in 2001-2002 was 0.28% and 0.39% in 2005-2006, according to the percentage distribution of students by religion/activity studies. Source: Statistics on Education in Spain at non-university levels, M.E.C. Office of Statistics. At other levels, such as secondary and nursery school, the percentage is insignificant.

problems that parents encounter when they try to arrange IRE classes for their children conform with both what is legally established, and also with the different points of view in the debate on whether or not IRE should be taught in schools.

3.2 Problems when it comes to teaching IRE

The first problem is **ignorance**. Most parents who sign their children up in primary schools do not know that, by law, they can choose the type of religious education that they want their children to receive. This is changing bit by bit, thanks to the work of different federations[23], but especially thanks to the work of the parents who are integrated into different local communities. This point has positive and negative aspects since, on the one hand, in an important number of cases, the measures adopted to demand IRE occur on the local, or even community, level, without contact with the rest of the Muslim communities in the city. This means that the demands focus on specific schools, by-passing neighbouring schools attended by children whose parents belong to another community or to a less organised Mosque:

> "*I found out that up there* [in a Granada neighbourhood] *they already have a teacher in the afternoon at the school and that it's just a matter of time before they start teaching classes ... our school is going much more slowly*" (Interv-Parents-ma20).

On the other hand, there is the problem of parents who, for various reasons, do not belong to (or regularly attend) a specific religious centre. The gulf between communities, the diversity of representatives and, especially, the lack of information provided outside the community circle intensifies the parents' ignorance:

> "*When we got to the school, we didn't know anything ... nobody had told us that there were classes in Islam. Our friends didn't know either, maybe because we don't go to a specific mosque where they would orient us ... because we don't belong to a specific one ...*" (Interv-Parents-fe36).

Added to this aspect is a **lack of interest** on the part of some parents with regards to the religious education of their children. Although this aspect cannot be generalised, in some sectors it is thought to be one of the main handicaps for students who want to take IRE but cannot. In some cases, this is due to the fact that children participate in the family migration process, meaning that their period of stay in any one school is often quite short. Therefore, this lack of interest, combined with ignorance, has created a certain apathy concerning some religious questions, which move into the background, behind the family's subsistence:

> "*There are more than 10 students* [the minimum to be able to request a teacher] *at school, but a lot of the parents aren't interested in having their children learn*

---

23 However, the low level of communication between the federations is a handicap that has increased the level of ignorance of the parents. We observed parents who are tied to some community – and most members of one or another federation – who are completely unaware of the IRE teaching staff and their right to demand education and even the type of IRE that the neighbouring school has.

religion at school [...] these are families that go back and forth looking for work, so they're here one year and gone the next. This happens a lot. Now we're more organised, giving more information out, but a lot of people don't want to get involved (Interv-Parents-fe31).

In other cases, it is simply because the parents are not believers/mosque-goers and do not want their children to profess a religion:

"there are also parents who are, let's say, atheists, who don't believe" (Interv-Parents-fe40).

Another possible problem is the **recognition or confirmation of the IRE teacher** according to his or her community of origin, nationality, speech and, in the furthest extreme, the suitability of their academic, pedagogical and/or religious education. Here there is also a wide diversity of opinions.

On one hand, some parents do not accept that the instructor teaching classes to their children might be a Spanish convert:

"In general, Arab Muslims think that non-Arab Muslims cannot achieve the same understanding of Islam that they have. They believe that they live it more intensely and understand it better than the non-Arabs. They think that you, as a Spaniard, cannot understand it as they do. They are here and you are below them. The opposite case is even more difficult, when a Spaniard does not want or has problems with their children attending classes with an Arab teacher". (Interv-Parents-ma24).

Also important here is the opinion, which is very widespread, that considers that only a 'good' Muslim can teach their children:

"Yes, if they were good Muslims, I wouldn't care if they're Spanish, French, American, whatever, but it has to be a good Muslim, a good Muslim who knows the religion" (Interv-Parents-fe31).

In a similar vein, there is an opinion that the teacher's discourse must be controlled:

"Look! We're talking about religion here, well...in the schools, too [...], since it's such a broad topic, it's so modern, now, we all talk about religion...there might be a religion teacher who imposes the ideology that he or she has on the students. If he's an extremist, he'll draw them to extremism. It could be a teacher who is against everything, just any religion, and focuses their attention on these ideas ..." (Interv-Parents-ma40).

Finally, it has been shown that there is some wariness according to the teacher's religious background. Here, the teacher's association with some federation or another is codified to identify the educational approach used with the students:

"in other regions, they have teachers who belong to the UCIDE or FEERI. This isn't really a problem ... but it is obvious that, depending on the community, a teacher who ascribes to one line or another is going to be preferred [...] Of course, this is at a very abstract level, because most parents don't stop and think about these questions" (Interv-Parents-ma20).

Furthermore, a discussion has been observed relating to **the suitability of the teaching staff in relation to their religious or non-religious affiliation**. In this context, it is interesting to note that the great majority of Muslims who were interviewed thought that IRE teachers had to be consistent with the material they taught. One example:

> *"they must be Muslim [...] This is fundamental. They must be Muslim because they are the only ones who know the true Din, the true religion, because now we can say that there is a true Islam and a false Islam and we have to be practicing Muslims"* (Interv-Parents-fe31).

However, it is interesting that, for an important number of Muslim students living in Melilla, whose experience with IRE is more extensive than most of the cases in other parts of Spain, the final objective of IRE classes should be educational, regardless of the religious affiliation of the teacher:

> *"Well, typically, the perfect teacher is nice, good and knows a lot about Islam. The teacher doesn't have to be of the same religion, just know Islam well, that's enough. There's no connection between your religion and what you teach, because in the end, they have to teach me my religion, not theirs"* (Interv-Student-ma13).

In addition to the religious affiliation of the IRE teachers, it is also important to note the recent debate about **their suitable academic and pedagogical training**. Here, the parents value the same things that they do in other subjects: efficiency, suitability, the capacity to adapt to the students, their knowledge, their experience, etc. Apart from this, the IRE teacher much have (or they require this) another series of specific connotations that are not imperative for most school teachers: they must be 'transparent' (aseptic) in their teaching of Islam and the culture, and they must be members of an Islamic community or be related to one of the existing federations (since it is, after all, the federations that choose the teacher – the CIE presents a single list, agreed upon by the federations, to the Ministry, which ratifies the teachers considered to be the most suitable). The teacher must (or is supposed to) have command of two languages (Arabic and Spanish). Also (cf. 1.2.2), the possibility of demanding a class on the Spanish legal code and constitutional values is being studied for teachers not born in Spain.

In addition to these problems, which are directly related to the specificity, heterogeneity and internal diversity of the different Muslim communities in the country, the **low level of interest and slowness of response on the part of the administration** is also important. This aspect has produced a widespread lack of enthusiasm in the communities (as the Muslim social agent) since, although they have the number (ratio) of students needed to request a teacher, the obstacles they face overwhelm their initial enthusiasm:

> *"My father was speaking with Muslims from here, who have a lot of contacts, of friends that have written ... they have translated the Koran and so forth. He talked to them and they got together so that they could do it, but nothing happened, they were told that they had to have a minimum of some percentage in each school to get an Islamic religion teacher. I don't know. They had stopped ... I mean, no, they didn't keep trying. It just didn't work"* (Interv-Student-fe17).

It is also important to consider here that administrative obstacles not only paralyze the interests of Muslim parents, but they also multiply day by day, making it necessary to go back and demand the right which has already been granted once again. One example of this is that, in order to formalise the situation of the IRE teaching staff, the parents have to write petitions and gather signatures to pressure both the school and the central or Autonomous Community administration:

> 'And the child has the right to have a teacher of the Koran by law. But there has to be a minimum of ten. But there are more than ten, gentlemen. No, no, no you have to write a separate petition about wanting the teacher. Why separate? On the sheet from the Andalusia government, it says that we have to write an X for the religion class that we want our children to take. So we chose it there. Why do we have to write a special petition? No, no, no this has been on the books for years. So, why do we have to write a special petition? No, you people from the Andalusia government just count: one cross, two crosses, three crosses, are there fifteen crosses? Well, just send the teacher and be done with it" (Interv-Parents-fe38).

This discussion about the crosses indicating religious affiliation revealed another series of points where a lack of trust in the system arose in the form of the questioning of not only the endless paperwork that has to be completed for their children to be counted, but also the assistance that they received from the school itself:

> "There were more bad than good things because the administration always put obstacles in our way [...] even in the schools, we have had to demand that they explain how to fill in the request forms [...] I think that some of them were acting in bad faith ... because if you don't know the language and you don't try to explain it, a lot of people have no idea that they can request religion for their children" (Interv-Parents-fe38).

Another significant problem concerns economic issues when it comes to hiring teaching staff. Although the central government and the different Autonomous Communities must pay the salaries of IRE teachers, in most cases, the lack of resources for hiring means that the same IRE teacher has to move from one school to another on the same day. This means that, depending on the schedules between the different schools in which they are teaching, they have to decide what class to give in each school and, conversely, also which schools are left without classes or are given only half of the pre-established course:

> "Because there's not enough time. They hire a teacher for X hours and these hours keep them busy in ... and what's more ... last year there were four schools because I requested them, three in Granada's capital city and one in some little town. And this year there may even be one more school. Maybe that's why he has to ... the classes, I don't know if that's why. But already last year, when I talked to him, and I asked him, he told me that they had told him that he had to fulfil the schedule, but look, [...] in this school, in that, it hasn't happened yet. What we want to find out now, if he can't do it this year, if next year he can work full time in each school. Two hours a week" (Interv-Parents-fe33).

Finally, this widespread lack of enthusiasm not only affects parents and communities, but also the students themselves, and, when they are older, they start to feel excluded from a system that does not respond to their educational needs. Indeed, it is increasingly common for students to be the social agents who criticise the administration's lethargy:

> *"Yes, especially this year. There are more than ten. I mean I think it's logical, right? Either all Moroccans or all Christians* [laughs]. *Why are they are going to give the class, I don't know, I don't see it happening ... Come on! If there aren't any other religions, get rid of them all and that's that. And what's more, not very many people take religion. Very few. In my class, at least, there are thirty of us and most are taking the alternative*[24]. *Ten or twelve go to religion class* [Catholic religion]. *But I really would have liked it* [IRE], *really"* (Interv-Student-fe17).

3.3 Why IRE should be taught in public schools

Having studied the main problems facing Muslim communities when it comes to having IRE in the public school, it is necessary to explore the extent to which the different social agents involved believe that IRE classes are necessary. In this respect, it is important to note *a priori* that not everyone is clear on the question of whether IRE classes are completely necessary. There are contrasting positions which hold different arguments: the need (or lack thereof) to give classes in Islamic religion in primary schools from the point of view of the Muslim social agent[25].

From listening to the thoughts of parents, students, religious leaders and teachers who think that teaching Islam in schools is absolutely necessary, it is clear that the issues that were most vehemently argued and are fundamental in the constitutional right of parents to ensure that their children receive religious and moral instruction in public schools in accordance with their own convictions are:

A comparative analysis of the social reality surrounding religious education in Spain. As noted above, the religion traditionally taught in school has been Catholicism and, until recently, IRE did not exist, regardless of whether or not there were Muslim students in the schools. Similarly, for the last several years, a laicist trend has been observed in certain sectors of the population that proposes the elimination of any type of religion in schools. In both cases, the Muslim community has been essentialised and formed a counter-reaction. In this respect, the most interesting response from some Muslim sectors originates in the confrontation and comparison with the CRE 'homonym'. This is seen in the words of a religious leader, who believes that IRE is demanded because of the existence of other religions (in this case Catholicism) in education. Therefore, the lack of existence of IRE would be a comparative and discriminatory affront to a minority religion:

---

24 Ethics, 'society culture, religion', citizenship, religion, etc., have been the only non-confessional alternatives.
25 From here on, the Muslim social agent is understood to be a group: mothers, fathers, IRE teachers, students and religious leaders. Other contrasting points of view which are currently evolving on a political and social level in Spain, such as the opinion of laicist groups and the Catholic Church itself, are not considered in this analysis.

> *"Really, the topic of teaching Islam in public schools arose because they were teaching the Catholic religion. It was people from the Catholic religion. We, it's not that ... because there was a group ... because the controversy arose and they said: well, let them teach it in the mosques! Let them go to a madrasah! Why in school? If it isn't taught, because of laic teaching, then they shouldn't teach it, but not any other religion either, not only Islam. Catholic religion shouldn't be taught in schools, either. It should be all or none"* (Interv-Leader-ma54).

As a result of this, regardless of the comparative aspect, a series of more socio-educational aspects or reasons were put forward to argue the absolute need for IRE. One of these is based on **non-discrimination against Muslim students**. Here, from the point of view of some parents and religious leaders, the fact that IRE exists now is very positive for students, i.e., if these IRE classes did not exist, the students might feel discriminated against with respect to their peers, the believers, even if they were Catholic. This would mean that, while the rest of the students attend the classes that they have chosen (ethics, Catholic religion, religion, etc.), Muslim students would have to attend a tutored class that does not correspond to their beliefs or convictions. Likewise, this type of alternative activity in primary school is not recognised, meaning that they have no type of academic requirement and/or evaluation:

> *"We always had to go to a tutored class where we went over our work or did senseless activities ... I mean that I had a religion, too, I wasn't an atheist like the others in the tutored class not doing anything ... and I felt different, I was the 'other', the weird one"* (Interv-Student-ma15).

This aspect can also be seen in the discourse of those students who did not have the opportunity to take IRE in school. In this case, the students' reflection is not comparative – 'I didn't have it before, but now I have it...' – but rather part of an inclusive reflection on the religion of the other. However, they do reveal that not having the IRE class in school provoked mockery and prejudice from their classmates:

> *"People taking Catholic religion should take it, with no fuss, but when it's that time, we Muslims should go somewhere else and a teacher who knows the Koran and Arabic should teach us Muslim religion and that way we'll be equal. Because it's not fair that I am in a school and that's all because I'm Muslim or the only one in the class that can't take religion and I have to go somewhere else to do other things [...] So it's better, because that way nobody can make fun of me"* (Interv-Student-ma11).

Closely related to this is the argument that IRE teachers serve as **psychological support or reference point for the students**. This moral support, as a reference point, goes beyond the classroom to become a model for intracultural mediation on different levels – between students and teachers, between parents[26] and teachers, and between the teachers themselves. A religious leader who began giving IRE classes in a rural school put it this way:

---

26 Some of them speak only Arabic and do not speak Spanish well and the IRE teacher is the only member of the faculty who speaks the two languages well.

> *"The first thing that I saw was that the children felt like they had psychological support, the psychological aspect, when they saw a teacher there in the school, inside this school organigram, and saw the presence of a teacher […] who spoke the main language that their classes were taught in and also spoke to them about the condition of being a Muslim, their culture. Of course, they are two cultures and a Muslim in a non-Muslim country learns two cultures, even in a Muslim country, because western culture is already in all the schools and has to be taught. This transcends to an individual level in a person. And then also for the non-Muslims ..."*
> (Interv-Leader-ma54).

A third argument to justify the need for IRE is that it is a **fundamental part of educating** a child, both in the cultural and religious spheres. In primary school IRE classes, the student begins to understand that Islam is a way of life and that it is based on daily religious practice. Learning how to pray, to perform one's ablutions, to recognise holidays, the life of the Prophet and of the Prophets contributes a deep knowledge of Allah, etc. to the student. And these are very positive reasons. In this respect, a teacher of Islamic religion explained why he thought that religion was fundamental for primary students:

> *"It is fundamental, it is very important from my point of view, because the child in primary school is going to begin to learn a little bit about his or her religion, because when a Muslim child grows up, he's going to see his family praying, right? And of course they don't know what the prayer is or why they are praying. Prayer is a pillar of Islam, every movement in the prayer is an adoration of God. When we pray we are adoring God. For us, God is closest to us when we are prostrate on the floor, this pose is the human-being recognising his submission to God and it is there that we ask for what we need most, our health ... the fast, for example, why do Muslims fast? In school, they are taught this with more detail, then the ablutions, really all of it, little by little, is explained, the life of the Prophet, the Shura, etc."*
> (Interv-Teacher-fe50).

3.4 Which educational model is considered the most appropriate

Throughout the different ethnographic interviews carried out in this study, the most widespread opinion expressed by the social agents involved corresponds to the existing model of religious education. Specifically, this means that the students should be separated by creed and that each one should receive the religious education that corresponds to his or her belief. The involved social agents believe that the education that they receive must be explicitly related to their own religion. A Muslim student, debating the prior choice of his parents and his own perception, expressed it thus:

> *"No, because if we are little and our parents tell us that we must follow the Muslim religion and parents of Catholic children tell them to follow the Catholic religion, then we shouldn't all be together. It wouldn't be fair because everyone couldn't talk about their own religion. For example: if we take Muslim religion, then the Christians and Jews aren't going to be there. They have their own religion"* (Interv-Student-fe13).

In this respect, there are arguments that *de facto* reject the policy of providing one common religion class or a 'history of religion' class, since disagreements in dogma and practice are thought to be incompatible. Joint classes would mean more conflicts than advantages:

> *If they taught religion to all the students regardless of their beliefs, there would be total conflict since, given that the belief systems are different, not everyone thinks the same or believes the same, so they should be separated by religion whenever it is time for religion classes"* (Interv-Student-ma17).

However, there are other educational models that are also considered to be appropriate by the different agents, although they are in the minority. Here, for instance, the intermediate position comes into play, that of **mixed non-confessional education**. This proposal arises in places where there is important religious and cultural diversity, such as Melilla, and sporadically in other regions in Spain. The proposed model is that used in other countries in the EU (cf. Knauth et. al. 2008), i.e., an 'intermediate' model for religious education in schools where students from different religions share one class about religions in general. In this case, the classes do not have to be given by teachers from a specific religion since they would be a type of 'Class on the History of Religions' or something similar.

> *"Yes, because that way, Christians would also learn our religion as we learn theirs. That would be even better"* (Interv-Studen-ma16).

With this type of proposal, the classes would be developed on the basis of the set of beliefs of the students involved. This means that a broad theoretical-theological education on each of the represented religions would be given by a religion teacher, and that the student would decide *a posteriori* to adopt the religion that best represented his or her way of thinking and social and/or family context:

> *"I think that there should be a teacher of religions, not of a single religion, who teaches students the different religions and ideologies that there are and what each group says. Teach what others say, not what he says. He would say, for example: Catholics say this, the ... Catholics, Protestants have a ... that they begin with ... something common that the whole world has, it's like this: Islam has this, that ... and teach a little about everything. And that way the students learn the topic and they can choose one thing or another, don't you think? They can choose their own path later"* (Interv-Students-ma15).

3.5 Alternative models to the IRE

With regards to the positions of the social agents who think that IRE is not necessary, it is important to note that a significant percentage of parents and students believe that Islamic religious education **should be taught at home, in the family** and, as a last resort, in mosques or madrasahs (cf. Rosón & Álvarez 2009, Dietz 2007). From the point of view of some Muslim agents, children's education is an extremely important aspect that must be kept separate from the arbitrary nature of choosing the teaching staff, the diversity of discourses and "opinions and branches" in Islam. Therefore, it must focus on the official discourse within the family, centring on the "values, ideas and interpretations" that the family has made from its own beliefs:

> *"In my opinion, religious education must be instilled by the parents, before letting such an important task fall to a teacher or a school. I was in a school and a secondary school and I think that it is not the right place to teach religion. I believe that it is better for the parents to be personally responsible for educating their children on the basis of their values and their ideas, because Islam today is very diverse and there are many opinions and branches and if you let just anyone teach it ..."* (Interv-Students-ma24).

At this point, it is important to summarise the opinion of those Muslims who think that **no religion should be taught in schools**, be it Catholic, Islamic or Protestant. The assimilation of their condition as minorities (which they see as a constant), the administrative obstacles, and a point of view that is diametrically opposed to what is put forth officially by the Catholic Church is fully expressed in the face of the existing social debate:

> *"From my point of view, I don't think that any confession should teach religion classes in school. Not Islamic or Catholic [...] this would be like a last resort [...] because I prefer that no religion be taught in school"* (Interv-Students-ma24).

3.6 Is informal religious socialisation an alternative to IRE?

Formal teaching of the Islamic religion is only one part of the group of initiatives for religious socialisation being developed in Muslim communities in Spain. Other times and spaces are also dedicated to socialisation, which, from a school perspective, takes place within informal spheres, but still plays an important role in the process of the community configuration of these groups. It is well known that the family sphere is the first space for religious socialisation serving, for younger generations, as the access point to basic knowledge of the principles of a belief that is transmitted as a family inheritance (generally in the form of religious sets of gestures and practices). Of interest here, however, are the community initiatives for religious socialisation (specifically, the educational activities that take place in community Koranic schools) regarding what is supposed to be a practice that is consolidated within the fold of these groups.

The socialising component constitutes a structural element within the definition and function of Muslim oratories in the context of the diaspora. In the first place, it is thought that one of the main purposes of these community spaces is to offer a set of initiatives in favour of religious socialisation for new generations, but also, by extension, for the group as a whole. The people who back these oratories, a large number of whom are parents who wish to meets the demands of worship that are generated by these groups, express it in this way. This socialisation is specifically understood in the context of a non-Muslim society in which the active maintenance of these references is a constituent element in maintaining community ties, as well as being fundamental to the power to construct differentiated belongings and identities with respect to this context. In the second place, these community spaces are understood to be extensions of the first sphere of socialisation, the family, complementing, and an extension of what has taken place there. The mosque becomes the community space that acts as an extension of – rather than a substitution for – the religious socialisation that began in the home. One of the interviewees expressed it thus:

> "*they learn the Koran, recite the prayers, perform the ablutions ... these are practical things, because a child who is seven years old already has to be shown inside his family to pray five times a day and everything that precedes the prayers*" (Interv-Leader-ma54).

In the third and final place, these spaces become informal spheres for socialisation that are legitimated by the group, filling the existing vacuum created by the absence in the group of it's own social institutions. However, the fact that they are legitimated does not mean that they cannot concur with other initiatives, whether in settings outside the group (Islamic religious education in the school for example) or inside it (such as proposals for the education of the mother tongue).

Group wishes are not always specified, i.e., despite the fact that the religious socialisation of new generations seems to be a fundamental priority in the desire to open a new Koranic schools, this need may not always be met. This is due to two different reasons: either because the appropriate person to carry out this education is not available (this task usually falls to the Imam in the Koranic schools, despite the fact that at times this person may be reluctant or incapable of taking on the responsibility) or because there is a lack of economic resources to guarantee the continuity of the education. These reasons have a common denominator in the lack of human or material resources in these groups, which are fundamentally made up of non-qualified immigrant workers. However, as the group stabilises and it becomes possible to guarantee greater economic resources to maintain the Koranic school and its activities, these educational activities become consolidated. It becomes possible to count on the resource of a responsible person (in the case of new generations, educated people or university students who assist the Imam of the Koranic school), as well as a teaching space for them, with a minimal infrastructure (chalkboard, shelves, pedagogical materials). This helps to make education an activity that is incorporated into the daily lives of these groups, making weekly attendance of these socialisation activities by young girls and boys a regular occurrence.

There also develops a principle of trust relating to the socialising capacity of the Koranic school as a community institution. This trust makes it possible for Muslim parents to leave the important task of connecting new generations to this community in the hands of responsible parties, who can help them to develop into 'social' Muslims. It also adopts a dimension quite different to the consideration that religious formation in a formal school setting receives. While the Koranic school is seen as their own institution and one oriented to maintaining these group references, the school continues to be seen as an alien institution which is at times identified as an acculturating agent. The difference in functions between the two institutions is clearly defined, as is made clear in this testimony:

> *"My children study ethics. In primary school, they take ethics classes and they do extra work, reading, doing homework, doing projects. And I think this is good, because they learn religion at home with their father and they go to the mosque to learn the Koran and to read and write"* (Interv-Parents-fe27).

Similarly, Muslim Koranic schools continue to act as points to connect the group with the reference points from their society and culture of origin. Being connected to this background that the students' origin represents means that religious socialisation in these informal contexts is carried out through a specific cultural heritage, and this represents one of the main distinguishing elements in relation to formal religious education which, apparently, focuses on doctrine and not on specific cultural variants. This means that there is a desire to reproduce the same traditional models of religious socialisation as those belonging to the society of origin (Koranic schools). This transplant, however, cannot be literal, given the determining factors that are present in the contexts of the non-Muslim diaspora which impart a different character to these community socialisation initiatives.

It is difficult to affirm that informal religious socialisation represents an alternative to IRE. It may contribute to meeting a set of demands for specific religious socialisation and education (in the sense of catechesis), and at the same time it may also form an important mechanism for maintaining the community tie with new generations. However, the continuingly precarious component of resources and qualified personnel (the Imams are not always willing or adequately trained), the pedagogical weakness (since an important portion is based on memorisation) and the lack of developed contents (since it focuses only on the copying and recitation of the Koran), limit public and social recognition of this education. Moreover, and within the context of the growing attention to activities that (it is thought) are carried out in mosques, as well as the roles that (it is suspected) the Imams play, certain declarations by Spanish political leaders which argue for the need to include IRE in the schools are not surprising. See, for example, the speech by the *Convergència i Unió* deputy, Josep-Antoni Duran i Lleida in the Congress of Deputies:

> *"There is an increasingly large presence of immigrants whose religion is different from ours. What do we prefer, for religious education to be given in the mosques or established in the schools? What do we prefer, education, if the parents have the right to request it, that can be given in public or private publicly subsidised schools or for religion to be withdrawn from schools and education be given in places that will not be controlled in the future?"*[27]

The paradoxical element in this case is that, despite the fact that the pedagogical principles that sustain informal religious socialisation have been questioned on more than one occasion from political spheres and formal educational institutions, the same discourses have shown themselves to be favourable to the incorporation of Islamic education in schools as a 'lesser evil', and as a way to replace the traditional education (which is interpreted as synonymous with obscurantism), which, it is believed, is taught in community Koranic schools. However, to suggest this argument is to be ignorant of the logic of organisational self-administration that

---

27 Congress of Deputies session diary (8th legislature), 3 November 2005.

these initiatives reveal and which the group wishes to use to respond practically to the needs of worship without having to depend on authorities and entities which they do not consider to be their own. In any case, the incorporation of Islamic education into the school would not mean the immediate replacement of religious socialisation, since its contents and orientation are very different.

4. Teaching Islam in school: pedagogical reflections

4.1 How IRE classes should be given

There is currently a debate about the type of contents that should be provided, *de facto* in religion classes, versus what is stipulated in the Cooperation Agreement and the official IRE curriculum that was agreed upon between the communities (the CIE as a last resort) and the Ministry. This debate – in some cases taking place outside the Muslim communities – does not only centre on the suitability of the discourse that the teacher should present in the classroom, but also on how, pedagogically speaking, the subject should be taught. To analyse this, it is important to consider the demands of the social agents involved. The debate focuses, on one hand, on **the primary meaning of religion classes** and on the other, specifically in the case of IRE, on the language in which the classes should be taught and on what basis. In this respect, it is possible to find different points of view, both complementary and contradictory.

In the first place, in reference to the 'primary meaning' of IRE, there are two principle positions. One holds that the classes must maintain traditional values, i.e., it should be taught at school, but within the parameters of the ELCO classes or as currently taught in Mosques, communities and/or associations. This means basically that it must be taught in Arabic and on the basis of the holy book, the Koran. The other position holds that IRE should be equated to the other subjects that are given in formal education.

From the point of view of some parents, IRE should only and exclusively be taught to students **in Arabic and using the Koran**. Together, as a set, they are sufficient to teach the religion. In most cases, this is a response to the fact that the Koran represents the basis of Islam and contains Allah's revelations to Mohammed. In this respect, regardless of the religious significance of the Koran, its importance stems from the fact that, in addition to being a theological text, it is also a legal, political and economic text. Furthermore, it is also considered to be the 'eternal and uncreated' word of Allah and must be transmitted in classical Arabic, without the slightest change to the original language. According to tradition, the Koran was revealed to the Prophet Mohammed in Arabic and for this reason, the language acquired crucial relevance. Thus, Muslims have traditionally taught Arabic to anyone who wants to know Islam, as the only correct way to teach the liturgy, since a translation has no didactic or religious value.

These points appear in the discourse of some Muslims living in Spain, not only those who arrived here – through different migratory processes – from Arab countries in which these issues are culturally assimilated, but also different communities of converts born in Spain, who sometimes resort to taking their children to

Arab countries that follow educational and cultural models that are appropriate to their interests. From this point of view, the reflection on the didactic value of what is taught in IRE makes no sense if it is not in Arabic and basically concerned with the Koran. However, this is not the only issue, because teaching their culture and way of life also means reflecting on the 'regulatory framework' of their own religion, i.e., the Koran and the teachings of the Prophet, all in Arabic:

> *"And I don't like it, when they are talking about things in Islam and they are speaking Spanish. I would like [it to be in Arabic], really, do you know why? Because the defence of Islam is not the language, but the way to reach children and teach children. For example, if you explain what an 'ayat' is in Spanish, it is not the same as if you explain it in Arabic"* (Interv-Parents-fe36).

However, on the other hand, for other interested parties, IRE classes go beyond what is traditionally understood to be Islamic religion. They should develop a series of practical values, beyond theory, which should be taught to the students in a critical way and not by rote. To do this, distance should be put between the classes and the 'traditional way', the community context, and the examples of education carried out inside Muslim communities (mosques, Koranic schools, etc.). For those who adhere to this argument, public schools are the best place to teach these classes:

> *"[…] here religion for them is learning the Koran. That is what religion is for them. And learning the Koran is not religion. It stops there. Because learning the Koran, reciting it by heart, you don't understand what it is saying, what it refers to, I'm sorry. This mentality has to change. More than learning it, it has to be practiced. Practice is understanding what is being said and following it every day"* (Interv-Parents-fe35).

Secondly, there is also the intermediate position, which is closely related to the Cooperation Agreement, and which contains a coherent interpretation of the way in which Muslims should teach religion classes. This interpretation assumes that it is not possible to teach certain things in the curriculum that was approved by the Ministry if they are not in Arabic. For this reason, the IRE teacher must "promote the spontaneous interest of the students in learning the rules for reading the Koran and, in general, the command of the Arabic language, in a simple and gradual way, as well as in identifying, analysing and memorising Koranic texts and the corresponding Prophetic Traditions"[28]. Here, Arabic must complete the student's education, although it should not be a priority in IRE:

> *"It's clear that there are some things that must be said in Arabic; the prayers are said in Arabic and there are some things that must be learned"* (Interv-Teacher-ma44).

In any case, having seen both positions, religious education must be adapted to the pre-established model in Spanish education and in turn, to what is established by

---

28 Cooperation Agreement with the Religious Denominations with *Notorio Arraigo* signed in 1992 with the Islamic Commission of Spain (CIE). For more details, see: http://religlaw.org/interdocs/docs/coagrspstislamiccom1992.htm (English version).

law. However, it is necessary to be conscious of the fact that this question is not an easy one since the teacher always focuses the education according to the intrinsic subjectivity that comes from being a human being. This means that although some parents demand education in Arabic (or more reading in Arabic in IRE), formal education must be done on the basis of what was agreed upon for the subject curriculum. Other aspects relating to religion, such as the reading and memorisation of the Koran in Arabic, must be carried out outside of the classroom, in most cases, and generally take place in the informal education of mosques and/or madrasahs. This does not mean that readings and/or prayers in Arabic cannot take place in the classes:

> "*We don't teach the Koran or Arabic. First because we are not authorised to do so by the Ministry of Education and Science and what's more, it is in Arabic, the Koran is written in Arabic and if you don't teach Arabic, how can you do it?...We have asked many times, to see if we can get authorisation, and parents tell us that they want us to teach the Koran and Arabic, but I tell them to take the kids to the mosque and to classes to learn it, because we can't do it here. The truth is that some of them come very well prepared, but in an hour I can't waste time on this because then, who will teach the syllabus? I can't follow the syllabus, can I? Because it consists of memorisation and the best place is the mosque*" (Interv-Teacher-ma35).

However, for a small part of the interested parties, the question of language should be secondary and/or nonexistent. In this respect, it is possible to find certain interviewees who refer to the students' lack of knowledge of Arabic or to the need for students to focus solely on the language of the country in which they live. This means approaching religious education on the basis of finding the best way to help students understand the country in which they live and in which they will work, i.e., in Spain and in Spanish:

> "[…] *My daughter doesn't live in an Arab country, she lives in Spain, so it should be in Spanish* […] *it should be a Spanish Muslim, but the main language of Spaniards is Spanish* […]. *Why should she learn Arabic or say things in Arabic and not in Spanish? How is she going to communicate with people in Arabic?*" (Interv-Parents-fe31).

4.2 From theory to practice: experiences of students who take IRE in public primary school

In focusing on the experiences of students who have already had the chance to take IRE, it is important to ask: what did these Islamic religion classes mean for the primary education students? And, what role did IRE play in their daily lives? In this respect, it is important to bear in mind both the **internal (emic) view of Muslims,** and also how this education influences them from an external **(etic)** point of view in their interreligious and cultural dialogue, and in their relationships with their peers.

Internally (emic), with regards to education in their own religion, we find a series of arguments that value the existence of IRE classes in public school positively, because:

> *"they teach students **how to obey** the religion that they want to take up"* (Interv-Student-ma14);

because it is "a very positive **encounter activity**" since the actors outside this religion begin to normalise it and become familiar with it; because it allows for **greater interaction between some parents and students** who would perhaps otherwise not have had this:

> *"I didn't have the opportunity to study much, but when my son comes home from religion class, we always enjoy ourselves ... he tells me and I tell him ..."* (Interv-Parents-fe35);

because it gives a more precise, ordered and reasoned content to their religion, as well as its moral demands, contents and bases, which in some cases are unknown to the parents and students:

> *"Yes, I learned a lot in school, because at home I told my dad: look! I did this and that and that! He corrected me sometimes: it's not like that! It has to be like this! Maybe the teacher was wrong? And I would ask the teacher about the things he told me: my dad says this and this ... whatever! And she corrected both of us"* (Interv-Student-fe15);

because the school provided the necessary daily routine, since it gave academic and regulatory value to aspects that could be routine or monotonous in daily life:

> *"A lot of times, they came to tell me that they had done this or that, when it was time to eat and they know everything and you can tell that they have interiorised what they learned in class. But a lot of times, they were lazy in this respect and we had to repeat it at home all the time so that our daughter wouldn't forget it. It's harder for her to learn things at home. [Why?] I think that since they are so relaxed with their parents they don't listen to them at all. I mean, at home they get bored, I start to teach them something and they say, I'm bored! I'm going to do something else! I'm going to the bathroom! ... There are more distractions at home and at school it's more formal"* (Interv-Parents-fe35);

and finally, because IRE **normalises one model of Islam, eliminating external differences**. This means that it constructs an orthodoxy and minimises popular beliefs which are considered superstitious, in which pre-Islamic concepts mix with orthodox or literal readings of the religion and ethnic and/or national practices. The IRE teacher and the classes provide the children with religious knowledge that goes beyond the criteria of their parents and even the Imams:

> *"There are people that think that these classes go against Muslim religion, that they are decaffeinated, that they could contain ideas that are contrary to the faith and etc., etc., all the ideas inside the Islamic religion, the parents ... the Imams were also a bit reluctant until we managed little by little to get them to accept this as a positive reality"* (Interv-Teacher-ma47).

Similarly, in IRE classes, students are **motivated by their own religion and increase their knowledge of it.** This means discovering new aspects of the religion that they practice, completing and at times being able to compare personal and family experiences with the praxis and 'official' dogma expressed both by the teacher and by the rest of the students attending the class:

> *"In class, you learn things about your religion, because there are things where you say: Oh! I didn't know this or that. And the other one* [the teacher] *is only teaching maths, maths and on and on ... and in your religion, well, wow! I didn't know that ... mum, look what they told me ...* [and mum answers] *Yes, yes! In those classes we always participate or we want to participate more than in the others. We're always waiting for religion class* [...] *Three hours a week: Monday, Wednesday and Friday and if it was the whole week, even better, and if there were private classes"* (Interv-Student-fe15).

School, in this respect, provides an ideal setting for learning and reflecting on one's own religion, and in turn, for learning about the religion of the 'other'. Although this is not a priority objective, IRE classes normalise a situation that once created tense relationships based mainly on mutual ignorance:

> *"It has a favourable repercussion both for the Muslim children and the non-Muslims. This favours the individual's own condition and then society's, naturally. It is nothing short of responding to the needs that are being produced spontaneously on a global level around the world. Because there is an inter-racial, intercultural connection that nobody can stop"* (Interv-Leader-ma54).

In this way, IRE seeks to contribute to *"the development of personality and education of the students as good citizens"* (Interv-Leader-ma54). **This aspect gives way to reflections on IRE's external influences (etic)** with respect to other students or classmates who attend the same school, i.e., how IRE promotes inter-religious and cultural dialogue and improves the relationships between groups of peers. This point is difficult to generalise, since in most cases the model that currently exists does not treat the religion of the other inclusively (cf. Dietz et al. 2008):

> *"We are separated into two classes, the only times that we work together is when we study inter-culturality, we study Christmas, Ramadan ... we put the classes together and work together between the other teacher and me, like that. This is Melilla* [...] *religion is a way of life but that doesn't prevent you from having relationships with others"* (Interv-Teacher-ma40).

However, the knowledge and the moral and religious values that are offered through IRE like *"culture, respect for yourself and others, the commitment to others, love, friendship, collaboration, etc."* (Interv-Student-fe14) help students to include the other. It is possible to observe examples of this, where ties are created which, in theory, should promote relationships between peers:

> *"The believing Muslim believes in all the prophets, right? That's what they say and they refer to it. There are divergences between Muslims and Christians but they are small and Islam teaches you the obligation to respect others"* (Interv-Teacher-ma41).

These values, or moral norms, constitute the first step to coexistence, since religious education in one's personal life teaches respect towards others:

> *"I think that cultures, religions and beliefs should be known better, since more and more barriers are forming between people and this impedes coexistence. What's more, they should learn to respect others, because you could offend someone, since they may not think as you do […] In the same way, people from different religions can live in harmony with mutual respect and tolerance. I think that respect and tolerance is taught with good education"* (Interv-Student-fe12).

This point should help to qualify the negative examples relating to IRE, since, from the point of view of most of the social agents involved, the processes of conflict and/or divergence have nothing to do with the religious affiliation of the students:

> *"they always tell you things, there are always problems, fights. But they aren't religious clashes as much as cultural ones"* (Interv-Parents-fe35).

Thus, in conclusion, the rather general idea was observed that religious affiliation is not a question which is usually discussed in class or between peers, but it is rather a private matter, which only rises to the public sphere of the classroom or the school in a few cases (cf. Rosón & Alvarez 2009). However, it appears that this trend slowly starts to change from the moment that IRE classes are normalised and accepted by the majority:

> *"The other children, the people, at the beginning, can be different. Some are surprised, others because it's new, because of their uncertainty, they want to see something new, others with added motivation: look this is different from me! And they want to learn, to speak with him: what did the Islam teacher teach you? Then they get closer, they strike up a dialogue and that is positive. I mean, the child expands, widens his circle and isn't left alone as if his condition were something secret from the school and his classmates ... their principles are a secret ... but when the teacher arrives, then...today we have the Koran, today we're going to see this other thing ... then this gives him to excuse to share it with his friends and schoolmates who aren't Muslim. So there is an interrelationship between the two. This calms the student down so that he can move beyond some of his own principles. In fact many of them move beyond them ... because, for example, they are going to look to see if it is sausage or chorizo and say, no thanks, I don't like it! But with mutual interaction, the child has the option of explaining why he doesn't want it ... then a closer relationship starts up. This then can promote more knowledge of Islam and the interrelationship with other religions"* (Interv-Leader-ma54).

4.3 Practical experiences beyond the curriculum

There is another set of points that go beyond the primary curriculum, themes like coexistence, interculturality, non-discrimination and the inclusion of the other, which are dealt with in IRE classes on certain occasions. These aspects are fundamental when it comes to observing how IRE classes try to promote processes of dialogue and coexistence between students attending IRE and the rest of the students in the school.

4.3.1 Coexistence

From the start, IRE education means a general education in the values connected to Islam. From this point of view, teachers try to inculcate the value of coexistence in daily life through their teaching. To do this, they reflect, from within their own religion, on the values and norms that should be followed:

> "Well ... with religious education ... we especially want to teach the children the values that they have to learn to coexist in daily life, education, respect. Because religion is not only about praying to God, not only about adoring God, but all the values that the love of God implies for a person from day to day in our religion, a smile is adoring God, for example. We often explain it to children like that" (Interv-Teacher-ma35).

In this context, emphasis is put on showing students that religion is a form of life and that, in turn, it has some intrinsic values which produce better citizens and better human beings with respect to their fellow men. This means a high degree of awareness-raising on the part of the students that, based on their religion, and within its framework, they can come to coexist with the people who surround them:

> "Religion is a way of life, a way of identifying yourself in your existence as well, in the case of Islam ... Islam is not a normal religion; it is a way of living with a person, with your neighbour, being moral, not stealing ... searching for the most honest life possible and all the love towards your parents and family ... all religions are the same, the message is the same, none tell you to do evil, not at all" (Interv-Teacher-ma42).

It can be seen, *de facto*, in the discourse of the students, that these values are interiorised when they begin to take IRE classes through daily practice. From this point of view, coexistence does not mean that the students are going to abandon their *Din*, their beliefs or their convictions. Nor does it mean the eradication of conflicts, but rather a step towards dialogue from the moment that one becomes conscious of the need to regulate and manage problems (or conflicts) that arise with the other:

> "Well, I don't mind that they have a different religion. What is important is that we are people and we have to coexist. We have the same heart, we are equals. We are equal but different, we have different religions and that is good, because I didn't force them to be in my religion. And they can't force me to be in their religion. We have to respect each other" (Interv-Student-fe13).

4.3.2 Interculturality

One of the goals reflected in most IRE classes involves promoting processes of interculturality between students. This aspect is rather abstract, seen from the perspective of pedagogy, since it means approaching cultural diversity both on the institutional level and the relational level (García Martínez 2007) (between students in the classroom and in school). Likewise, it can lead to pedagogical reductionism from the moment that cultural diversity is essentialised from the other. However, this study mainly found that, until recently, the longed for and supposed intercultural processes have not taken place in mono-cultural/mono-confessional schools. Indeed, most of the examples observed at this time required leaving behind the classroom or the school during its formal hours so that students can use examples based on daily life. When the knowledge of the other has been consolidated and the values and examples needed for this desired interculturality are inculcated, the student can return to the classroom. In this respect, it seems that, for now, the classroom is not the best place to develop this objective.

However, it is possible to find exceptional cases where the existence of interpersonal relationships has made mutual knowledge and appreciation of the other possible. One example can be seen in Melilla[29], through a study of the different religious holidays and celebrations that take place in the city, starting in the classroom, but without forgetting the external context. The students reflect on and study Ramadan (the end of the fasting period)[30], Hanukkah, Christmas (Christmas Eve), etc., and the events are used to provide a set of practical information to the students which they would otherwise find rather difficult or boring:

> *"Four years ago, I started working in a little school in Melilla called Hipódromo [...] There was a Jew, two Christians, twenty-six Muslims and two kids from mixed families in my class ... There are a lot of religious holidays, but all of them have a common denominator [...] We began working with Hanukkah, which came first and then, with the children, we started to look for points in common. It went very well and Christmas and Ramadan came and we prepared for the end of the fasting period and began to study as well in class, looking for information and whatnot. We also began to study the days within the month of Ramadan and ended up with the end of the fasting period. With the focus that we wanted, we did a kind of religious retreat, inviting parents, teachers and children. An area in the classroom was set up for praying and Abdelazis led the prayers. We also ate dates [...] and ate harira soup afterwards and all of this was explained. When Christmas came, we celebrated that and the parents helped, we all worked. Because Muslim children also study Christmas: what do Christmas Eve and Christmas night symbolise?"* (Interv-Teacher-ma44).

This aspect raises the need to consider learning strategies tied to the different (inter-)group interaction dynamics and procedures in which the desired communication takes place. Here, the intervention and mediation of the teaching staff, as well as the rest of the social agents involved, is very important.

---

29 It is estimated that approximately 56% of the population in Melilla is Catholic, 40% are Muslim and the rest of the population is made up of Jewish and Hindu minorities (Ministry of Education and Science 2006/2007). For more details, cf. Rosón & Alvarez 2009.
30 "The Ramadan contest awards students from the four denominations. 'I have a lot of friends who do Ramadan and want to talk about what this custom consists of'". (El Faro Digital, 08/11/2008). This is a contest that has been held in Ceuta since 2003 in which students from different schools produce drawings and essays about this rite.

4.3.3 Non-discrimination and the inclusion of the 'other' in daily practice

There is another set of case studies that convey the important role which the educational system plays, in relation to IRE classes, in achieving a desired encounter between 'minorities and majorities', i.e., collaborating in the fight against racism and xenophobia and, of course, against any type of discrimination. Clear examples can be seen in those activities that take place in the classroom which are focused on non-discrimination, both on a religious and relational level (between peer groups).

Regarding religion, the aspect most often noted by teachers is the attempt to promote respect and tolerance towards the different Prophets, insofar as respectful knowledge of different aspects of another person's religion reduces problems of discrimination:

> "We always talk about not doing ... not discriminating for example, when we take up the topic of the Prophets since we are dealing with different prophets, with Abraham and David and Jesus Christ, and the Holy Books as well, with respect and tolerance towards others" (Interv-Teacher-ma42).

Similarly, there is a set of values which teachers try to inculcate in students from a religious perspective, such as being respectful when speaking of Catholicism, since there are points in common that must be valued from the Muslim point of view. This is the case with the Virgin Mary, monotheism (the concept of God for Catholics and Allah for Muslims), the Bible, Jesus as a prophet who is similar in rank to Mohammed, etc. Although this inclusive analysis of the other is always done on the basis of the student's own religion, i.e., from the Islamic point of view, it constitutes positive knowledge assimilated by the student when he or she, on the basis of prior knowledge, is encouraged to engage in a dialogue about religion with students of different creeds.

With respect to the type of relationships between equals, one of the wishes expressed by teachers is that the students in their classes learn and put into practice the value of tolerance and love for their fellow men:

> "This is inculcating values, tolerance, respect, love for your neighbour, especially tolerance and love for your neighbour, regardless of whether they are different, that they don't think like you, you have to tolerate this and ask them to tolerate you. I try to focus religion from this point of view" (Interv-Teacher-fe40).

Similarly, values of "coexistence with the neighbour related to positive morality: not stealing, searching after an honest life, being kind to elders, the family, etc." are encouraged (Interv-Teacher-ma42). These aspects are a part of all religions, and they promote values for coexistence:

> "How can religions help people coexist? Well, the fact is that they are giving children values, their religion teaches them values every day. I, personally, think that all religions have positive values. Someone in another religion can see them and accept them and I think that helps coexistence, that they don't have to label them as Muslim or Christian, that they are first and foremost people who profess a religion, very good! [...] Religion should encourage values of coexistence, to

respect and especially know your neighbour. I don't think this is or should be a source of conflict" (Interv-Teacher-ma40).

4.3.4 Reaffirming one's identity

Islam, as expressed by Muslims, is much more than a religion. It is a way of life and constitutes one of the most important markers of identity both for immigrants coming from mainly Islamic countries and for those born (or who have converted) in Spain. In this respect, IRE classes reaffirm this Islamic identity in several ways. On the one hand, the separation of the students into different classes for religion confirms the differences between the different believers and, in turn, the non-believers. This contributes to the construction of a differentiated identity, based both on the separation of spaces (each group goes to a different classroom) and of the material studied. This reinforcement of identity does not have to be constructed as discriminatory in a multicultural society (it is the contents and interrelationships between groups that create discrimination). On the other hand, IRE classes can serve as a reinforcement for intercultural activities, insofar as they are a clear demonstration of respect and the coexistence of different belief systems and religious practices, when the time comes to reinforce the hallmarks of identity for each one.

However, it is necessary to point out that not all of the examples obtained in the fieldwork were completely positive. This is due to the processes of 'essentialisation' and in some cases stigmatisation which, regardless of the religion professed, are argued and defended out of the mutual ignorance of the different groups.

Here it is important to note the general ignorance regarding what Islam is (practice and dogma) among non-Muslims, who attribute stereotypes and prejudices derived from the social-historical context of the past to them:

> *"People don't know a lot of things, they don't know their side. If they don't know their side they're going to know ours even less. So, there's a lot of ignorance. But ok, a lot of ignorance, maybe the way of asking about it isn't the best. But when you start to talk and you answer them – they listen to you. I realised that they listen. Maybe they don't understand what you're explaining and all, but at least they listen – oh, maybe it's that I didn't know and whatnot. But there is a total ignorance about Islam. But that is also our fault, I mean, a bit of it is our fault. Because most Muslims don't mix with others. That's true"* (Interv-Parents-fe35).

This ignorance and essentialism can be experienced by Muslims as a symbolic aggression which leads them to counteract it, intensifying their Muslim identity, both in practice and in their hallmarks of identity.

In turn, on the other hand, there is widespread ignorance among Muslims relating to the religion of the other. This, in the cultural framework in which it occurs, creates conflicts which can lead, on the one hand, to certain tensions between a feeling of belonging to the country of origin and a feeling of belonging to the host country (Elbaz and Helly, 1996:87):

> "it is so simple, we're in Spain and the religion there is Catholic. It's normal that they don't give classes on Islamic religion, just like in Arab countries they don't teach Catholicism" (Interv-Student-fe22).

And other cases reveal a disdain towards non-Muslims:

> "It's just that ... how can you respect people who dress up dolls and drag them out onto the street ... they are polytheists, and that is highly forbidden ... my grandfather says that that's why they'll never go to Paradise" (Interv-Student-ma11). "Uggh ... the things that ... Christians ... can't you see that these things are bad for you, like alcohol, tobacco, pork, which also has a lot of cholesterol, that they're bad and we, I don't know, for us it's not good to eat that because it's bad for your health. And they also adore dolls, which doesn't make sense to me. And to say that God had a son, I don't see the logic. There. And it's like they don't have limits or ... they don't do anything but live life and they don't think that we are going to die and after we die, there's another life. Well, it's like that" (Interv-Student-fe17).

These cultural 'misunderstandings' which create the need to reaffirm identity on the part of both sides can, in the long run, produce intransigent positions within peer groups that look down on or demonise the religion of the other:

> "I haven't had many experiences, but those that have occurred, the racism of some of my classmates when I was really little, insulting me and my religion and my God and everything that I believe [Allah]" (Interv-Student-fe14).

This, in short, is one of the greatest challenges facing both schools and religion classes, including IRE: to produce mutual respect based on the knowledge of oneself and the other which, in turn, can construct multiple identities capable of coexisting without becoming conflictive.

5. Concluding remarks

When we talk about religious education in contemporary school, in the majority of cases we think of the Catholic religion, due to its long tradition. However, other religious minorities also exist – among them the Muslims – whose presence is more and more visible, both in the religious and the educational landscape of contemporary Spain.

It could be observed that an approach to Islamic religious education needs a better contextualisation. It is essential to reflect on pre-established regulations and jurisprudence in and by the state, on whose educational framework the development of Islamic religion classes specifically depends. This, in turn, should be complemented with observable data of social reality, which means listening to the individuals involved in the educational process – parents, children, professors, religious leaders etc., who have gone unnoticed for scientific community and political managers. This would be the only way to understand the "ambivalent" practice which, in fact, is carried out in the Spanish educational system. Despite the Islamic religion having, in theory, the same legislative force with equal rights as other religious minorities, in daily reality we can observe contrasts in its implementation, social perception etc.

In the case of Islamic religion there are various elements at play. On the one hand, there is a lack of dialogue between the Muslim authorities. On the other hand, there is also a certain idleness of the competent state and autonomous institutions in applying current legislation, and they often only react when there is a strong and explicit demand in a determined place; meanwhile, religious pluralism is only exercised on paper.

Such lack of common parameters implies the significant differences between minority confessions (Tarrés & Rosón, 2009), as well as uneven availability of professors, provision of training, or existing didactic material suitable for students.

All this contributes to situations of restlessness and, to a great extent, to an inability of all social agents involved in it to manage both the religious pluralism and the seemingly isolated conflicts. ranging from the lightest *praxis* to the proper legal use. That is to say, ranging from: 'What should I do to give my children Islamic religious education?', to: 'What should be done when religion is becoming explicit through religious symbols in the classroom?', or: 'What should be done when the tendency of a part of the society defines its position, questions the fundaments of a "traditionalist point of view" or existence/non-existence of any religion in the educational space?'

The attitudes toward religious diversity, as well as those towards religious education, which are held in society still reflect the historical divisions, fears, phobias and conflicts which prevent young people or future generations of citizens from fulfilling the opportunities offered by interreligious or even intercultural dialogue. In this sense, both laïcists and Catholic mono-confessionalists share an essentialist notion of religion which equals it with culture, language and even nationality.

Such is the essentialism which "avoids and detests 'blending', 'blurring the borders'" (Dietz et al., 2008) or hybridizing identities and religious practices as a point of departure from which we could overcome the everlasting dichotomy between confessionalism and laïcism. Only by overcoming this ethnocentric essentialism we will manage to "deal" with the future diversity and heterogeneity in terms of religion, ethics and culture.

References

Alvarez Veinguer, A. & Rosón Lorente, F. J. (2009) Pupils, Teachers and Researchers: Thinking from Double Hermeneutics – An Ethnographic Approach to a Triadic Methodology, in: Avest, I. ter, Jozsa, D.-P., Knauth, T., Rosón, J. & Skeie, G. (Eds.) *Dialogue and Conflict on Religion. Studies of Classroom Interaction in European Countries* (Münster, Waxmann), 225-245.
Cornelius, W. A. (2004) Spain: The Uneasy Transition from Labor Exporter to Labor Importer., in Cornelius, W. A., Martin, P. L. & Hollifield, J. F. (Eds.) *Controlling immigration: a global perspective* (Stanford, Stanford University Press), 385-428.
Dietz, G. (2007) Invisibilizing or Ethnicizing Religious Diversity? The Transition of Religious Education Towards Pluralism in Contemporary Spain, in: Jackson, R., Miedema, S., Weisse, W. & Willaime, J.-P. (Eds.) *Religion and Education in Europe. Developments, Contexts and Debates* (Münster, Waxmann), 103-132.
Dietz, G., Rosón Lorente, J. & Ruiz Garzón, F. (2008) Religion and Education in the View of Spanish Youth: the legacy of mono-confessionalism in times of reli-

gious pluralisation, in: Knauth, T., Jozsa, D.-P., Bertram-Troost, G. & Ipgrave, J. (Eds.) *Encountering Religious Pluralism in School and Society: a qualitative study of teenage perspectives in Europe* (Münster, Waxmann), 21-49

Elbaz, M. & D. Helly (1995) Modernidad y postmodernidad de las identidades nacionales. *Revista Internacional de Filosofía Política* 7, 72-92

Escudero, M. (2006) El Islam, Hoy, en España: El Resurgir de una Esperanza, in: Ministerio de Justicia (2006) *La nueva realidad religiosa española: 25 años de la Ley orgánica de libertad religiosa* (Madrid, Ministerio de Justicia), 159-196.

García Castaño, F. J. (2001) Algunos datos aproximativos a la presencia de extranjeros en España, Andalucía y Granada, in: F. J. García Castaño (Ed.) *Inmigración Extranjera en Granada* (Granada, Ayuntamiento de Granada), 41-56.

García Martínez, A. et al. (2007) *La interculturalidad: desafío para la educación* (Madrid, Dykinson).

Gasol, B. (2005) Cultura religiosa a l'escola. El cas de Catalunya, in: Forteza González, M. & Gómez Segalà, J. (Eds.) *Cultura religiosa a l'escola* (Barcelona, Generalitat de Catalunya), 17-20.

Gil Araujo, S. (2004) *Documento de trabajo: Inmigración latinoamericana en España. Estado de la cuestión* (Alcalá de Henares & Miami, Instituto Universitario de Estudios Norteamericanos de la Universidad de Alcalá & International Florida University).

González Barea, E. (2007) *Estudiantes marroquíes en España: educación universitaria y migraciones* (Sevilla, Editorial Doble J).

Izquierdo Escribano, A. (1992) *La inmigración en España. 1980-1990* (Madrid, Trotta).

Jiménez-Aybar, I. (2004) *El Islam en España. Aspectos institucionales de su estatuto jurídico* (Pamplona, Navarra Gráfica Ediciones).

Knauth, T., Jozsa, D.-P., Bertram-Troost, G. & Ipgrave, J. (Eds.) (2008) *Encountering Religious Pluralism in School and Society – A Qualitative Study of Teenage Perspectives in Europe* (Münster, Waxmann).

López García, B. (Ed.) (1996) *Atlas de la inmigración magrebí en España* (Madrid, Ministerio de Asuntos Sociales-Universidad Autónoma de Madrid-Taller de Estudios Internacionales Mediterráneos).

López García, B. & Berriane, M. (Eds.) (2004) *Atlas de la inmigración marroquí en España* (Madrid, Ministerio de Trabajo y Asuntos Sociales-Universidad Autónoma de Madrid-Taller de Estudios Internacionales Mediterráneos).

Lorenzo, P. & Peña, M.T. (2004) La enseñanza religiosa islámica, in: Motilla, A. (Ed.) *Los musulmanes en España* (Madrid, Trotta), 249-279.

Martín Muñoz, G. (Ed.) (2003) *Marroquíes en España. Estudio sobre su integración* (Madrid, Fundación Repsol YPF).

Mijares, L. (2006) *Aprendiendo a ser marroquíes. Inmigración, diversidad lingüística y escuela* (Madrid, Ediciones del Oriente y del Mediterráneo).

Moreras, J. (2005) La situation de l'enseignement musulman en Espagne, in: Willaime, J.-P. (Ed.) *Des Maîtres et des Dieux: écoles et religions en Europe* (Paris, Belin), 165-179.

Planet, A. I. (2008) Islam e inmigración: elementos para un análisis y propuestas de gestión, in: Planet, A. I. & Moreras, J. (Eds.) *Islam e Inmigración* (Madrid, Centro de Estudios Políticos y Constitucionales), 9-52.

Rodríguez, M. (2005) La enseñanza de la religión en la escuela pública española 1979-2005, in: *Observatorio delle libertà ed istituzioni religiose*. Available on-line: www.olir.it.

Rosón Lorente, F. J. (2008) *¿El retorno de Tariq? Comunidades etnoreligiosas en el Albayzín granadino (Tesis doctoral)* (Granada, Departamento de Antropología Social; Universidad de Granada).
Rosón Lorente, F. J. & Alvarez Veinguer, A. (2009) Spanish youth facing religious diversity at school – findings from a quantitative study, in: Valk, P., Bertram-Troost, G., Friederici, M. & Beraud, C. (Eds.) *Teenagers' Perspectives on the Role of Religion in their Lives, Schools and Societies – A European Quatitative Study* (Münster, Waxmann), 357-388.
Tarrés, S. (2006) "Inmigrantes extranjeros asentados en Andalucía. La religión como estrategia de adaptación de una comunidad magrebí de Sevilla, in: Junta de Andalucía, Consejería de Cultura (Ed.) (2006) *Anuario Etnológico de Andalucía, 2002-2003* (Sevilla, Junta de Andalucía, Consejería de Cultura), 385-409
Tarrés, S. et al. (2007) *Pluralismo religioso e inmigración: la enseñanza de la religión en la escuela, el caso de Andalucía*, paper presented at IV Congreso sobre las migraciones en España, Valencia.
Tarrés, S. & Rosón, J. (2009) La enseñanza de las religiones minoritarias en la escuela. Análisis del caso de Andalucía (Minority religions Entering Mainstream Schools: The Case of andalusia), *'Ilu, Revista de Ciencias de las religiones*, nº 14, 83-98
Tatary Bakry, R. (1995) Libertad religiosa y acuerdo de cooperación del estado español con la comisión islámica de España, in: Abumalham, M. (Ed.) *Comunidades islámicas en Europa* (Madrid, Trotta), 165-172
Trujillo, F. (2008) Plurilingüismo en el aula: las lenguas de los estudiantes, in:.Actas de las I Jornadas sobre Lenguas, Curriculo y alumnado inmigrante. Universidad de Deusto, Bilbao, 61-70. Available online at: http://www.segundas lenguaseinmigracion.es/ense_ anzal2/Trujillojornadas.pdf.

Acronyms used

- (Interv-Leader-[female/male]age). Religious Leader's interview.
- (Interv-Teacher-[female/male]age). Religious Education Teacher's interview.
- (Interv-Parents-[female/male]age). Parents' interview.
- (Interv-Student-[female/male]age). Pupil's interview.
- **ELCO:** Teaching the Language and Culture of Origin. Enseñanza de la Lengua y Cultura de Origen.
- **FCJE:** Federation of Hebrew Communities in Spain. Federación de Comunidades Judías de España.
- **FEERI:** Spanish Federation of Islamic Religious Entities. Federación Española de Entidades Religiosas Islámicas.
- **FEREDE:** Federation of Evangelical Religious Entities of Spain. Federación de Entidades Religiosas Evangélicas de España.
- **IRE:** Islamic Religious Education.
- **LOE:** Organic Law on Education. Ley Orgánica de Educación.
- **LOGSE:** Law on the General Organisation of the Educational System. Ley Orgánica General del Sistema Educativo.
- **LOLR:** Organic Law on Religious Freedom. Ley Orgánica de Libertad Religiosa.
- **UCIDE:** Union of Islamic Communities of Spain. Unión de Comunidades Islámicas de España.
- **UNED:** National Distance Education University. Universidad Nacional de Educación a Distancia.

Anna van den Kerchove

Islam within the Framework of "Laïcité"
Islam and Education in France

1. Introduction

The issue of Islam's relationship to education is a difficult one because it assumes the past and present relation between Europe and Islam; it is also a pressing one, especially since September 11th 2001. France does not escape this comment, and many books about Islam and Education have been written since the 1990s, most of which are intended to give advice and cultural information to the teachers. This paper is written with the same intent as these books, although perhaps with the new impulse of the REDCo project. Indeed, two perspectives are adopted here. The first one is that of the Muslim teenagers themselves, investigated through the quantitative and qualitative enquiries made by the French team of the REDCo project during 2006-2008, in different schools throughout France. For the first time, we have an insight into the thoughts of teenagers aged 15-16, and in particular those of Muslim teenagers. The second one is the perspective of the teachers, and their views on how they can and should teach Islam in classrooms; here, we have to stress that the English translation does not convey all the subtleties of the French language: indeed, the French language distinguishes between "*i*slam" and "*I*slam", the first being the term for the religion, the second for the civilization. Before dealing with each perspective in turn, a brief overview of the history of Islam in France and in the French education system is needed in order to understand better the rest of the paper.

2. A brief overview of Islam and Muslims in France

2.1 Short survey of the relationship between Islam and France[1]

From the beginnings of the spread of Islam in the 8th century, the south of what is present-day France has been in contact with Muslims. Since that time, the French kingdom has been in touch with the Muslim world, through wars as well as through cultural and commercial exchanges. Few Muslims lived in France then, and when Napoleon I. established the system of the "recognised cults" (*cultes reconnus*) with the 1801 Concordat and the 1802 Organic Articles, three '*cultes*' were mentioned: the Catholic (which was no longer recognised as the state religion but as the religion of the majority of the French population), the Protestant, and the Israelite. No mention was made of Islam.

Because of the French colonial conquests after 1830, especially that of North Africa, France ruled over many Muslims, and French colonial policy was con-

---

[1] For more details, see Billon (2003, 109-115).

fronted with the issue of Islam. It oscillated between repression, with the governor-general of Algeria Thomas-Robert Bugeaud (1784-1849), whose conquest of Algeria was very harsh, with destruction of villages, and respect and admiration, as with Louis Lyautey (1854-1934). The latter thought that the Europeans were not welcome. Trying to soften the French presence, he recommended the preservation of the privacy of the Muslim religion.

In 1905, the Third Republic enacted the law on the Separation of the 'Churches' (Catholic, Protestant and Jewish) and the State, establishing the so-called "laïcité". Since then, the French Republic does not recognise the religions nor subsidize them; rather it ensures the freedom of religion and religious practices.[2] As what are now the Alsatian and Moselle *départements* were at that time part of the German Empire, the 1905 law did not apply there and it still does not. Neither did it apply in the French colonies at that time, such as North Africa. After the First World War, in order to honour the Muslims who had died for France during the war, the French government took some liberties with the law; it created a Muslim institute and funded the Great Mosque of Paris.

However, the French Republic had already forgotten its strong relationship with Islam before the Second World War. This attitude is clearly attested by the way it saw the massive Muslim immigration after the 1950s. As was the case in the rest of Europe, France invited legal workers during the "Glorious Thirty" years, up until the beginning of the seventies; most of them came from the former French colonies, and from the newly independent Maghreb. They were perceived by the French government, as well as by the population, as temporary workers only, and not as Muslims. With the economic crisis in the seventies, immigration was limited to family reunion. Since the eighties there has been a rise in illegal immigration and in the number of political refugees. The new immigrants were urban and literate. The number of regularisation was increasing. At the same time there were several crises involving Muslims in France and in the wider world: 1) the long conflict from 1975 to 1980 where immigrants reacted against the direction of Sonacotra[3] because of rent increases; 2) the denunciation by the French Prime Minister Pierre Mauroy of the influence of Muslim extremists in the 1983 Renault strike; 3) Ayatollah Khomeini's political take-over in Iran 1979; 4) the increase in hostage taking throughout the world. Islam thus emerged into the open, mostly for negative reasons. Consequently the perception of the Muslims changed. Since then, there have been more and more publications and television programs about Islam, mostly with alarmist connotations. The Islamization movement, particularly that among young Muslims born in France, is viewed through the prism of fundamentalism, and the question of the capacity of Muslims to integrate within the French society

---

2   1905 Law, article 1: "The Republic assures the freedom of conscience. It guarantees the free exercise of the religions (*cultes*) under the only limitations promulgated below, in the interests of law and order"; article 2: "the Republic neither recognises, nor provides a salary nor subsidizes any religion (*culte*)".
3   Sonacotra, "Société nationale de construction de logements pour les travailleurs" now named Adoma, was established in 1956 in order to remedy the problem of the insalubrious housing of the Algerian immigrants. Since the beginning of the seventies, conflicts have increased because of the rapid decay of the accommodations and because the residents did not have the status of tenants.

and "laïcité" is regularly debated. Islam is also regularly accused of having inherent flaws.[4]

2.2 The organization of Muslims in France

The number of French Muslims has increased since the seventies. They are split into different movements and every previous attempt to form a federation was in vain, until the French Government decided to act directly. The first political intervention was that of Pierre Joxe, then Home Secretary, when he established the Reflection Council about Islam of France (Corif) in 1990. This was unsuccessful but it inaugurated a governmental action which followed the same line, whatever the political party in power. Indeed, the government became aware that anarchy was viewed just as negatively by Muslims as by the public authorities.

In 1997, under Lionel Jospin, the government took more direct action: a consultation with French Muslims was set up with the help of the state, which organised the logistics and guaranteed impartiality and transparency. The consultation had three objectives: the insertion of Islam into the French religious landscape; the establishment of a representative authority for the Muslim religion; and the solving of some old problems such as the practice of the Muslim religion and the construction of new mosques. The first objective was attained in January 2000 with the text *Principes et fondements juridiques régissant les rapports entre les pouvoirs publics et le culte musulman en France*; the Muslim religion now shares the same legal status as the other religions, within the framework of the "laïcité" established by the 1905 law. The second objective was attained with the *Accord-cadre sur l'organisation future du culte musulman en France* in 2001 and, despite a short polemic due to the events of September 11th, so was the creation of an association, the CFCM (French Council of the Muslim religion), which was first elected in 2003 (and thereafter every two years). The current president, elected in June 2008, is Mohammed Moussaoui, a Mathematics lecturer at Avignon University (in the South of France). This Council, whose main task is to unite the different Islamic currents, is a forum for debate, and it seeks to tackle the following issues: the construction of mosques, the organisation of religious celebrations, the nomination of chaplains in hospitals, prisons and secondary schools,[5] the training of imams, etc. However, the CFCM is a contested organisation, and some claim that it is a political rather than a religious one, and that it is therefore not representative of all French Muslims.[6]

---

4 The bibliography on the subject is abundant. Here is only a selection: Kaltenbach & Tribalat (2002); Etienne (2004); Roy (2005); Vaïsse, Laurence, Roy & Dreyfus (2007).
5 The 1905 law authorizes the different religions to have chaplains in establishments such as secondary schools, prisons, hospitals. Cf. the 1905 law, article 2: "the Republic neither recognises, nor puts on a salary nor subsidizes any religion. (...) However, budgets for expenses relative to the services of chaplaincy can be registered to the state and intended to assure the free exercise of the religions in public institutions such as upper schools, middle schools, primary schools, homes, asylums, and prisons."
6 Its legitimacy is also sometimes contested by some Muslims and its powers are not so great as some Muslims would have imagined.

2.3 The Socio-demographic situation of French Muslims

France is the European state with the largest number of Muslims, with about 4-5 millions Muslims from a population of 62 millions, representing about 6-8%. Islam is therefore the second religion in France, after Catholicism. However, this number alone does not mean much because it is only an estimate[7] and it has to be correlated with other items, such as the distinction between practising and non practising Muslims, the number of mixed couples, converts, etc.

The majority of French Muslims originate from North Africa and 49% are less than thirty years old. More than a third of them (38%) live in the Parisian suburbs, particularly in the Seine-Saint-Denis *département*, and 13% live in the Marseilles-region. Although most of the Muslims are urban, almost all rural *départements* have a Muslim community and at least one place of prayer[8].

At first, many lived near their place of work. Following the urban renovation and the rehabilitation of town centres since the 1960s, the poor population, many of which are Muslims, had to live in the suburbs. These are now often immigrant districts, and many of them are Muslim districts.

The Muslim presence is now an everyday fact of life, and two thirds of them are French. Despite these two facts there is still a degree of fear among other sectors of the population. There are many misconceptions and misunderstandings about Islam in the population overall, as well as among pupils. Two misconceptions in particular are worth highlighting. 1) Generally, people perceive Islam as a religion which is situated in tradition and opposed to modernity; this point of view is very important in France because of the colonial past when Islam was conceived as a resistance to modernisation.[9] 2) People also perceive Islam as one religious entity and not as plural and diverse, thus reducing Islam to a fundamentalist discourse.

2.4 Islam in education

Because of "laïcité", as is the case for other religions, there are no specific lessons dedicated to Islam as a religion.[10] The Alsatian and Moselle *départements* are the exceptions to this: as these *départements* are still under the 1801 Concordat, they still have religious education in primary and secondary schools, which nowadays is a cultural and religious education rather than catechism. This religious education is not compulsory. However, this does not concern Islam because this religion has not obtained the statute of "recognised cult" yet, as is the case for the Catholic,

---

7 It is illegal for the French government and its various departments to include religious categories in its statistics. The statistics related to religious categories come from polling groups and cause controversy, especially with regards to the percentage of Muslims. The researchers seem to agree with a number of around 5 millions Muslims in France. However, they generally admit that Islam is the second religion in France. See *L'atlas* (2007, 124-125); for the problem of number: Kaltenbach & Tribalat (2002).
8 Cf. *L'atlas* (2007, 125).
9 See Guénif-Souilamas (2003, 97).
10 For more details on the French context, cf. Willaime (2007, 60-69) and Borne (2007, 97-100).

Lutheran, Calvinist and Jewish religions, even if, in 2006, some voices proposed the inclusion of the Muslim religion in the statute.

In order to find Muslim religious education, which is not compulsory, it is necessary to go to Muslim private schools. Indeed, French education is divided between state schools (for more than 80% of the pupils) and private schools. Most of the private schools have a "contract of association" with the state, a possibility allowed by the 1959 Debré law. The Debré law regulates the relationship between the private school and the state: the state pays the teachers; the private school has to respect the official instructions concerning education, and the teachers should have qualifications. The contract may be signed between the school and the state after at least five years of functioning. It is an advantage for the school: the fees to enter the school are low, since the state pays the teachers. There are only four Muslim private schools for the time being and they are very recent. The first one is the Medersa Taalim oul-Islam primary school in Saint-Denis in the Réunion Island, under an association contract with the state since 1990. There are three secondary schools: one is a middle school, "Collège Réussite", in Aubervilliers (north-east suburbs of Paris) which opened in 2001 but which has not yet obtained a contract. In 2003, the first private Muslim upper school opened in Lille: the "Lycée Averroès", which signed the association contract in June 2008. Another upper school opened in March 2007, the al-Kindi Lycée, in Décines, near Lyon. Because there are so few Muslim schools, it was not possible to do enquiries in these schools at the time of the REDCo project, while enquiries were made in some Catholic and Jewish private schools.[11]

However, even if Muslims pupils are in these four private schools, they do not only hear about Islam in religious education. Indeed these schools have to respect the national program, the same as in the state schools. This program is under the supervision of the state. The French Republic has made the choice to teach about religions within the framework of already existing school subjects: History, Civic Education, French and Foreign Languages as well as Arts[12]. History is the subject where pupils hear the most about Islam. Because of the REDCo project, we will focus only on the secondary school curricula. Islam is mostly present in the second level of the middle school ("cinquième": twelve/thirteen year old pupils) and the first level of the upper school ("seconde": fifteen/sixteen year old pupils). The new official instructions for the second level will be applicable in September 2010. Like the former instructions, they focus on the origins of Islam ("islam" in the French language), with an emphasis on the cultural and historical context of Mohammed and the Qur'an and Hadith texts, as well as on the cultural and religious diversity of Islam ("Islam" in the French language). Islam is also dealt with when teachers have to cover the *Reconquista*, the crusades, and Africa between the eighth and sixteenth centuries. In the first-level of upper school, Islam is dealt with in the chapter dedicated to "The Mediterranean during the twelfth century: Crossroads of three civilisations"; the main idea is to bring into light the diversity of exchanges

---

11 For these specific enquiries, see Willaime & Béraud (forthcoming).
12 For a general overview, Borne (2007, 100-112), Saint-Martin (2007, 139-172).

between the Catholic, Byzantine and Muslim worlds. In the other levels of secondary school some time is also dedicated to speaking about Islam.[13]

It is noticeable that more space is given to the study of Islam in the past than to the present. If the diversity of Islam and the impact of Islam in European history are covered, more can be done. However, one should say that the curricula are very short texts. The educational authorities are increasingly aware of the shortcomings of the curricula, and they complement them with other educational tools. We will speak about them latter. Moreover, one cannot compare the quantity of "religious stuff" in the French curricula to that in other European countries where one hour a week is dedicated to Religious Education.

3. Empirical findings related to Muslims teenagers

3.1 Comments about the quantitative study

For the quantitative study of the French team, 851 questionnaires were completed in 18 schools throughout the country.[14] One of two teenagers declares membership of a religious community, and 24% of them claim that they are Muslims. Muslims teenagers are thus over-represented in our sample in comparison with the national average (6-8%). The French team makes the assumption that this over-representation could be associated with an equally higher proportion of students of immigrant origin.[15]

As far as the different regions in the sample are concerned, there is also an over-representation of Paris and its suburbs.

Table 1:   Geographical classification

	Complete sample		Muslims	
Region	Frequency	Percent	Frequency	Percent
Paris Region	238	28	64	58.2
Northeast	71	8.3	9	8.2
Southeast	163	19.2	23	20.9
Northwest	220	25.9	8	7.3
Southwest	159	18.7	6	5.5
Total	851	100	110	100

95% of the Muslims teenagers are in state schools. As the only private schools represented in the sample are Catholic, the 5% of Muslims who attend a private school therefore go to a Catholic one. Indeed, there are only four private Muslim

---

13   Particularly during the last year of middle-school, when teaching the cultural changes that have taken place in France since 1945.
14   For the methodology used, and for more comments regarding the sample, see Béraud, Massignon, Mathieu & Willaime (2009, 132-135).
15   See Béraud, Massignon, Mathieu & Willaime (2009, 134).

schools in the whole of France. The choice of a private Catholic school rather than a state school is mainly due to the perception of the higher scholarly standards of this type of school; parents who wish the best for their children will often send them to a private school. For some Muslims, the choice can also be due to the fact that Catholic schools allow students to wear visible religious signs, such as the hijab for the girls.

Before presenting the results, I would like to make one comment on the reactions.[16] Only one headmistress did not allow the enquiry to take place in her school: she feared that the questions about religious symbols would give rise to a debate and that she would have some difficulty to control it. She obviously had in mind the fact that her school had an important proportion of Muslim pupils.

The results of the survey are rich and informative, and I will focus on three topics only: the religious involvement, the position regarding the principle of "laïcité", and the interaction between Muslims and non-Muslims. These topics have been chosen in relation to the general perception of Muslims in the wider society.

3.2 Religious involvement

Although "religion is not one of the main concerns of French students" there is, however, a connection between teenagers' beliefs and their religious background.[17] This statement is particularly true for the Muslim teenagers. 87% of them consider religion to be important, and think about it at least once a week, while 68% think of it every day. This is more than for teenagers from other religious backgrounds / worldviews, and more than for teenagers in general. This positive conception of religion in general implies a strong religious involvement. 57% of Muslims consider that religion determines their way of life, whereas only 15% of Christians agree with this statement; it is coherent with the fact that 91% of Muslims disagree with the item that religion is nonsense. This involvement goes beyond simply thinking and speaking about religion. Muslim students are also more involved in religious practices than the students in general, and more than those with a different religious background. They read more sacred texts (36% at least once a month, whereas only 9% of Christians do so, and no student from other religious backgrounds do); 48% of them pray every day, while only 14% of students and 15% of Christians pray every day. However, one can notice that whereas 26% of Christians never go to a religious service, 45% of Muslims never go, which is the same percentage as for the complete sample.[18] This can be explained by the fact that it is more difficult for Muslims teenagers to go to Friday prayers, with it being a work day, than it is for Christians to attend church on Sundays. All schools with Muslims

---

16 For the general presentation of the comments and reactions, I refer to Béraud et al. (2009, 135-137).
17 Cf. Béraud et al. (2009, 137-138).
18 We can compare these percentages with the percentages given by the "Society's analysis center" (Centre d'analyse de la société) in relation to the religious practices of French Muslims as a whole: 88% observe the fast during Ramadan; 43% pray five times a day; 20% read the Koran once a week; and 17% go to the mosque at least once a week. Cf. L'atlas (2007, 125).

have a high degree of absenteeism in the school canteen during Ramadan and in the class during Eid[19].

3.3 Position regarding the principle of "laïcité"

Islam is generally perceived as being opposed to the principle of "laïcité". When people think this principle is in danger, they think that the threat comes from Muslim pupils. The over-representation in the media of some cases involving young Muslims confirms this negative perception. Moreover, one cannot ignore the negative impact of international tensions involving Muslim states. From the point of view of the Muslim teenagers, the regulations of "laïcité" can be perceived as partisan: in the school canteen, the absence of meat on Friday compared to the absence of Halal meat in general; the fact that Roman Catholic feasts are official holidays while none of the Muslim feasts are. Although non-Muslim teenagers have generally lost sight of the religious meaning of these customs, some Muslims consider them as demonstrating a sort of inequality.[20] In this context, it is interesting to study how Muslim teenagers deal with the principle of "laïcité". This study will be conducted through looking at the statements regarding the different manners in which religion could appear at school.

84% of Muslims think that "at school meals, religious food requirements should be taken into account" and 87% think that "students can be absent from school when it is their religious festival". By comparison, regardless of religious background / worldview, 65% (58% of teenagers with no religious background) agree with the first statement and 63% (40% of teenagers with no religious background) with the second one. In each case, there is a major agreement with the two statements but for Muslims the agreement is more pronounced (accordingly, the disagreement is also less pronounced: for the first statement only 5% of Muslims disagreed, compared to 20% of teenagers with a religious background and 27% of teenagers with no religious background). The Muslims might have in mind the absence of Halal meat, the lack of choice when there is pork on the menu in the school canteen, and the fact that the main Muslim feasts are not official holidays unlike the Christian ones; this is considered as an injustice. In some schools, many Muslim parents ask for Halal meat and for more choice when pork is on offer. Over the past few years, schools have taken these requests into account. Furthermore, there is also an official recommendation to pay attention to this question, providing that the principle of "laïcité" is respected, i.e. that the school does not propose only Halal meat or only pork meat. Moreover, when it comes to the absenteeism of Muslims during their religious feasts, there is in general a tacit tolerance: the teachers generally tend not schedule examinations on these days and they do not penalise the missing pupils, only ask them to make up the lesson.

With regards to wearing discrete religious symbols, the Muslim teenagers do not distinguish themselves from other teenagers: 80% of Muslims agree with the statement "the students should be able to wear discrete religious symbols at

---

19 This data comes from the empiric experience of the teachers. There is no scientific inquiry about such absenteeism.
20 "Atelier n°4" (2003, 196).

school", a percentage very similar to that for Christians, for teenagers with other religious backgrounds / worldviews, and for all teenagers in general, regardless of whether they have a religious background / worldview or not: 78/79%. As for the possibility for praying or following religious services in schools, we also notice the same trend in the complete sample, regardless of religious background / worldview. There is a slightly larger number of Muslims who agree that it should be possible to pray: 27% of them, compared to 18% of Christian teenagers and 13% of teenagers in general.

Concerning more visible religious symbols, the difference is more pronounced. For the whole sample, the majority (54% of teenagers with religious background / worldview and 66% of teenagers with no religious background / worldview) disagree, whereas only 17% agree (21% of teenagers with religious background / worldview and 13% of teenagers with no religious background / worldview). By contrast, the Muslims are more divided: a third agree, a third disagree. We can notice a similar result with the statement: "students should be excused from taking some lessons for religious reasons". These two results, which are difficult to interpret, may show, on the one hand, that some Muslim teenagers accept the principle of "laïcité", and in particular the 2004 law about religious symbols, and on the other hand that others are a little upset by the same law. We might correlate this with the feeling of the lack of recognition and with the lack of Muslim private schools.

At this stage, we can make three remarks. 1) There is no real opposition between the complete sample and the group of Muslims. The same trend is noticed in the two groups. 2) However, we can also notice that some issues seem more delicate for Muslim students, such as the absence of Halal meat and the possibility of missing school for religious feasts. These issues are mainly concerned with practices which the Muslims see as part of their religious or cultural identity, and where they therefore perceive an injustice. These same points are also those which are tolerated by the school community. 3) The Muslim teenagers are divided about points which are seen as a threat to the principle of "laïcité" and to the laws: e.g. the wearing of the hijab and the challenge it poses to the 2004 law, the missing of certain lessons for religious reasons, and the principle of compulsory education.

Behind this, there is a question of identity, one facet of which is Muslim identity. The affirmation of this identity mainly expresses itself through visible practices, such as the observance of the fast in Ramadan and the celebration of some major feasts. Occasionally it may also express itself through prayer, as it sometimes the case during a school trip.

The question of "laïcité" is also expressed in the way in which French schools handle education covering religion. Most French teenagers (82%) think that a course dealing specifically with religion should be optional. "This attitude is due to the absence of mandatory religious education in French public schools".[21] A majority of Muslims also agree with this statement, albeit a smaller one: 61%. We notice that 23% of them are hesitant when it comes to this statement, a hesitation which is more pronounced than for other teenagers.

---

21 Béraud et al. (2009, 146).

For the other statements pertaining to a religious education, we can make the same remarks as the French team made for the complete sample: the results are difficult to interpret;[22] like their classmates, the Muslims feel, that in case religious education would be available, teenagers should not to be separated according to their religious background for religious education classes, a feeling stronger in their case (68%) than in the complete sample (59%). At the same time, only 24% agree the statement "Religious education should be taught to students together, whatever differences there might be in their religious or denominational background". The final remark concerns the statement "there is no need for the subject of Religious Education. All the relevant topics are covered by other school subjects (e.g. literature, history, etc.)". In the whole sample, 45% of teenagers agree with this statement; the students with a certain religious background or worldview, however, are more divided (one third agrees, one third disagrees, one third has no opinion); Muslims are more in favour of a religious education (50%) but it is noticeable that the percentage of the Muslims with no opinion on this question is relatively high: 37%. As for the other teenagers with a religious background / worldview, there is no overwhelming desire for a course dealing specifically with religion.

3.4 Socialisation and interactions between Muslims and non-Muslims

For the purpose of the analysis, we will distinguish between three circles of socialisation and interactions: the family and the community, school friends and other friends, and the school conceived here only through its relation between teachers and students.

The family is the traditional source for information about religion (95%, percentage combining the answers for the item "very important" and "important"). We can correlate this with the fact that, for most Muslim teenagers, their families have the same religion (74%) and the same views about religion (81%), and with the fact that, for the majority, "religion is something one inherits from one's family" (52%). This last percentage is higher than that for teenagers with a certain religious background or worldview (46%), and with that for teenagers having no religious background or worldview (30%). Consequently, the family is the first place where religion is discussed (84% of Muslims[23]). The importance of the community as the first source of information is to be underlined, whereas religious leaders are not really seen as people with whom to speak about religion. For around half ("not important" and "not important at all") of Muslims, the media is not seen as a source of information, whereas documentation or books are. This is a particularly interesting result when we bear in mind that most of the teenagers spend more time on the internet or in front of the television than they do reading books! This result does not mean that they read many books but rather that they seem to be more confident about finding correct information about religion in books than in

---

22 Béraud et al. (2009, 147).
23 To facilitate the comparisons with the analysis of the complete sample in Béraud et al. (2009, 140-141), we adopt the same rule for this part: the percentage combines the answers "about every day", "about every week", and "about every month".

the media. All of these results tend to show that, in this first circle of socialisation, the Muslim students remain among themselves, where the same religion is practiced.

However, there is also a second circle of socialisation, that of friends. If friends are not really seen as an important source of information in comparison to the family, the community or books, they are not neglected: 50% of Muslims think they are an important source of information. For 66% of Muslims, friends are mostly people with whom they can speak about religion.[24] We can correlate this result, as for the family, with the fact that most of their friends share the same views about religion. However, that does not mean that Muslims only have Muslim friends. 89% of Muslims have "friends who belong to different religions". The great majority of them socialise "with young people who have a different religious background" at school (90%) and after school (73%).[25] Indeed, most of them (56%) say, "it doesn't bother me what my friends think about religions" and only 23% think that "I have problems showing my views about religion openly in school".

As for the third circle of socialisation, the school is not really seen as an important place of information: only 28% agree with this statement, a result coherent with the complete sample. This could be due to the fact that lessons relating to religion are not frequent. Because teaching about religion is done through different disciplines, there are only a few hours devoted to this topic and it is difficult to compare France with other countries where one hour a week is devoted to Religious Education. Consequently, 50% of Muslims – compared to 41% in the complete sample – never speak of religion with their teachers. However, we can notice that a third of them (the same percentage for the complete sample) speak at least once a month with a teacher: probably with the history teacher, as he/she is the one who speaks more about different religions during the year.

If the first circle of socialisation is not really diversified in terms of religion, the second is more so and there are more interactions between Muslim and non-Muslim teenagers. Furthermore, Muslims are more inclined to talk about religion with friends rather than with other people.

4. Teaching Islam at school: pedagogical remarks

When it comes to the teaching of religious issues in general, Islam is perceived by teachers as being particularly difficult.[26] This is not due to the novelty of such teaching, which has existed since the end of the 19th century, but rather to the evolution of mentalities and attitudes. Initially, the teaching of religious issues was also a problem when it concerned Christianity, whereas Islam, which was considered as an exotic religion, was taught without raising objections. The present difficulties come from the awareness of the importance of Islam in French society

---

24 For this percentage and the following ones, see the previous footnote.
25 Both percentages are coherent with the answers to the following statement: "at school, I prefer to go around with young people who have the same religious background as me" and "in my spare time, I prefer to go around with young people who have the same religious background as me": only 6% of Muslims agree both whereas 94% disagree.
26 Cf. Borne (2007a, 131-137).

and from the generally negative opinions about Islam. Teachers fear that their teaching might cause trouble or even rejection. This situation is sometimes highlighted in the media, but it should not be generalised. The history teacher Alain, interviewed by Bérengère Massignon within the framework of the REDCo qualitative study, speaks of the particularly critical attitude of a class where Muslim students were the majority; but "he refuses to generalise and he lays the blame for the difficulties he had on that particular class, that year, in that school, stressing that it was only one example which had not occurred again".[27] Having myself taught in similar schools, I agree with Alain. The teacher should not fear some reactions providing that he/she takes some precautions. These concern, first of all, the professional attitude of the teachers and, secondly, the teaching methodology.

4.1 The professional attitude of the teachers

There is no specific professional code of ethics for teaching about Islam: it is identical to the teaching of other religious issues and other school subjects such as literature, mathematics, etc. When speaking about Islam, however, teachers need to be more cautious about their own attitudes. Indeed, more than is the case when teaching other topics, the legitimacy of the teacher is placed under question by some pupils from time to time. They claim to be believers and may oppose the teachers with some parts of the Qur'an unknown to them. They are on the level of belief, and no longer on the level of the school subject, where the teachers' legitimacy cannot be doubted. Therefore the teachers have to be very careful not to pass from one level to the other. Their goal is neither to propose a religious education as such, nor to present some exegesis or interfere in the sphere of belief, but rather to educate about religious issues from a historical and cultural standpoint. This implies that they put faith in the background. They talk about "facts"[28] and make a distinction between knowledge and belief, without, however, placing them in opposition to one another. They have to be respectful, therefore, and they should not offend. Muslims can claim that the Qur'an is an inspired text and that it comes from God; in the classroom, the teachers do not dispute this claim, but what they teach is different. It is not in contradiction with belief but it is on another level. There are several truths, one being religious, another historical,[29] but they are not in opposition. The teachers' main goal is to build up and develop a critical attitude in their pupils, not by denying their belief, but rather by helping them to exercise rational thought.

Another attitude which the teacher has to adopt within the framework of "laïcité", is an avoidance of deducing the religious identity of their pupils from their attitude or other visible signs. The religious diversity of the pupils is not denied, but neither is it taken into account. The teachers interviewed by Bérengère Massignon first point out the learning abilities of their pupils, then the socio-economic inequalities, followed by their ethnic or national origin and, only then, in

---

27 Massignon (2009, 61).
28 We understand this term in a sociological sense; for this sense and the French expression "faits religieux", cf. Willaime (2007, 37-57).
29 Cf. Borne (2007b).

fourth position, their religious identity.[30] Since the March 15, 2004 law, "ostensible religious signs" are prohibited in schools. Discrete signs are tolerated. These signs give some indications to teachers, but their religious connotation is not always obvious, e.g. the hand of Fatma. Another sign is the level of absenteeism in the school canteen during Ramadan or in the classroom during Eid, the feast celebrating the end of Ramadan. Some hasty connection is sometimes made between national background or last name and religion. Most teachers however, bypass these vague categories in order to concentrate on the individual.[31]

4.2 The training of the teachers

The teachers need to be very well informed in order to avoid being contested in their legitimacy. The better they are trained, the better they will be able to adopt a correct deontological attitude and a correct discourse. Teacher training takes place in universities, with an extra year in a specific institution: the *Institut Universitaire de Formation des Maîtres* or *IUFM* (University Institute for Teacher Training). This training is often inappropriate for the real needs of the teachers, and religious issues are only a non-compulsory part of the curriculum. This is particularly true for Muslim religious issues. However, since the 1990s, the CAPES[32] has set more subjects related to religious issues. This trend encourages future teachers to train themselves in these topics.[33]

When someone becomes a teacher, it is possible for them to deepen his/her previous training while teaching. They can attend some specific courses at the *IUFM* during the school year (three per year). Many are dedicated to religious issues, in which Islam is taken into account. For example, in 2009, the Paris *IUFM* proposed a course about the three monotheistic religions and their founding texts; the Arras *IUFM* offered a course about the sources of the three monotheistic religions: the history of the Qur'an was presented, as was the religious figure of Mohammed (what do historians know about him? What does he mean/represent for the Muslims? How can the teacher speak about him?); The Creteil *IUFM* programmed a lecture "Islam and Islamisms" during a two day course; in 2010, the Caen *IUFM* plans to schedule a two day course about Islam. In addition to these courses, many books have been published to help teachers, giving them some scientific knowledge and pedagogical help. For example, the magazine edited by the Documentation française, *La documentation photographique*, recently

---

30 Cf. Massignon (2009, 60).
31 See the example given by Massignon (2009, 61).
32 CAPES, *Certificat d'aptitude au professorat de l'enseignement du second degré*, is a certificate which is required in order to be able to teach in secondary schools. It is a very selective exam.
33 For example, in 2001, the programs were « State, Society, cultural and religious life, economic life in France under Louis IX" (medieval history) and "Athens during the 5th BC: political life, economical, social, religious and cultural aspects" (ancient history). For 2009, the program in modern history is "the religious conflicts in Europe from the beginnings of the 16th c. to the middle of the 17th c."

published an issue written by Pascal Buresi, *Histoire de l'islam*, with a short text, many documents and commentaries[34].

4.3 The objectives of the teacher

Since the end of the 1980s, religious issues have come back openly into the school curricula, not in opposition to "laïcité" but as an integral part of it. France is moving from a "laïcité" of ignorance to one of intelligence[35]. The Joutard report in 1989 explicitly stated that: "knowledge of the religious cultures is necessary to the intelligence of our societies, of their past and present, of their artistic and cultural heritage, of their juridical and political system". The Debray report in 2002 stressed the importance of a "laïcité d'intelligence"[36] and put the accent more on civic aspects. Thus, the goal of French educative policies about religious issues since the 1990s has been threefold: cognitive, patrimonial and civic. All these three objectives are present, to different degrees according to the lesson and the discipline, whereas national programs seem to stress factual knowledge in particular, its main aim is to educate citizens. Knowledge is also know-how and 'knowledge-being'. The teaching of Islam, just like the teaching of other religious issues, has to conform itself to this threefold goal.

Therefore, the first objective remains the cognitive one. The better we know, the better we understand a cultural heritage, which will help to build a constructive dialogue with people from various backgrounds. To attain the cognitive goal, the teachers have to build knowledge. Therefore, before this, it could be useful to "deconstruct" some "knowledge" and to be aware of the pupils' misconceptions and prejudices. The teachers can achieve this awareness through enquiries with multiple choice questions, or through posing open questions such as "give five expressions which characterise Islam for you". The latter is the easiest and the more spontaneous way of carrying out such research. It generally reveals that the knowledge of the pupils is both limited and erroneous (particularly for younger students)[37], even for pupils with a Muslim background (at least with regards to the knowledge which interests the teacher; the pupils following a religious education in the mosque could have another kind of knowledge concerning what we could call legends, mystic etc.). They can name the Qur'an, Mohammed, some of the five pillars, the main feasts, and their knowledge is more ritual than historical[38]; however, the same could be said for pupils from other religious backgrounds: how many Catholic pupils are really able to list the seven sacraments? As is the case with many adults, pupils confuse religion and state, Islam and fundamentalism, Islam and war, Muslim and Arab. This preliminary examination allows the teacher to see on which ground they will construct his/her lesson: how they will complete

---

34 See also Ferjani (1996); *L'enseignement* (2003); Bouzar (2006).
35 See Willaime (2007, 63). The expression « laïcité d'intelligence » goes back to Régis Debray, Debray (2002).
36 Debray (2002, 43).
37 Cf. Cusenier (1996, 185-187).
38 "Atelier n°5"(2003, 202).

the knowledge already acquired by the pupils, and correct their erroneous conceptions and representations. One question, then, is "how to do it?".

4.4 The way of teaching

Like the pupils, teachers have clearly integrated the principle of "laïcité", but some questions remain. For example, the literature teacher sometimes asks him-/herself when and how long he/she should speak about Islam, because the official program gives them some liberty. The history teacher has a different question: how to make the pupils understand that their perspective is both scientific and respectful of the pupil's beliefs. Many teachers fear disputes when speaking about Islam, a fear which is less apparent when they speak about Christianity or Judaism. One solution may be not to avoid this question, and to explain the manner in which Islam will be spoken about. This is related to the problem of the relationship between knowledge and belief.

The teachers can use the personal knowledge of pupils, but they have to be very cautious: they should not ask a Muslim pupil to explain to his comrades what Islam is. As Dominique Borne says, there are two reasons: a believer does not always master knowledge related to his religion; the objective of scholarly education is not to instil belief.[39] Moreover, the teachers can face some negative reactions. For example, a teacher in an under-privileged school in Seine-Saint-Denis (north-east suburbs of Paris) wanted to build his lesson on the family background and the Muslim culture of most of his pupils; he asked them to bring some objects related to Islam to the school. This was not a success and pupils said it was forbidden by religion to do so, especially to bring the Qur'an, because the school was not a religious place. Here, against the intention of the teacher, two levels were finally opposed to each other: the one of the pupils, religious; the other of the teacher, scientific. It would perhaps have been better if the teacher had himself brought a translation of the Koran from the *CDI*, *Centre de documentation et d'information*, saying that this volume is a book of study in the school, and not one of belief.

Teaching is based on documents of diverse nature – mainly texts and iconography in literature and history, as well as maps and charts for the history teacher – and on their study through the tools and methodologies specific to their disciplines. The history teacher contextualizes the documents and treats every document in the same way, whether it be an extract from the Qur'an or a financial account. Such an attitude is not always well understood and could be qualified as rationalist, but it does not imply an opposition between "historic truth" and "religious truth". Some teachers make such oppositions but luckily they are few. Some say nothing about a difference between various kinds of truth, sometimes in the hope that the question will not be asked; others say a few words about it. Between the two latter positions, we can only recommend the second one, because they may depend on the previous training of the teacher and on the relationship he has managed to establish with his classroom.

---

39 Borne (2007a, 134).

The different points of view, believer versus rationalist, are also marked through the way of speaking. Muslims consider the Qur'an to be an inspired text; the historians discuss this belief, and neither reject nor confirm it; the historians talk about the context of writing of the text, how one version was finally chosen from many, and what the belief of the Qur'an as an inspired text implies for Muslims and for their religious practices. Teachers should not use a confessional language. At the same time, they should have the possibility to speak about the cultural and religious content of an issue. They can evoke this content with expressions such as: "Muslims believe that …", "the Tradition says …", "according to Muslims, …". These ways of speaking reveal a certain distance between the teachers and the studied topic, while still respecting this topic.

The teachers lead pupils to distinguish between what is related to history and what is related to myth, and how the latter is meaningful for a society and its beliefs. They help them to recognise the religious forms and manifestations in different events, as well as to be very aware that the borderlines are sometimes so fragile that it is nearly impossible to see them.

All the previous remarks could also apply to other religious issues. The following remarks concern a lesson about Islam more specifically. Indeed, there are many misconceptions about Islam which have an important impact on societal (and political) discourse. The teachers should correct these misconceptions. They have an important civic function.

Firstly, it is imperative to present Islam in a historical context and in its diversity in both the past and the present, and not as something rigidly fixed on the five pillars. Second, the teachers should not teach about Islam as if it was an exotic topic but should present it as an integral part of European history, and establish its relation with European history. The teachers should deal with the contribution of Islam to the cultural and religious history of Europe in the past and the present. This is clear during the 12th-13th centuries when the increasing exchanges, alongside the crusades, allowed occidental scholars to obtain knowledge of ancient texts translated in Arabic, which in return transformed Christian culture, religious language and European culture in general. The teachers should give more space to Islam in their lessons related to contemporary issues and events. When dealing with cultural developments in France since 1945, it could be useful to speak about Islam in France, which is also an "Islam of France", different from that of other countries with its specific organisation. At the end, the teachers should manage to make it clear that there is no incompatibility between Islam and "laïcité" (the French one and/or the European one). The objective of "laïcité" in France in 1905 was not meant as a choice between Christianity (mainly Catholicism) and "laïcité"; and therefore nowadays, neither is it between Islam and "laïcité". "Laïcité" does not imply being in favour of a secularised Islam, but rather it aims at a civic tolerance by everyone.[40]

---

40 Bauberot (2003, 151-152).

5. Conclusion

For several years now, Islam has enjoyed the same legal status as the Christian and Jewish religions, with regards to the 1905 law. In the field of education, if we compare it with the Christian and Jewish religions, Islam has less private schools of its own. However, since a few years, there has been a trend towards the establishment of more private schools, even if the process is a lengthy one. The Muslim teenagers seem to have integrated the principle of "laïcité", even if they sometimes feel upset by what they consider to be injustices. Moreover, the question of identity is not to be neglected. Their relation with their family is important, but there is also space for openness to other religions through the friends in school or outside the school.

These comments tend to confirm that the teachers should not have too much to fear when speaking about Islam, providing that they are well trained and that they exercise their teaching with a correct professional code of ethics. Their attitude should be the same as the one they adopt when speaking about other issues, whether these issues are religious or not. However, it is perhaps important to be more cautious. They should not be servants of the world actualities nor of the misconceptions which are current in society. Their civic function is as important as their cognitive function.

References

"Atelier n°4" (2003). "Atelier n°4. Islam et école à Marseille", in: Borne, D. & Levallois, L. et al. (Eds.) *Europe et islam, islams d'Europe. Actes de l'université d'été, Paris, 29-30 août 2002* (Paris, Direction de l'Enseignement scolaire), 194-200.
"Atelier n°5" (2003). "Atelier n°5. Islam et école dans « le 93 »", in: Borne, D. & Levallois, L. et al. (Eds.) (2003) *Europe et islam, islams d'Europe. Actes de l'université d'été, Paris, 29-30 août 2002* (Paris, Direction de l'Enseignement scolaire), 201-203.
Baubérot, J. (2003) La secularisation de l'islam et la recherche d'un nouveau pacte laïque en France, in: Borne, D. & Levallois, L. et al. (Eds.) *Europe et islam, islams d'Europe. Actes de l'université d'été, Paris, 29-30 août 2002* (Paris, Direction de l'Enseignement scolaire), 145-154.
Béraud, C., Massignon, B., Mathieu, S., Willaime, J.-P. (2009) The School – an Appropriate Institution in France for Acquiring Knowledge on Religious Diversity and Experiencing it Firsthand?, in: Valk, P., Bertram-Troost, G., Friederici, M., Béraud, C. (Eds.) *Teenagers' Perspectives on the Role of Religion in their Lives, Schools and Societies. A European Quantitative Study* (Münster, Waxmann), 131-163.
Billon, A. (2003) "À la recherche d'un islam de France", in : Borne, D. & Levallois, L. et al. (Eds.) *Europe et islam, islams d'Europe. Actes de l'université d'été, Paris, 29-30 août 2002* (Paris, Direction de l'Enseignement scolaire), 109-115.
Borne, D. (2007) "L'enseignement des faits religieux, quels contenus?", in: Borne, D. & Willaime, J.-P. (Eds.) *Enseigner les faits religieux. Quels enjeux?* (Paris, Armand Colin), 97-119.

Borne, D. (2007a) "Quelles approches pédagogiques?", in: Borne, D. & Willaime, J.-P. (Eds.) *Enseigner les faits religieux. Quels enjeux?* (Paris, Armand Colin), 121-137.

Borne, D. (2007b) *Enseigner la vérité à l'école? Quels enjeux?* (Paris, Armand Colin).

Borne, D. & Levallois, L. et al. (Eds.) (2003) *Europe et islam, islams d'Europe. Actes de l'université d'été, Paris, 29-30 août 2002* (Paris, Direction de l'Enseignement scolaire).

Borne, D. & Willaime, J.-P. (Eds.) (2007) *Enseigner les faits religieux. Quels enjeux?* (Paris, Armand Colin).

Bouzar, D. (2006). *Quelle éducation face au radicalisme religieux?* (Paris, Dunod).

Cusenier, D. (1996) Stratégies pédagogiques. 1- Les representations des élèves sur l'islam, in: Ferjani, M.-C. (Ed.) *Les voies de l'islam. Approche laïque des faits islamiques* (Paris, Cerf), 185-188.

Debray, R. (2002) *L'enseignement du fait religieux dans l'école laïque, Rapport au ministre de l'Éducation nationale* (Paris, Odile Jacob).

Etienne, B. (2004) *La France et l'islam* (Paris, Hachette).

Ferjani, M.-C. (Ed.) (1996) *Les voies de l'islam. Approche laïque des faits islamiques* (Paris, Cerf).

Guénif-Souilamas, N. (2003) Les jeunes musulmans en France, in: Borne, D. & Levallois, L. et al. (Eds.) *Europe et islam, islams d'Europe. Actes de l'université d'été, Paris, 29-30 août 2002* (Paris, Direction de l'Enseignement scolaire), 95-107.

Kaltenbach, J.-H. & Tribalat, M. (2002) *La République et l'islam : entre crainte et aveuglement* (Paris, Gallimard).

L'atlas (2007) *L'atlas des religions* (Paris, La Vie).

L'enseignement (2003). *L'enseignement du fait religieux. Actes du séminaire national interdisciplinaire organisé à Paris les 5, 6 et 7 novembre 2002* (Paris, Direction de l'Enseignement scolaire).

Massignon, B. (2009) Teaching Diversity in the French Secular School – Between Deontological Distanciation and Personal Commitment, in: van der Want, A., Bakker, C., ter Avest, I., Everington, J. (Eds.) *Teachers Responding to Religious Diversity in Europe. Researching Biography and Pedagogy* (Münster, Waxmann), 55-67.

Roy, O. (2005). *La laïcité face à l'islam* (Paris, Stock).

Saint-Martin, I. (2007). "Approche par les oeuvres (texts et images)", in: Borne, D. & Willaime, J.-P. (Eds.) *Enseigner les faits religieux. Quels enjeux?* (Paris, Armand Colin), 139-172.

Vaïsse, J., Laurence, J., Roy, O. & Dreyfus, J.-M. (2007) *Intégrer l'islam. La France, ses musulmans : enjeux et réussites* (Paris, Odile Jacob).

Willaime, J.-P. (2007). "Qu'est-ce qu'un fait religieux?", in: Borne, D. & Willaime, J.-P. (Eds.) *Enseigner les faits religieux. Quels enjeux?* (Paris, Armand Colin), 37-57.

Willaime, J.-P. (2007). "Enseigner les faits religieux à l'école. Le débat français et sa mise en perspective", in: Borne, D. & Willaime, J.-P. (Eds.) *Enseigner les faits religieux. Quels enjeux?* (Paris, Armand Colin), 59-91.

Willaime, J.-P. & Beraud, C. (Eds.) (forthcoming). *Les jeunes, l'école et la religion. L'approche française en perspective européenne* (Paris, Bayard).

Marjoke Rietveld-van Wingerden, Wim Westerman & Ina ter Avest
Islam in Education in the Netherlands
History and Actual Developments

1. Introduction

Islamic education and Islamic primary and secondary schools only recently came to the fore in the public debate in the Netherlands. It appears as if the Islam is a novelty in Dutch society since the arrival of migrant workers in the 1960s. However, Holland has a long historical relationship with Islam, starting in the late Middle Ages. In this chapter we describe the history of Islam in the Netherlands, and in particular Islam in education, by addressing the following questions: To what extent has Islam been part of public debates as early as Medieval times and, more recently, in our post-modern society? Can we speak of a new era in the perception of the Islam after the immigration of Muslims into the Netherlands in the second half of the last century? If so, what was the reception of this religion by native Dutchmen, and in what ways did Muslims themselves cope with the problems of integration and identity formation? What has been the role of education in this respect? Has education been seen by the policy makers as a precondition for Muslims' identity formation and citizenship education?

In this contribution, we focus firstly on Dutch interests in Islam since the late Middle Ages. This first section ends with the recent history and the actual position of Islam in the Netherlands. While the Islam in the Netherlands is rooted in a wide variety of national, ethnic and cultural backgrounds, it is impossible to sketch the Islam unequivocally. So, we focus on the Dutch perception and recent reception of the muslim newcomers and their 'strange' – in the eyes of the common Dutchman, the man in the street – religion. Subsequently, in the second section, we investigate how Muslims explored the Dutch 'pillarized society' and describe how they adapted to the typical Dutch educational system. In the third section, we observe how Dutch Islamic primary and secondary schools integrate the necessary adjustment to Dutch citizenship and the wishes of migrant Muslim parents with regard to the religious nurture and education of their children. Since the Islam in the Netherlands can be characterized as plural, the same is applicable for the identity of Islamic schools. In the final (fourth) section we come to the conclusion that these schools have to cooperate in a far more intensive way with parents and with neighbourhood organisations concerned with leisure time activities. The school is central in these processes, and the teacher is pivotal.

2. The perception of Islam in the Netherlands

2.1 Late Middle Ages and early modern times

It was by means of literature and commerce that the Dutch had their first encounters with Islam. Medieval educational texts in the Dutch and Flemish language already described the relationship between Christianity and Islam. Romances of chivalry, like an epic poem about Charles the Great, sang about the skirmishes between small Christian and Muslim armies in Spain and the Southern part of France. The poet Diederic van Assenede (±1230-1293) translated from the French language 'Floris ende Blanchefloer', a love story of a Muslim prince, who preferred a beautiful Christian female slave to become his princess. In the thirteenth century Jacob van Maerlant, author of an extensive amount of didactical and historical books, wrote his *Spiegel Historiael* [Historical Mirror] and *Van den Lande van Oversee* [About the Country from Overseas]. In both publications he made an urgent call to liberate Jerusalem from the Muslims. This summons was articulated by presenting Islam as the arch-enemy of Christianity, which was the only true religion. He described Mohammed as a disgusting man who used his knowledge about Christianity and Judaism to brew a perverted cocktail: Islam (Van Oostrom 1998, 357-360). Contrary to the Jews, Van Maerlant saw Muslims as pagans and, above all, as the military enemies of the Christians during the Crusades (Harper 1998, 71-97). Clashes between Christians and Muslims, originally sketched as tribal fights, received a negative religious flavor. Older stories and verses about skirmishes were transformed into religious wars (Wessels 1978, 45). Religion became politicized.

Since then negative views on Islam dominated, and previous positive memories of good relations between Muslims, Jews and Christians were forgotten. The period of the mutual understanding of Spanish philosophers like the Muslim philosopher Averroës (1126-1198) and the Jewish scholar Maimonides (1135-1204), as well as the fact that Muslims, Jews and Christians all traced their philosophies back to the early Greek philosophers, disappeared behind the horizon (Kraemer 1960, 34-37) and persistent caricatures on Islam became dominant. An example of this is provided by the Amsterdam theologian Cornelis Uijtenhagen who, in 1666, tried to prove that Mohammed was the Anti-Christ personified (Slomp 1984, 421).

This negative perception was greatly influenced by the Turks who, being the occupiers of the Holy Land, were seen as the enemy during the Crusades. After the conquest of Constantinople by the Turks (1453) a stream of pamphlets and books were published in which the wrong-doings of the Turkish people became a synonym for Islamic misdeeds. Most of the Dutch publications were translations from foreign printed materials. Although the designation 'Turkish' had a strong negative connotation, a certain admiration for the Ottoman Empire existed, because of its freedom of religion. Moreover, one stated that the Turks had 'qualities Christians did not have. They were simple, faithful and disciplined, patient and brave, while the Christians were extravagant, disobedient, frivolous and frightened' (Theunissen 1989, 37-38). The attribution of good qualities to the Turks went into reverse in order to articulate the threat of the Muslims. For instance, in his *Consultatio de Belle Turcico* (1530) [Consultation on the Turkish War], the Dutch philosopher and theologian Erasmus of Rotterdam depicted the rise of the Ottomans as God's punishment for the moral decline of the Christians.

Soon, however, commercial contacts would affect the perception of Islam. From 1613 onward Dutch business offices were established in Turkish cities like Smirna, where the Dutch experienced freedom of religion and could even build their own churches (Samberg 1928). As a result of the commercial links between Holland and the Ottoman Empire, the Dutch perception and reception of Islam changed and even became more positive than elsewhere in Europe. Although a great number of anti-Islamic pamphlets still were printed in the Netherlands, Dutch Calvinist businessmen and many politicians preferred the Islamic Turks to the Roman-Catholics. In the period 1568-1648, when Calvinistic Holland fought the war of independence from the Roman-Catholic Habsburg Empire, Martin Luther's statement: 'Better Turkish, than Popish', was more or less a nationalistic battle cry (Theunissen 1989, 43). It was at the end of this war of independence that the Qur'an was translated into Dutch for the first time (Theunissen 1989, 42).

Since the middle of the sixteenth century Flemish and Dutch merchants had contacts not only with Turkey but also with Morocco (Benali & Obdeijn 2005, 17-51). The commercial links stimulated the study of the Arabic language and the religion of Islam. Since 1586 both subjects have been taught, with a few short interruptions, at the University of Leyden (Brugman & Schröder 1979, 3; Slomp 1984, 421). For a long period commerce and humanities went hand in hand in Holland. For instance, in 1622, Gollius, professor in Arabic language at Leyden University, joined a business trip to Morocco (Slomp 1991, 69). Muslims came to Holland for commercial reasons and lived together with many other foreigners in the Dutch cities. Until the present day, the University of Leyden has been an important centre for Islamic studies, both in the Netherlands and abroad, and it is where, since the middle of the nineteenth century, the 'Encyclopedia Islamica' has been published.

When the British traveler Andrew Marvell visited Amsterdam in the seventeenth century, he could observe the city as 'the place for Turk, Christian, heathen, Jew; staple place for sects and a lot of schisms. It is one 'bank of conscience', where no one opinion is too strange to find credit or exchange' (cf.: Boxer 1973, 143). He saw a cultural climate with a relative freedom for theological and philosophical discourses in the public space, a domain characterized by global commercial and scientific relations, the absence of an official state religion and a high percentage of migrants. Amsterdam, and Holland at large, appeared to be a laboratory for the development of plurality. Holland was known for its relative freedom of religion, thought, speech, printing and conscience. 'Relative', while there were still certain restrictions, but in general there was more freedom than in other European countries, because in Holland books could be published that were not allowed to be printed elsewhere. Foreign philosophers like René Descartes (1596-1650), Pierre Bayle (1647-1650), John Locke (1632-1704), Wilhelm Leibniz (1646-1716) and Voltaire (1694-1778) experienced that censorship was nowhere so mild as in the Netherlands (Westerman 2008, 13-15). According to the Princeton University historian Jonathan Israel, the Enlightenment, having laid the foundations for the modern Western political and liberal world, is rooted in this relative cultural Dutch freedom, a freedom that led to the development of such human rights as equality, democracy, secular values and universality (Israel 2001, 2006).

Although freedom prevailed, there was still some censorship, as the Jewish philosopher Baruch de Spinoza (1632-1677) experienced. His interpretation of the Torah and the Bible, his rationalistic approach and pleas for freedom of speech and opinion, resulted for him in a conflict with the board of the Sephardic Synagogue opposite his home, as well as with the Calvinist churches in Amsterdam (Kaplan 1995). Many Christian theologians, in Holland and abroad, saw Christianity as the 'only path to the one God' (D'Costa 1986, 22). In their opinion plurality and dialogue with persons belonging to other religions was a threat to the Christian testimony. Even in the relative freedom of the Netherlands, pleas to learn from other religions only had an apologetic intention.

2.2 A seventeenth century school book on Islam

Despite the commercial, theological, scientific and commercial interests in Islam, this knowledge did not affect textbooks for (primary) education. However, there is one exception. Its author is the famous pedagogue and theologian Jan Amos Komenský (1592-1670), better known by his Latin name Comenius. After many peregrinations through Europe, he spent the last years of his life in Amsterdam. Comenius was seriously concerned about the religious plurality of his time, but only from a Christological perspective (Van der Linde 1979, 212). He implemented his ideas in schoolbooks and pedagogical handbooks. According to Comenius, children should be taught about the history of religions from their fifth year onwards. This same motivation could also be found behind his *Orbis Sensualium Pictus* [The world explained in pictures], the world's first illustrated encyclopedia for children and the most widely distributed textbook. It appeared in more than 254 editions in at least twenty languages (Kok 1992, 12). The book begins with a lesson about God the Creator and ends with the Last Judgment. The second lesson teaches about Christianity, Judaism, Islam and Heathendom. Comenius emphasized that Christianity had to be taught in an open and honest way to Jews and Muslims. Then, he was convinced, they would accept Christianity as a better religion than their own (Van der Linde 1979, 195-212). Comenius wrote the *Orbis Sensualium Pictus* (1658), during a few years' stay in Hungary, close to the then border of the Ottoman empire. However, he got his information about Islam from books published in the Netherlands and not directly from Muslims in his neighbourhood. He explicitly referred to the Flemish Nicolaas Clenard, professor of Eastern languages in Louvain, who had visited North Africa in 1535. From such outsider perspectives Comenius learned how Islamic education was organized. In his educational advisory guide, the *Opera Didactica Omnia* (1657/1658) [The complete didactical works], Comenius uttered his admiration for the characteristic Islamic way of teaching, exemplified with Muslim children who had to learn the Qur'an by heart over a two years' period (cf.: Westerman 1994, 28). This would prevent that the contents would be forgotten later in life. Moreover, the holy book could be lost by fire or in situations of sudden escape, an argument that was appealing for Comenius, since he knew what it was to flee (many times during his life he had been forced to do so (cf.: Tworuschka 1983, 27; Van der Linde 1979, 208-209).

Although Comenius lived and worked in the Netherlands at the end of his life, he had no decisive influence on the educational practices in Dutch schools (Groenendijk & Sturm 1992, 60). His information about Islam, as presented in the *Orbis Sensualium Pictus*, did not reach many Dutch children. With his dialogical approach Comenius was a precursor among Dutch theologians. There was, however, one important difference. Theologians used to know facts about other religions in order to refute them. Their polemic approach even formed a special discipline within theology, the so-called *theologia elenctica*, or apologetics. One of the apologists was the Leyden theologian, professor Johannes Van Hoornbeeck (1617-1666), who was dedicated to resisting Jews, Muslims, Roman-Catholics, Libertines, Lutherans and others (Brienen 2008, 19-42; Van Amersfoort & Van Asselt 1997, 111). He even intended to found a *'Congregatio de Propaganda Fide'* [Congregation for the Promotion of the Belief], focusing on the rejection of Islam (Juynboll 1931, 222). The excluding and one-sided character of the *theologia elenctica* was soon noted by other theologians like Relandus (1676-1718). He is one of the first authors who provided a more or less fair and unprejudiced presentation of Islam in his *De Religione Mohammedica* [About the Mohammedan Religion] (Steenbrink 1991, 45). This book was translated into many languages, but never into Dutch (Slomp 1984, 422).

A book on Islam, published in Holland in Latin, a language that only academic scholars could read, is symbolic for the results of Islamic studies after Relandus. That became more clear when, from the 1960s onwards, many Muslims immigrated into the Netherlands. Despite commercial contacts with Muslim countries, colonial ties with the world's largest Islamic country (the East-Indies), and the long and rich history of academic Islam studies, Islam was still a strange phenomenon in the public and educational domain. In spite of Comenius' *Orbis Sensualium Pictus*, schools had only seldom taught about Islam. The few moments that teachers paid attention to this religion were in the setting of lessons about the work of Christian missionaries who tried to convert 'the poor, but polygamous, and ignorant Mohammedans' (Ligthart 1917, 165). Information about Islam in children's literature was even worse (Westerman 1994, 30-31). One of the probable causes is that academic Islam studies had mainly focused on the regions in the East Indies and the Middle East and not on the religion of Islam in the more nearby countries like Turkey and the countries in North Africa.

2.3 Islam in Dutch society after 1960

The post-war streams of migration show a wide diversity of countries of origin, resulting in an Islamic population in the Netherlands with a broad variety of national, ethnic, linguistic and cultural backgrounds. Some Muslims were citizens from former Dutch colonies, others were visiting students, migrant workers and refugees. Nowadays nearly all Islamic law schools and ethnicities are represented in the Netherlands. This is an important difference to several other European countries, like Germany, where the majority of Muslims adheres to the same law school. They come from, among others, the former Yugoslavia, Albania, Turkey, Kurdistan, Iraq, Palestine, Morocco, Tunisia, Egypt, Sudan, Nigeria, Somalia, Iran,

Pakistan, Afghanistan, Indonesia, Bangladesh, The Philippines, and Surinam. The estimated number of Muslims in the Netherlands grew rapidly after 1975, from 50,000 in 1971 to 628,000 in 1995, and 946,000 in 2004, from a total population of 16.5 million (Rath et al. 1996, 4-5; Shadid & Koningsveld 2008, 33).

Although the majority of Muslims arrived as foreign workers after 1960, it was Indonesian students who had earlier founded the first Islamic organization in Holland in 1932 (Rath et al. 1996, 3). Likewise, the first mosques were established before the huge influx of Muslim immigrants. Already before the Second World War, a mosque had been established in The Hague. In 1951 former soldiers of the Dutch East Indies Army immigrated into the Netherlands, mostly from the Moluccas, because the newly established independent Indonesian government considered them as collaborators with the former colonizer. Most of them were Christians, but a small minority was Muslim. The Dutch government provided houses, schools, and – in spite of the separation between state and religion – places of worship, like a small mosque in Balk, in the Northern part of the Netherlands (Rath et al. 1996, 270).

The first immigration wave in the 1960s and 1970s was the result of the Dutch post war industrial expansion. Low paid labourers were needed for those jobs which the Dutch themselves did not apply for, like line work, garbage collecting and spinning and weaving in the textiles industry. They came from Mediterranean regions like Spain, Italy, Turkey, Morocco and Tunisia. Initially it was only the men who came, intending to stay for a few years and to return after having earned enough money. Therefore, they were called 'guest workers'. They were hardly stimulated to integrate into Dutch society, since they were expected to return to their home country in due time, and by consequence they lived rather isolated. Despite their original intentions, the Muslim men did not return to their home countries. After several years they were finally allowed to invite their wives and children to the Netherlands. Once they were aware of the permanence of their stay, these migrant groups began to value their cultural and religious heritage for their children, attending Dutch schools and forming the new generation of the 'new' religion of Islam in the Netherlands (Shadid 2006, 14-16). During the 1980s and 1990s, the Dutch Muslim population increased and became more diverse through immigration from the former Dutch colony Suriname and refugees from African, Asian and East-European countries. Because of the wide variety of ethnic backgrounds Islam in the Netherlands has first of all, similar as in Britain, to be characterized as religious and cultural diverse.[1]

The designation 'guest worker' reflects the original Dutch perception of these newcomers, which was ignorant concerning their religious background and not interested in it. That changed after the Iranian Revolution (1979) and Khomeini's fatwa concerning the writer S. Rushdie because of his *Satanic Verses* (1989). Soon a public debate about Islam started. Gradually, the debate polarized, and focused more and more on the possible dangers and extremist tendencies of Islam, neglecting the average Islamic perception of the Qur'an and shared values like tolerance and respect (Shadid, 2006, 16). This negative perception was stimulated by the extremist attack on the twin towers in New York in 2001. On a national

---

1   Compare the chapter of Inga Niehaus this volume.

level, the Dutch media focused on the increase in minor criminality amongst Moroccan youth, mainly boys. This negative publicity about Muslims stimulated right wing politicians to portray themselves as opponents of the introduction of Islamic values in the Netherlands. One of them was the ex-Muslim Ayaan Hirsi Ali, a refugee from Somalia, who became a member of the Dutch Parliament. She blamed the Prophet Mohammed for, among other things, marrying a young girl (Westerman 2007, 388-390). She and her right wing colleague Geert Wilders were utmost worried about what they called the 'islamization of society'. Both politicians used the media film to convince the Dutch society of the dangers of Islam. In 2004 Hirsi Ali and Theo van Gogh produced the movie *Submission*. This was so offensive that a young man, a Muslim fundamentalist, killed Van Gogh. Wilders' short movie *Fitnah* (2008) blamed Islam for radical hate-sowing texts and suggested tearing 'cruel' sections out of the Qur'an. The political critics of Islam, who consider themselves as neo-liberals in the tradition of the Dutch eighteenth' century Enlightenment, make the principle of freedom of expression absolute and diminish the right of freedom of religion (Westerman 2007, 391).

3. Islam and the Dutch educational system

3.1 Muslims and the Dutch pillarized society and education

When 'guest workers' were allowed to reunite with their wives and children in the Netherlands in the 1970s and explored the school system, they were confronted with an educational system that was very unfamiliar to them. The entire Dutch educational and social system is, unlike in many other countries, based on the so-called 'pillars' of religious and non-religious worldviews (Ter Avest et al. 2007). Large religious and non-religious groups have created their own press, trade unions, political parties, sport clubs, libraries and broadcasting companies. Some of these groups also established schools. That was the Dutch way of coping with diversity: living in peace together, but separated into groups. The extraordinary situation of the educational system is not that it consists of two types of schools: the public and private ones, but that both are fully subsidized by the government. In 1917 this financial equalization was attained after half a century of Roman-Catholic and Protestant agitation against the government's favoring of public schools.

Private schools are governed by school boards, originally consisting of parents and often supplemented with professionals. In the case of public schools, the local municipalities are usually the formal body. In addition to this formal responsibility, many public schools also have a school advisory board of parents for more practical reasons. Contrary to public schools, private schools are free in their policy concerning the admittance of pupils, appointment of teachers and in providing religious education (RE) as a curricular subject. Although public schools are not permitted to teach religion, they are free to offer optional extra-curricular education in more than one religious and non-religious worldview during school hours. These lessons should not be taught by the school teacher but by special teachers appointed by religious denominations and non-religious groups like the Humanist Union (Kuyk 2007, 137). To obtain subsidies, private schools have to meet certain quality requirements, controlled by the school's inspectorate. Before the process of secularization began in the 1960s, most liberals and socialists chose to attend public schools, while Roman-Catholics and Protestants opted for private Roman-Catholic and Protestant schools. The result is that two thirds of the Dutch school are denominational. Only half a percent of these denominational schools was not religious-orientated, but based on a specific pedagogical program or educational theory, such as those of Maria Montessori and Rudolf Steiner. Despite the secularization after 1970 the proportional relation between the two types did not change, and neither did the low proportion of religious-neutral private schools. To avoid confusion with the concept of private schools in other countries, where 'private' often means that parents have to pay for the education and as a consequence such schools are for the elite, we speak of denominational schools instead of private schools (Rietveld-van Wingerden, Sturm & Miedema 2003, 104-105).

Schools and municipal authorities reacted in different ways to the arrival of Muslim pupils and their adjustment to the Dutch educational system. Some claimed that public schools were the most appropriate for them, because of their 'neutral' position in religious affairs (Van Rijsewijk 1984). However, because of their neutral stance towards religion, most of these schools ignored their pupils' religious backgrounds. An option was that public schools added Islamic education as an extra-curricular subject. It is symptomatic for the acceptance of Muslims and their involvement in Dutch society that only a few public schools started Islamic religious education. Advocates of these lessons experience a lot of opposition. That happened in 2008 with the Muslim chairman of one of the Amsterdam city councils, Ahmed Marcouch. He was told that public schools should be religiously 'neutral' (Westerman, 2009). Quite a number of his opponents were afraid that such education could only raise fundamentalism in the children's minds.

Right wing politicians reacted with a plea for stopping all of the few optional Islam lessons at public schools. Others reacted that such requirements should be adjusted to all other groups that taught religion and worldviews in public schools. Opponents sought requirements that all 'out-door' RE teachers should be qualified and able to speak Dutch, which was not always the case with Muslim RE teachers. Ironically, the Dutch parliament decided in December 2008 to pay the salaries for all RE teachers in public schools, Islamic teachers included (Westerman, 2009). In the meantime a teachers' training institute in Amsterdam, the IPABO (Inter-confessional Pedagogical Academy for Basic Education) has started the training of Islamic RE teachers. For imams and secondary education teachers, the VU-University in Amsterdam also started a Masters program on Islam.

The position of religious education in denominational schools was and is totally different. In the 1980s some Protestant and, to a lesser extent, Catholic schools, mostly in the country side, did not want to have Muslim pupils in their classes for religious reasons. But later on more and more Christian schools began to accept non-Christian children, including Muslim pupils, and now nearly all do. A few of the Christian schools were even forerunners in the development of 'interreligious education' (Gerritsen 1990, 12-14; Ter Avest 2003, 2009a).

3.2 Muslim children in Dutch schools

While the first generation of Muslims lived rather isolated from the Dutch communities, their children made Islam visible in the wider society, and especially in schools. Schools became the 'laboratories' for a multicultural and multi-religious society (Westerman 2006, 205-206). Initially, some parents sent their children to public schools, unacquainted as they were with the Dutch educational system. Moreover, they were advised to do so when the first-generation Muslims had their newly arrived children registered by the municipality, which often considered the public school's neutral religious stance more appropriate for them. Soon, however, most Islamic parents preferred Protestant and Roman-Catholic schools, because of the school's discipline and positive attitude towards religious education and moral values. But there is also a pragmatic reason. Because denominational schools form the majority, the chance for a Muslim family to have such a school in the neighbourhood is greater than the possibility of having a public school around the corner.

Dutch denominational schools were therefore confronted with an increase in Muslim pupils. The percentage of these pupils in primary education grew from only a few percent in 1980 to thirteen percent in 1995/1996 (204,810 children) and fifteen percent in 2004/2005 (240,720 children) (Van Koningsveld & Shadid 2006, 77). Despite the establishment of Islamic schools after 1989, the large majority of Muslim children (94 per cent in 2002 and afterwards) attended non-Islamic schools. The government and the schools themselves were forced to find ways of coping with the educational, cultural and religious differences between the students in previously ethnically homogeneous classes. The government's main aim was to reduce educational disadvantages. Therefore, schools received extra financial aids for every child belonging to an ethnic minority. This money could be invested in extra teaching facilities, extra teachers, language education and programs for cognitive socialization (Leemans & Pels 2006, 65). Primary schools were stimulated to provide programs in which the children's own language and culture formed the starting point for learning Dutch. Such programs were called OETC (Onderwijs in Eigen Taal en Cultuur) (Extra & Yağmur 2006). OETC teachers were recruited from the population of ethnic minorities. However, OETC was meant only for certain groups: children of guest laborers, refugees, Roma and Moluccans. Other groups were excluded. For instance, Pakistani expats living in Amsterdam could not send their children to OETC classes during school hours. They and other groups often organized weekend classes for their children to learn Urdu, Chinese or other languages.

The participation of Turkish and Moroccan children in OETC was rather high, respectively eighty and seventy percent in 1987 (Shadid & Van Koningsveld 1990, 108). What was not foreseen was that language problems would destroy the good intentions. An increasing number of children born in the Netherlands did not speak their parents' language. A further complication was that the national languages were not always the children's mother-tongue, like for the Berbers from Morocco. Moreover, the Arabic of national languages differ from the Classic Arabic of the Qur'an lessons which was used as the official language for OETC lessons (Otten &

De Ruiter 1991, 95). Therefore many young Moroccan children struggled not only in learning Dutch but also in learning Arabic in more than one version.

Furthermore, the cultural component of OETC also became problematic. Dutch teachers and school-administrators, not understanding the language used in OETC, soon became suspicious that the lessons were being used for the promotion of nationalistic ideas and religious instruction. The latter happened only incidentally. In 1987 religious education was part of the instruction in 53 per cent of the Turkish and 60 percent of the Moroccan lessons (Shadid & Van Koningsveld 1990, 108). Moreover, Dutch politicians were more inclined to prioritize assimilation, especially after '9/11'. They considered native languages and cultures as hindrances to a successful integration into Dutch society. Citizenship education appeared on the political agenda as the way to stimulate social cohesion (Leeman & Pels 2006, 70-71). Therefore, OETC lessons during school hours were stopped in 2004. Of course, it is still possible to organize OETC during the weekend and after school hours, as well as to provide Qur'an lessons in the mosque.

OETC lessons were designated to the specific groups of newcomers, but were of no value for the school population as a whole. How could schools be helpful in integrating non-native Dutch children into society? A new Primary Education Act (1981), implemented in 1985, forced schools to adopt a more intercultural approach. Instruction about religious and ideological movements became a compulsory subject for all schools. This subject was called 'Geestelijke Stromingen' (literally: Spiritual Movements) that should be taught in an objective, neutral way. This new subject was therefore separated from religious education. The legislator made a clear distinction between 'teaching about religions' and 'teaching into religions'. The 'objective – subjective' duality raised many theoretical and practical questions, which cannot be discussed here (Westerman 2001, 207-221). Unfortunately, the great number of questions curbed the development of Geestelijke Stromingen. In the case of Islam, the new educational materials did not exceed the standard information about the Islam, like the five pillars and five prayers a day, and they ignored the children's own religious experiences. An analysis of textbooks in 1994 showed that most of the materials presented incomplete and above all incorrect information about Islam (Westerman 1994). Moreover, a lack of motivation hindered the implementation of this new subject. Some twenty years later the subject seems forgotten. It is only recently that aspects of this subject have been included in citizenship education, a new and compulsory subject since 2006.

The awareness of the differences between religions and the tensions between Islam and Western culture (see paragraph 1.3) motivated some school boards, both Christian and Islamic ones, to find new educational concepts in which differences are not considered as a threat but an opportunity. Some Christian schools opted for interreligious education, while a group of Islamic schools used the diversity within the Islamic world and the confrontation between the Islam and Western values as a basis for working out a school program. In the next paragraphs we discuss these concepts, first by focusing on interreligious education at denominational Christian schools (2.3), followed by the initiatives of Islamic schools (3.2).

3.3 Denominational schools and interreligious learning

The events of September 11th 2001 ('9/11') stimulated reflections on the role of religion in society and a critical approach towards Islam, fed by the above mentioned politicians Hirsi Ali and Wilders. However, in the more relaxed climate of the 1980s, the Protestant and Catholic educational pillars had already started deliberations about the opportunities and hindrances presented by interreligious dialogue. Initially the Christians feared the potential for religious syncretism in Christian-Muslim dialogue (cf.: Kraan 1987, 1990; Gerritsen & Westerman 1990). This was in the period that worldwide Christian theologians, stimulated by a growing global awareness and new church-related orientations such as the Second Vatican Council, discussed new theological positions towards other religions. The intention was to reconstruct the traditional theology from a *'theologia extra ecclesiam'* (a theology that excludes religion outside the church) into a *'theologia religionum'* (a theology that includes all religions) (Westerman 2001, 78-83). Still, within this climate, several Protestant and Catholic schools took the Islamic background of the pupils as a starting point and developed programs to promote mutual understanding of Christianity and Islam (Bierlaagh 1988). A well known example of such an interreligious approach is the Juliana van Stolberg school in the small town of Ede, which served as an example for elsewhere.

In 1989 the board of the protestant primary school Juliana van Stolberg decided to offer Islamic religious classes to Muslim pupils, at the request of the Islamic parents. A committee of Christian theologians, parents' representatives, teachers and an imam had extensive deliberations on the religious narratives that should be implemented in RE, separately for the Muslim and Christian pupils. It was important to pay attention to the pupils' existential life themes, like the beauty of creation, the birth of a new born baby brother or sister, and the inevitable sorrow and pain when one has to say farewell to a significant other. The decision to teach Islamic next to Christian religion signified the inception of the first Dutch interreligious primary school. The reasons behind this initiative were based on the positive significance of religion as an important aspect of the individual's life view in a multicultural society (Ter Avest 2003, 2009). 'Encounter' became the central concept. Religious Education was included in this curriculum in two ways. Firstly, the children attended RE classes in line with their religious socialization at home, either Christian or Islamic. These lessons were given separately to Christian and Islamic children. The class teacher taught Christianity and the imam taught Islam. Secondly, every child had a weekly 'lesson in encounter', taught by the class teacher. The Christian and Islamic lessons and the 'encounter lessons' were finetuned to the developmental phases of the children. According to the age of the pupils, they were introduced to stories common to both the Bible and the Qur'an, like those of Joseph/Yusuf and Moses/Musa, and to the different articulations of both religions, like fasting and the person Jesus/Isa. The children learned from their classmates, 'the others', the good reasons for behaving differently. The pupils noticed and learned from the authentic way in which their classmates experienced the rituals of their religion as meaningful. The school has served as an example for other Christian schools, but had to close its doors, in 2002, due to socio-geographical reasons. The population of the school's neighbourhood changed from young migrant families into mainly elderly and aging people.

A comparable initiative started in the city of Rotterdam in 1999. A group of twenty-four Protestant primary schools, most of them with a population of over ninety percent of Muslim pupils, implemented a process of interreligious learning. Firstly, the teams of teachers – being (secularized) Christians –, reflected on the inclusion of Muslim children in RE lessons (Bakker & Ter Avest 2009b, 2010). This Structural Identity Consultation (SIC; Ter Avest, Miedema & Bakker 2008; Ter Avest & Bakker 2009a) was of pivotal importance. In these team meetings the teachers discussed their commitment to the Christian identity of their school in correspondence to the school population. At the start of this SIC-process teachers described individually an example of good practice, a 'critical incident' in which according to their view the school's Christian identity was at stake. The conversations that followed made each teacher more aware of her/his personal relation to the Christian tradition and to the school's 'situated Christian identity'. The SIC enables the teachers to reflect both on others' positioning in relation to the Christian tradition and on the school's identity. Aware of the differences and communalities, within the team, in relation to the Christian tradition, the teachers are invited to take the other's perspectives and to explore the differences between the Christian and Islamic tradition. In SIC-processes the concept of 'interreligious education' is highlighted in situated 'practical wisdom' in the classroom, for example by a teacher allowing her Muslim pupils to pray in their own way during morning prayers, or inviting Muslim pupils to inform their classmates about the ritual of breaking the Fast at the end of each day during Ramadan.

In 2007, three primary schools in the Bijlmer district of Amsterdam took up the mental legacy of the interreligious Juliana van Stolberg primary school. These schools interpret the 'inter-religiousness' as an encounter between pupils from different religious backgrounds, which at the same time strengthens the roots in their own tradition, in RE classes in their own school context, according to the school's identity. The three schools for primary education, a liberal Roman-Catholic, an Islamic and a public school, coordinated their efforts for the education of their pupils living in a world of diversity (Ter Avest & Clement 2008). In the Roman-Catholic school Bible stories are told during RE lessons. In the Islamic school *sura's* from the *Qur'an* are recited every week. In the state school the curriculum is imbued with a humanistic world view. Keeping to their own cultural school climate, and to religious and non-religious worldviews and related educational concepts, the principals of the schools decided to cooperate in those fields which, in their view, most easily allowed for doing things together, like the festivities on the Queen's Birthday. They follow their own lines of thought in those fields which call for a tradition-related approach, like celebration of Christmas in the Roman-Catholic school and the performance of the sacred duty of Ramadan in the Islamic school. Central in the mission statement of each of the three schools is that they wish to prepare their pupils for a future in a multi-cultural and multi-religious Dutch society by 'learning to live together'. The boards and teachers perceive the school as a learning environment in between their children's families and society, and the school as a participatory community and a place of encounter. Each school has its own catchword as an expression of the core of the school's identity. The motto of the three schools together is: *'Het meervoud van samen in toekomst'* ('the plural of cooperation is future').

4. Islamic schools

4.1 Adjusting to the Dutch society and educational system

It took a long time before Muslim parents could grasp the complexity of the pillarized Dutch society (Van Bommel 1990, 49-51). It must have been confusing that there was a secularization process on the one hand and that, on the other hand, most schools were religiously affiliated. Initially, a rather small number of Muslim migrants were so confused about the Dutch educational system that they did not send their children to school at all. Some Amsterdam Christians noticed it and warned the Amsterdam municipal officials. Because the council did not respond, they founded the Bouschrã School in 1978 ('Good News' School) (Westerman forthcoming). The school provided education in Arabic and Islamic religion, alongside the general Dutch school subjects. Actually, this school was the first Islamic school in the Netherlands, although managed by a Christian school board (Hagen 1988, 42). After some very successful years the Bouschrã School had to close because of opposition from city officials who considered public schools as the most ideal school for Muslim children.

As soon as the Muslims became familiar with Dutch society they started their own organizations. They founded mosques where children were welcome to learn the Qur'an and Arabic after school hours (Karagül 1987). Some mosques also took up social and educational tasks in youth care, homework classes and advice for parents concerning the upbringing of their children. Later on, other societal organizations were founded like Islamic broadcasting stations, social work organisations and primary schools. All these local and even national initiatives showed the Dutch that Islam was present. Moreover, Muslims became active in political parties, liberal, socialist, and also Christian democratic parties. This political participation had already started in the 1980s, when the first Muslims were elected to municipal governments. Recently (2008) this development arrived at a new peak with the appointment of an Islamic Moroccan mayor Achmed Aboutaleb in the city of Rotterdam, Holland's second biggest city. Municipal bodies have great power in applying the Constitutional right of freedom of education at the local level. It could therefore happen that two Muslims, representing different political parties, stood opposite each other when the approval to start an Islamic school was on the agenda of their municipal board. This was the case, for instance, in the city of Eindhoven (in the Southern part of the Netherlands), where the Turkish socialist councillor F. Cansilar objected, because he thought such a school would increase the children's backlog, while his Christian democratic colleague C. Toprak, also a Turkish Muslim, defended the Islamic school. Toprak believed that Islamic self-organization would increase emancipation and integration (Hagen 1988, 39-46).

The practice of a strict neutrality concerning religions in general, in particular by public schools, awoke Muslim parents' desire to have schools for their children where Islam is integrated into the curriculum. The importance of the public schools' attitude is shown in Belgium where, in 1974, Islam was officially recognized as a religion, allowed to be taught in the public schools. Here the need for Islam schools was much smaller than in the Netherlands (Karsten 2006, 26-28.) The dream of Muslim's own Islamic schools was intensified when the OETC lost its cultural component. However, it was not only for purely religious and cultural reasons that Muslims wanted to have their own schools. Muslim parents often experience neglect and discrimination against their children, according to Hoesein Nanhekhan, principal of an Islamic primary school in the city of Utrecht. Moreover, Nanhekhan emphasized that his school paid more attention to language acquisition and cognitive development, adjusted to the situation of Muslim children. In this way, Islamic schools want to improve the pupils' development and output to higher levels of education. According to Nanhekhan, Muslim parents choose for quality first and then for the Islamic identity (Nanhekhan 2002, 63-68).

Initially, the establishment of Islamic schools met little resistance, accustomed as the Dutch were to the pillarized school system. Soon however, political adherents of public education in particular began to object. One of them was the alderman for education of the city of Utrecht, who feared that such schools would stimulate the segregation of ethnic minorities (Sikkes 1989). Public opinion about the desirability of Islamic schools was and is still strongly divided. In January 1992, for instance, 57 percent of the Dutch population was in favor of such schools (Rath et al. 1996, 58). The percentage in favor has dropped the last few years because of an increased fear of a radical Islam (Shadid & Van Koningsveld 2006, 258-260).

The first Islamic primary school in the Netherlands was the Al Ghazali primary school in Rotterdam (1987). In 1994 there were 29 Islamic primary schools, from a total of 8.139 primary schools (Rath et al. 1996, 64) and in 2004 there were 41 primary schools and two secondary schools. They form only 0.6 percent of the total number of primary schools (Shadid & Van Koningsveld 2006, 77). So, like in Britain, the majority of Muslim children in the Netherlands are educated in non-Muslim schools.[2]

Like their Christian counterparts, these schools also have their organizations on the national level to assist individual schools, stimulate reflection and develop school materials. The first and largest one is the Islamitische Scholen Besturen Organisatie (ISBO [Organization of Islamic School Boards]), founded in 1990. The main aims of the ISBO are the advocacy of the interests of Islamic schools and the provision and stimulation of good conditions for Islamic education in accordance with the Qur'an and the Sunna (Shadid & Van Koningsveld 2008, 245-247). Other comparable organizations were founded alongside the ISBO, such as the Islamitische Stichting Nederland voor Onderwijs en Opvoeding (ISNO [Islamic Foundation in the Netherlands for Schooling and Education]) and, specifically for Rotterdam schools, the Islamitische Onderwijsgroep Nederland (INO [Group of Islamic Education in the Netherlands]) (Dumassy 2008, 73; Shadid & Van Koningsveld 2008, 245-247). Recently a new union was established, the Stichting voor Islamitisch Onderwijs in Midden en Oost Nederland (SIMON [Foundation of

---

2 See also the chapter of Inga: Niehaus in this volume.

Islamic Education in the Middle and the Eastern part of the Netherlands]), to function as the board of eight Islamic primary schools.

For most of the Islamic schools the start was not easy going. Although Islamic schools fit into the pillarized educational system, many regulations had to be adapted to. Most of the Islamic school board members had no experience with school management, while there was no tradition of non-governmental religion based schools in their countries of origin. For most of them the regulations of the Dutch pillarized system were difficult to interpret, because of the complexity of the Dutch educational system and corresponding requirements. Due to a strict separation of state and religion, one of the preconditions was that the school board should not consist of the same people as the board of the mosque. Some school boards also struggled with the requirement that a teacher of their school(s) cannot be a school board member. Moreover, it was difficult to find enough qualified school headmasters and teachers. That is the reason why, until today, many non-Muslim teachers work in Islamic schools, and why most of the headmasters do not have an Islamic background.

A core problem for Islamic school board members is the status of the school curriculum. Contrary to Britain the Netherlands has no national curriculum.[3] Schools are so-called relative-autonomous. That means that officially every school is responsible for its own curriculum. However, this responsibility is bordered by general national educational standards as global educational objectives and partly centralized national exams. Individual schools have the freedom to organize their own curricula within these borders. Usually the Islamic school boards lacked the skills and knowledge for their own schools' curriculum construction. In most of the Muslim schools the great number of non-Muslim teachers developed substantial parts of the school curriculum, at least for the non-religious subjects. For the subject Religious Education Islamic school boards are assisted by the Stichting Leergang Ontwikkeling (SLO [National Foundation of Curriculum Construction]). As a result of their efforts the majority of Muslim schools have good academic qualities. The few schools with low academic standards are mainly schools with board members who do not recognize the freedom of teachers to formulate their visions on a curriculum that fits in the Dutch educational context.

Like Roman-Catholic and Protestant schools, Islamic schools have to cope with a wide variety in traditions with respect to their religious backgrounds. There are several interpretations of the educational needs of Muslims in a Western society such as the Netherlands. What a 'good Islamic education' is, is not a foregone conclusion. As there is a common presumption that some people try to use the freedom within this variety of Islamic educational traditions to preach radical Islamic fundamentalism, nowadays many Dutch people – especially some politicians – do not fully trust the Islamic educational pillar in our society. However, the report of a school-inspection conducted shortly after '9/11' and subsequent researches some

---

3   See the chapter of Inga Niehaus in this volume, comparing the British and Dutch educational tradition, Niehaus states incorrectly that the government funded schools in the Netherlands are obliged to teach the national curriculum. This obligation does not even exist for 'governmental' schools, while in the Netherlands resulting from article 23 of the Dutch Constitution, there is no national curriculum. Every school is, within certain national directions, responsible for its own curriculum,

years later, showed that nearly all Islamic schools promote an open attitude towards Dutch society and stimulate their pupils to participate in Dutch society and to cooperate in the creation of social cohesion (Inspectie 2002, 5). Nevertheless, the reports did not convince adherents who continue to object to Islamic schools as a danger to society and a hotbed for fundamentalism and radicalism. In the midst of the various reactions to Islamic education, Muslim educators themselves reflected upon and explored the (im)possibilities of adjusting to the requirements of the Dutch educational system as well as adapting to Dutch society.

4.2 Islamic education 'on the move'

The process of raising awareness of differences and commonalities between traditions represented by their pupils is not only at stake in Christian interreligious schools with a considerable part of Muslim pupils. In 2008, the above mentioned SIMON corporation, the board of eight Islamic primary schools, started a process of reflection on the tensions that they experience between living and educating according to the Islamic tradition and the context of a westernized Dutch society. The presence of Christian and secular teachers in their schools articulated both the possible discrepancies and commonalities between religious worldviews. SIMON organized consultations with principals and encouraged their eight schools to form identity committees. These came up with inductively-achieved topics of information and discussion, which were used in official documents, formulating the mission statement and drawing up the rules and regulations for its eight schools (Aktaran et al. 2008b). Taking their starting point in Islamic values, these documents seek to incorporate local Dutch habits, like birthday celebrations, and also governmental decisions on aims for primary education. Moreover, these SIMON schools and their boards discussed the subject Geestelijke Stromingen (Spiritual Movements), physical education, and official documents on Human and Children's Rights (see also Bakker & Ter Avest 2008a, 2008b).

The starting point for the SIMON foundation is 'respect for diversity', and an awareness of diversity as an authentic characteristic for Islam with its different law schools (*fiqh*) and interpretations (*aqidah*). Moreover, the board is aware of the variety among pupils concerning their religiosity – they come from confessional and secularized Islam families – and ethnicity. The board of SIMON has decided to explore the ways in which Dutch Muslims can respond, both to differences within Islam, and to the diversity in opinions on how to be a Muslim in Dutch society. With regard to 'coping with diversity', SIMON is aware of a special responsibility for children who are socialised in their Muslim families and are educated in the Dutch educational system.

Diversity within the framework of the Dutch educational system is the leading principle in SIMON's mission statement. This serves as a framework for each of the participating schools to develop their own 'practical wisdom' in relation to their own neighbourhood and specific population of pupils and parents. There is a spirit of respect, loyalty and tolerance for diversity in the mission statement that might stimulate the participants (governors, principals, teachers, parents, pupils) accordingly, despite differences in interpretation of the sources of the Islamic tradition. Differences are seen as enriching and are valued accordingly. 'Unity in diversity' serves as a catchword (Aktaran 2008a).

Concerning the aims of the Dutch education, like those in the field of language acquisition, mathematics and geography, most of them are religiously affiliated. That is not the case with respect to subjects and aims to, among other things, encourage orientation in the world the students live in, social-emotional development and orientation in the field of arts. A goal description like: 'pupils learn to respect the generally accepted values and regulations' offers a lot of deliberations within the SIMON group. What is 'generally accepted'? What is acceptable and tolerated within the Islamic value system? And if so, are there contrasting and conflicting values within this system? For such items, sensitive to Islamic interpretation, the board consulted several Islam scholars. They reflected upon a variety of themes in which Dutch values and Islamic interpretations are at stake and might cause tensions. The board elaborates these topics in the mission statement. We will go into some of these themes in detail, as an example of the way in which Dutch Muslims develop their own 'polder Islam' on how to be a Muslim in the Netherlands, and to provide students with an education as future citizens of a multicultural, multi-ethnic and multi-religious Dutch society. We will first elaborate on the issues seen as debatable in primary schools, and then we will highlight some issues raised in Islamic secondary education.

4.3 Reflection on differences between Islamic and Western values

In the SIMON schools, but also in other fields of the Islamic society, the reflections and discussions about cultural and religious differences between Islam and non-Islamic habits and traditions are increasing. That is especially important for schools as places of religious and cultural transformation. For a long time much had been taken for granted, but recently a more (self-)critical attitude has evolved. The deliberations concern the celebration of religious festivals, birthday and national festivities. Furthermore, issues that determine school life are also discussed, such as those of headscarves for girls, drama and music (Aktaran 2008a). Some of these topics will be discussed here.

Like Christmas and Easter are the main religious feasts in Christianity, Islam has two as well: *Id al Adha* and *Id al Fitr*. The first one is the commemoration of the willingness of Abraham to sacrifice one of his sons for God: Isaak or Ismael, depending on the story, biblical or koranic. *Id al Fitr* is the end of the fasting period *Ramadan*. These main Islamic festivals are celebrated in all Islamic schools in the Netherlands. Even many non-Islamic schools allow their pupils some days off to celebrate these days with their families and sometimes a Christian school invites Islamic parents to organise a celebration during school hours.

However, although these celebrations are obvious in Islamic school, this is not the case with personal feasts like birthdays. This celebration, so common in Dutch society, meets resistance among Muslims because of the position of man towards God. According to Islam every man and woman is dedicated to subordinate himself to God's will and plan. Man is not seen as the centre of creation. Egocentric thoughts should be transformed into altruistic behaviour towards others. The celebration of a birthday is not in harmony with this obedient and modest attitude. Instead, the child should learn from early childhood to focus on the relationship with God.

For children, the discrepancy between Islamic family traditions and societal habits like birthdays, and mother's day and father's day as well, might be difficult to understand. It formed the subject for reflection among Muslim educators in the Netherlands, who are aware of this problem. They took into account psychological theories on the cognitive and affective development of the child with regard to the possible understanding of conflicting worldviews leading to a variety of solutions (Aktaran 2008a). One group of Islamic educators advised to adhere to the Islamic tradition and religious values by forbidding celebrations of birthdays, mother's day and father's day. Obedience and modesty towards God, but also the confusing results for the child were their main arguments. In their view it is impossible to clarify to children that the birthday, forbidden in the Islam, could be celebrated at schools. Opposing this is another group, who presented arguments based precisely on the bicultural context of the children (Ramadan 2004, 128-135). They take their starting point in the Western Christian habit of celebrating birthdays. By articulating its difference with the Islamic notion of the attitude towards the Creator, the child's birthday formed an opportunity to reflect upon its comings and goings and put to the fore the Islamic notion of being God's guardian of the world. In RE lessons the child's birthday could be related to the concept of 'submission' and presented as its concretisation (Aktaran 2008b). A *halal* approach is favoured in all cases, that means that nothing should be done that can not find favour in the eyes of God.

Whereas the Queen's Birthday is a national holiday of pleasure and joy underpinning the unity in diversity, the commemoration of the dead on May 4th is also a moment of shared feelings of sadness and sorrow.[4] Much effort is made to include ethnic minorities in the commemoration of the dead by pointing out the contribution of Muslims to the liberation of Europe from dictatorship and the tyranny of the Nazi regime in the Second World War. The recently developed curricula on citizenship education aim to strengthen the power of shared feelings of Dutchness (Westerman 2008).

In discussions on the permissibility of festivals, the expression of joy in dancing, for example, has been thoroughly discussed, in particular with regard to drama lessons, that are regularly included in the curriculum of primary schools. In these deliberations the focus has been on the consequences of drama and music. In earlier times drama, music and dancing have been associated with drinking, dancing, sensuality and sexuality. These aspects of life are considered to distract from obedience to God. That was the reason why music and drama has been declared to be not permissible (*haraam*). Other thinkers considered music and drama permissible (*halaal*) under certain preconditions. The debate on music and drama lessons (part of the core aims of the Dutch compulsory curriculum in primary education) focuses on the consequences of these subjects. Texts of songs

---

4   Originally this day of commemoration was dedicated only to the Dutch victims of the Second World War. Nowadays it has been broadened in two ways. Not only Dutch victims of the Second World War are memorised, but all victims of war all over the world.

and the consequences of dancing should be pure (*halaal*) from an ethical point of view. Characteristic for drama lessons and music should be the supportive role with regard to other subjects in the curriculum. This topic is very urgent in the Dutch context, since it is a national habit that at the end of primary school a musical is performed by the pupils leaving school and continuing their education in secondary school.

The starting point for dancing is that folk dancing is a part of culture. However, the usual regulations with regard to contact between boys and girls, in particular boys and girls older then ten years of age, should be taken into account (Aktaran 2008b; Ter Avest 2009).

One particular aspect of the 'usual regulations' in the contact of boys and girls is the dress code, in particular the wearing of the headscarf (*hidjaab*). In Islamic schools different dress codes apply. In some schools, all female teachers (whether Muslim or not) have to wear a headscarf. For girls, the schools feel a responsibility, in close cooperation with the parents, to stimulate them to wear a headscarf. For male teachers in those schools it is preferable to have a beard. In other schools a headscarf is compulsory only for Muslim teachers, and in yet another group of schools not even all Muslim teachers wear a headscarf. Headwear which covers the face completely is not allowed in any of the Islamic schools. Parents wearing such head coverings have to identify themselves when entering the school.

4.4 Islamic secondary education

Recently two Islamic schools for secondary education were established in the Netherlands, one in the city of Rotterdam (2000) and the other one in the city of Amsterdam (2001). Awareness of the 'situatedness' of Islamic RE has been increasing not only in Islamic primary schools, but also in Islamic secondary schools. In a sweeping statement at the REDCo conference in Amsterdam (2008) on the role of religion in the life of youngsters aged 14-16, one of the directors of these secondary schools pleaded for a reflection on Islamic RE. He stated that, due to the fact that his pupils are born in the Netherlands and intend and are bound to live in the multicultural and multi-religious Dutch society, he himself had started consultations with his teachers on the interpretation of the Islamic identity of his school and its consequences for the curriculum, and for RE classes in particular. In his view, the 'encounter with the other' is necessary to learn to live together. He sees the development of what he coins the 'answer-ability' from an Islamic perspective to the Dutch post-modern context, as an important aspect of his responsibility with regard to the enculturation of his pupils and the development of their religious identity. In this principal's view the *iman*, as a 'significant other' with regard to educational topics for Muslim parents, is of pivotal importance in the development of a situated Islam. This is despite contrasting and sometimes even conflicting differences in beliefs (Kasri, in: Ter Avest & Bertram-Troost 2009).

The Amsterdam Islamic secondary school, the ICA (Islamitisch College Amsterdam) is an example of the adaptation of Islamic pedagogical principles to the Dutch context (see also Meijer 2007). The ICA recognises that the family is important for the pupils during their adolescence. The board is aware of this and, consequently, emphasises the particular role of the school as an institution of education. Parents are seen as co-educators who are important informants for the teachers. The parents know their child best, and they can inform the school about the way they socialize their child in the Islamic tradition. According to the board of the ICA, school and parents should be complementary in their educational activities, emphasizing that the school is the place to get knowledge about topics such as literature, mathematics, economy, citizenship and also religion. A special role is given to the religious communities. In Islam, the imam speaks with authority when it comes to educational problems. Fully aware of the diversity in Islam, the ICA calls in imams to inform and discuss with the parents new developments in the curriculum with regard to topics that might be touchy for the parents, for example when it comes to Islamic values. An example of this might be a one week's excursion with a mixed group of pupils (girls and boys) to London, or the intention of the board to add introductory lessons on sexual behaviour to the curriculum. Another touchy topic is the dress code, in particular the headscarf. This is compulsory for girls. 'But what about the female teachers?' This question is discussed extensively, resulting in different solutions in different schools. In some schools all teachers (including the Dutch non-Muslim teachers) have to wear a headscarf, and in other schools only the Muslim teachers are obliged to cover their hair. Since most of the teachers are not Muslims, there is also a discussion about being a role model and representing the variety of religions in the Netherlands. In close cooperation with an advisory group on education (Capabel), the ICA board discusses any new initiative. By doing so, the ICA establishes a trustful relationship with the parents as partners in the education of their children. In their view, teachers should be an example of belief. There is a noticeable tension between the needs of the parents for Islamic education, and the needs of the pupils for knowledge about different religions as they are represented in Dutch society. Besides the contacts with parents and a variety of religious communities, the board of the ICA also has regular consultations with Islamic organisations in the field of education, such as the ISBO (Organization of Islamic School Boards) and the organisation of mosques in the Netherlands.

The population of the ICA is mixed with regard to Islamic law schools. Most of the pupils (Moroccans as well as Turkish) belong to the *Suni*, a smaller part to the *Sjiit-Salafit* law school. The board of the ICA allows Muslim pupils from different law schools to register at the school, 'we want to be a school for every Muslim in the Netherlands; a school in the midst of diversity'. The board emphasises, however, that the pupils of the ICA are Dutch children, born in Amsterdam. The board weighs up for its pupils the rights and obligations of Dutch citizenship and Islamic belief, taking into account that these pupils are the citizens of the future. A modern website underlines the 'situatedness' of this Islamic secondary school in the Dutch westernised context. According to the board of the ICA, Islam is not a hindrance for integration. 'Islamic values correspond to and support citizenship values and regulations'. RE in the ICA is 'work-in-progress'; the teachers develop their own teaching materials, since no material has been published yet for a 'situated Islam in the Dutch context'. The peers of the ICA pupils are also Muslims, like the pupils themselves. They do not have frequent contact with native Dutch youngsters, which is a consequence of the composition of the population of the neighbourhood where the ICA is situated, the same part of the city where the pupils live. The neighbourhood is not a natural environment for intercultural and inter-religious encounters. "Pupils don't travel half an hour to the other side of the city to meet 'the other'", the chair of the board of directors says as an understatement. "Learning to live with differences has to start with learning from the varieties of Islamic law schools and its adherents", according to the chair of the ICA (Ter Avest & Bertram-Troost 2009).

5. Discussion and conclusions

Although the Netherlands was the world's largest Muslim country until 1950, because of its colony of the East Indies, and although Leyden University was (and still is!) a world centre for Islamic and Arabic studies, ordinary people like 'Joe the Plumber' in the Netherlands were not well prepared for the immigration of large groups of Muslims after 1960. Their experiences and knowledge were not integrated into everyday practicalities, and ideas on education and literature. Therefore, it looked as if Islam was a new phenomenon in the second half of the twentieth century. This was mirrored in the fact that people initially spoke of Turks and Moroccans instead of Muslims. Muslims became visible as adherents to a non-Western religion only after the family reunions in the eighties, when their children went to school in the pillarized educational system. The Iranian Revolution (1979) and the Salmon Rushdie Affair (1989), gave rise to some feelings of fear for Islam, which resulted in a kind of segregation of society. This became worse after 9/11. Suddenly, many Dutch citizens perceived all Turks, Tunisians, Moroccans and refugees from Africa and the Middle East first and foremost as dangerous Muslims. These migrants who came to Holland as laborers or refugees, without any intention of fighting Dutch society, suddenly had to learn how to react to these negative stereotypes and prejudices. Their children experienced problems at school because of educational backlogs and segregation in the schools between native and migrant children. These backlogs motivated the government and schools to provide extra language lessons for these children. Likewise, the introduction of the subject Spiritual Movements was meant to reduce intolerance and segregation (1985). Muslim parents who became aware of the constitutional right of freedom of education decided to enter into the Dutch pillarized educational system, and started their own schools. At the same time, in 1989, a Christian school in the middle of the country started inter-religious education and functioned as an example for other schools.

Although schools are important as cradle for the future society, we have to be careful not to overestimate their role, and schools cannot compensate for wrongdoings in society. In order to respond to processes of segregation, and to stimulate encounters with 'the others', more is needed than efforts in the context of education. The principal of the ICA underlined the findings of the REDCo research that, despite the stimulation of intercultural encounters in schools, peers continue to meet in their own ethnic groups outside of school. One of the teachers interviewed in the REDco project commented on this: 'My pupils won't travel to the other side of the city to have an intercultural encounter. Their leisure time is spent in the neighbourhood they live in, a neighbourhood of migrants. Learning in school about different religious and non-religious worldviews is only part of the answer to the challenges of the multicultural society. The pupils of the REDCo research, in the Netherlands as well as in the other participating European countries, are convinced that at the end of the day, knowing about each other will result in respect and tolerance, in peacefully living together (Ter Avest 2009). In these processes, the teacher is of pivotal importance, since she is the gatekeeper between the micro-system of the family and the macro-system of the public domain, as a meeting place – and this is true in Islamic schools all over Europe.

References

Aktaran, E. (2008a) *Worden wie je bent, ontwikkeling van identiteit en onderwijsconcept SIMON scholen* (Leusden, interne publicatie SIMON scholen).
Aktaran, E. (Ed.) (2008b) *SIMON kaders voor de smalle identiteit* (Leusden, interne publicatie SIMON scholen).
Bakker, C. (2006) Van encyclopedie naar authentiek gesprek. In: S. Miedema (Ed.) *Religie in het onderwijs. Zekerheden en onzekerheden van levensbeschouwelijke vorming* (Zoetermeer, Meinema), 167-192.
Bakker, C. & ter Avest, I. (2005) De organisatie van een structureel identiteitsberaad, in: Hermans, Chr. (Ed.) *Perspectieven op vakontwikkeling en schoolontwikkeling*, IKO reeks deel 5 (Budel, Damon), 165-184.
Bakker, C. & ter Avest, I. (2005) Schoolethos and its religious dimension, in: *Scriptura, International Journal for Bible, Religion and Theology in South Africa, 89*, 350-362.
Benali, A. & Obdeijn, H. (2005) *Marokko door Nederlandse ogen 1605-2005* (Amsterdam: Arbeiderspers).
Bierlaagh, C.J.C. (1988) Leerlingen met een ander geloof in de katholieke basisscholen. *Samenwijs,* 9 (3), 90-91.
Boxer, C.E. (1973) *The Dutch Seaborn Empire 1600-1800.* (Harmondsworth, Pelican).
Brienen, T. (2008) *Johannes Hoornbeeck (1617-1666) eminent geleerde en pastoraal theoloog* (Goudriaan, De Groot).
Brugman, J. & Schröder, F. (1979) *Arabic Studies in The Netherlands* (Leiden, Brill).
D'Costa, G. (1986) *Theology and Religious Pluralism. The Challenge of Other Religions* (Oxford: Basil Blackwell).
Extra, G. & Yağmur, K. (2006) Immigrant minority languages at home and at school. A case study in the Netherlands. *European Education,* 38 (2), 50-63.
Gerritsen, J. (1990) Zeven jaren in de ban van de ring? 1981-1988 – de Stuurgroep P.C. Onderwijs en Culturele Minderheden, in: Gerritsen, J. H. & Westerman, W. E. (Eds.) *Ontmoetingen in het onderwijs. Onderwijs en vormingswerk in een multiculturele en multireligieuze samenleving* (Kampen, Kok), 9-19.
Gerritsen, J. & Westerman, W.E. (Eds.) (1990) *Ontmoetingen in het onderwijs. Onderwijs en vormingswerk in een multiculturele en multireligieuze samenleving* (Kampen, Kok).
Groenendijk, L.F. & Sturm, J.C. (1992) *Comenius in Nederland. Reacties op een grote Tsjechische pedagoog en hervormer (17^e – 20^e eeuw)* (Kok, Kampen).
Hagen, P. (1988) De school met de Koran'. *De Tijd.* 14 (April 8), 39-42.
Harper, R. (1998) *Als God met ons is … Jacob van Maerlant en de vijanden van het christelijk geloof* (Amsterdam, Prometeus).

Inspectie van het Onderwijs (2002) *Islamitische Scholen en Sociale Cohesie* (Den Haag, Inspectie van het Onderwijs).
Israel, J.I. (2001) *Radical Enlightenment. Philosophy and the making of Modernity. 1650-1750* (Oxford, Oxford University Press).
Israel, J.I. (2006) *Enlightenment Contested. Philosophy, Modernity, and the Emancipation of Man. 1670-1752* (Oxford, Oxford University Press).
Juynboll, W.M.C. (1931) *Zeventiende-eeuwsche Beoefenaars van het Arabisch in Nederland* (Utrecht, Kemink).
Kaplan, Y. (1995) De joden in de Republiek tot omstreeks 1750. Religieus, cultureel en sociaal leven. In: Blom, J.C.H. (Ed.) *Geschiedenis van de Joden in Nederland* (Amsterdam, Balans), 129-173.
Karagül, A. (1987) Een Turkse imam over koranschool en islamitisch godsdienstonderwijs, in: Wagtendonk, K. (Ed.) *Islam in Nederland. Islam op school* (Muiderberg, Coutinho), 77-88.
Karsten, S. (2006) Freedom of education and common civic values, in: *European Education*, 38 (2), 23-35.
Kok, J.R. (1992) Op zoek naar de theologische aspecten van de Orbis Sensualium Pictus, in: Kok, J.R. & Molnár, A. (Eds.) *Kinderen zijn God-geleerd – theologische vertrekpunten van Jan Amos Comenius* (Gorinchem, Narratio).
Kraan, J. (1987) *Bijbel en Andersgelovigen, naar een bijbelse basis voor de ontmoeting met andersgelovigen* (Kampen, Kok).
Kraan, J. (1990) Islamitisch godsdienstonderwijs op een christelijke school?, in: van Lin, J. (Ed.) *Ontmoeting van moslims en christenen. Grensverleggende verkenningen* (Hilversum, Gooi & Sticht). 10-45.
Kraan, J. (1991) Ontmoeting met moslimleerlingen binnen het christelijk onderwijs, in: Reesink, P. (Ed.) *Islam – een nieuw geloof in Nederland'* (Baarn, Ambo), 91-108.
Kraemer, H. (1960) *World Cultures and World Religions: the Coming Dialogue* (London, Westminster Press).
Kuyk, E. (2007) Religious Education in The Netherlands, in: Kuyk, E., Jensen, R., Lankshear, D., Löh Manna, E. & Schreiner, P. (Eds.) *Religious Education in Europe. Situation and current trends in schools* (Oslo, IKO Publishing House), 135-140.
Leeman, Y. & Pels, T. (2006) Citizenship education in the Dutch multiethnic context. *European Education*, 38 (2), 23-35.
Ligthart, J. (1917) *Verspreide opstellen ll* (Groningen, Wolters).
Meijer, W.A.J. (2007) *Traditie en toekomst van het Islamitisch onderwijs* (Bulaaq, Amsterdam).
Nanhekhan, H. (2002) Verantwoordelijk en eerbiedig leven: een islamitische school, in: Miedema, S. & Vroom, H. (Eds.) *Alle onderwijs bijzonder. Levensbeschouwelijke waarden in het onderwijs* (Zoetermeer, Meinema), 61-69.
Otten, R. & de Ruiter, J.J. (1991) De Marokkanen, in: de Ruiter, J.J. (Ed.) *Talen in Nederland. Een beschrijving van de taalsituatie van negen etnische groepen* (Groningen, Wolters-Noordhoff), 91-128.
Rath, J., Penninx, R., Groenendijk, K. & Meijer, A. (1996) *Nederland en zijn Islam. Een ontzuilende samenleving reageert op het ontstaan van een geloofsgemeenschap* (Amsterdam Het Spinhuis).
Rietveld-van Wingerden, M., Sturm, J.C. & Miedema, S. (2003) Vrijheid van onderwijs en sociale cohesie in historisch perspectief. *Pedagogiek*, 23 (2), 97-108.

Samberg, J.W. (1928) *De Hollandsche Gereformeerde Gemeente in Smirna. De geschiedenis eener handelskerk* (Leiden, Eduard Ijdo).
Shadid, W.A. (2006) Public debates about over Islam and the awareness of Muslim identity in The Netherlands. *European Education,* 38 (2), 10-22.
Shadid, W.A. & van Koningsveld, P.S. (1990) *Moslims in Nederland. Minderheden en religie in een multiculturele samenleving* (Alphen aan den Rijn, Samsom Stafleu).
Shadid, W.A. & van Koningsveld, P.S. (2006) Islamic religious education in The Netherlands. *European Education,* 38 (2), 10-22.
Shadid, W.A. & van Koningsveld, P.S. (2008) *Islam in Nederland en België. Religieuze institutionalisering in twee landen met een gemeenschappelijke voorgeschiedenis* (Leuven, Peeters).
Sikkes, R. (1989) Wethouders sceptisch over komst Islam- en Hindoescholen. Pot: 'Scheiding Nederlanders en buitenlanders gevaarlijk'. *Het Schoolblad,* 24 (3), 21- 23.
Slomp, J. (1981) Christenen en Moslims in Nederland. *Wereld en Zending. Tijdschrift voor missionaire informatie en bezinning,* 10 (4), 275-286.
Slomp, J. (1984) Islam in Nederland, in: Waardenburg, J. (Ed.) *Islam. Norm, ideaal en werkelijkheid* (Weesp: Wereldvenster), 419-440.
Slomp, J. (1991) Het begon al met Karel de Grote. Moslims in de vaderlandse geschiedenis. *Voorwerk,* 8 (2), 65-77.
Steenbrink, K.A. (1991) *De islam bekeken door koloniale Nederlanders* (Utrecht, Interuniversitair Instituut voor Missiologie en Oecumenica).
Ter Avest, I. (2003) *Kinderen en God verteld in verhalen. Een longitudinaal onderzoek naar de ontwikkeling van het godsconcept van autochtone en allochtone kinderen in een multiculturele en multireligieuze onderwijscontext* (Zoetermeer, Boekencentrum).
Ter Avest, I. (2008a) Religieuze burgerschapsvorming. *Al Nisa, Islamitisch maandblad voor vrouwen,* 27(6), 6-19.
Ter Avest, I. (2008b) Religieuze burgerschapsvorming als uitdaging. *Lessen. Periodiek van het Nationaal Onderwijsmuseum,* 3(4), 21-27.
Ter Avest, I. (2009a) Dutch children and their God, *British Journal of Religious Education,* 31(3).
Ter Avest, I. (2009b) Teachers responding to religious diversity, Impression of everyday practice and recommendations for teacher training, presentation at the Council of Europe, March 19.
Ter Avest, I. & Bakker, C. (2009) Structural Identity Consultation: Story telling as a Culture of Faith Transformation. *Religious Education,* 104 (3), 257-271.
Ter Avest, I. & Bakker, C. (2010) Self-understandings of (RE-)teachers in SIC, contributing to school identity, in: de Souza, M., Engebretson, K., Durka, G. & Gearon, L. (Eds.) *International Handbook for Interreligious Education* (London, Springer)
Ter Avest, I., Bakker, C. & Miedema, S. (2008), Different schools as narrative communities; Identity narratives in threefold. *Religious Education,* 103 (3), 307-323.
Ter Avest, I. & Bertram-Troost, G.D. (Eds.) (2009) *Geloven in samen leven* (Amsterdam, Science Guide).
Ter Avest, I. & Clement, D. (2008) *Samen school maken in DE Bijlmer, Culturele diversiteit en/in schoolcultuur* (Amsterdam/Utrecht, Unpublished Annual Report 2007-2008).

Theunissen, H. (1989) Barbaren en ongelovigen. Turcica in de Nederlanden 1500-1800, in: Theunissen, H., Baleman, A. & Meulenkamp, W. (Eds.) *Topkapi & turkomani. Turks – Nederlandse ontmoetingen sinds 1600* (Amsterdam: De Bataafsche Leeuw), 37-53.

Tworuschka, U. (1983) *Die Geschichte nichtchristlicher Religionen in christlichen Religionsunterricht* (Köln, Böhlau).

Van Amersfoort, J. & van Asselt, W. J. (1997) *Liever Turks dan Paaps? De visies van Johannes Coccejus, Gisbertus Voetius en Adrianus Relandus op de islam* (Zoetermeer, Boekencentrum).

Van Aarsen, E.K., Hoffius, R.G.H. & Verberne, B. (2007) *Godsdienst en humanistisch vormingsonderwijs. Onderzoek naar huidig lesaanbod en verwachte vraag* (Leiden, Research voor Beleid).

Van Bommel, A. (1990) Moslims in Nederland. Wat verwachten zij van het onderwijs? in: Gerritsen, J.H. & Westerman, W.E. (Eds.), *Ontmoetingen in het Onderwijs. Onderwijs en vormingswerk in een multiculturele en multireligieuze samenleving* (Kampen, Kok), 49-58.

Van der Linde, J.H. (1979) *De wereld heeft toekomst. Jan Amos Comenius over de hervorming van School, Kerk en Staat* (Kampen, Kok).

Van Oostrom, F. (1998) *Maerlants Wereld* (Amsterdam, Prometeus).

Van Rijsewijk, T. (1984) Islamitisch godsdienstonderwijs op Nederlandse lagere scholen. Verdeelde meningen bij christelijk en openbaar onderwijs. *Samenwijs,* 4 (7), 196-198.

Wessels, A. (1978) *De Moslimse Naaste. Op weg naar een theologie van de Islam* (Kampen: Kok).

Westerman, W.E. (1993) *Achtergronden van geboortegronden. Multiculturele zorgverbreding in het basis- en (voortgezet) speciaal onderwijs* (Nijkerk, Intro).

Westerman, W.E. (1994) *Een eenvoudige godsdienst? De Islam in Nederlandse leermiddelen* (Kampen, Kok).

Westerman, W.E. (2001) *Ongewenste objectiviteit. Onderwijs in geestelijke stromingen in historisch en vergelijkend perspectief* (Kampen, Kok).

Westerman, W.E. (2006) Intercultureel onderwijs en geestelijke stromingen, in: Miedema, S. & Bertram-Troost, G. (Eds.) *Levensbeschouwelijk leren samenleven. Opvoeding, Identiteit & Ontmoeting* (Zoetermeer, Meinema), 201-212.

Westerman, W.E. (2007) The Netherlands: A cultural crisis about tolerance, in: Lähnemann, J. (Ed.) *Visionen wahr machen. Interreligiöse Bildung auf dem Prüfstand* (Hamburg, EB Verlag), 387-392.

Westerman, W.E. (2008) Citizenship Education in The Netherlands, in: Howarth, R. B. (Ed.) *Citizenship Education in Europe* (Essex, EAWRE), 9-25.

Westerman, W.E. (2009) Dankzij islam geld voor godsdienstonderwijs openbare school. *Centraal Weekblad.* 13 (2), 8-9.

Westerman, W.E. (Ed.) (forthcoming) *De Bouschra School: de tijd vooruit* (Amsterdam).

Damian Breen

A Qualitative Narrative of the Transition from Independent to Voluntary Aided Status
A problem for the Concept of the 'Muslim School'

This chapter draws on in-depth life history interviews which were conducted with a head teacher who had seen two Muslim primary schools through the transition from independent to voluntary aided status as part of the original research for a PhD thesis. The life history interviews are not based on the life course of the head teacher, but rather they focus on the historical narrative of one of the schools that, as a head teacher, she led through the transition from independent to voluntary aided status. In accordance with her inclination to adopt instrumental roles at independent Muslim schools in pursuit of state funding the head teacher will be referred to throughout this chapter as Nasira (meaning 'victorious' or 'helper.')

The chapter will largely draw on the narrative of the first school which Nasira saw through the transition to voluntary aided status as head teacher. To simplify discussions in this chapter the term 'School A' will be used as a pseudonym to refer to the school. Throughout the chapter Nasira occasionally refers to consistencies in her experiences at School A with her experiences at a second school that she later led through the transition to voluntary aided status, also as head teacher. In those instances the latter school will be referred to as 'School B' in the text. Although primarily drawing on life history narratives, observation will also inform the narrative of School A. The chapter will describe the narrative of School A's transition from independent to voluntary aided status, initially outlining the school's background and history before discussing processes and changes which took place over time. Having demonstrated that acquiring voluntary aided status resulted in fundamental changes to School A's infrastructure over time, the chapter will conclude by arguing that such fundamental changes raise questions as to what the concept of the largely under-researched 'Muslim school' actually refers to in the wider faith schools debate. In line with the aims of the EU sponsored 'Religion in Education: A contribution to dialogue or a factor of conflict in transforming societies of European Countries?' (REDCo) project, this chapter, along with the thesis from which it is derived, aims to offer insights into Muslim schools in England and Wales. Drawing on the above, cultures or religions could be explored in-depth through the medium of faith schools as a bridge between belief systems (Breen 2009, 106), promoting dialogue in the context of European development (Jackson 2008, 155). Responsibility for learning about other faiths should not lie exclusively with children in schools, and so, as researchers, insights drawing on qualitative research should inform our knowledge about Muslim schools.

1. The context of England and Wales

Faith schools in England and Wales predominantly take two forms, those that are independent, and those which are voluntary aided. Independent schools are entirely privately funded through charitable status and receive no financial support from local or central government. Under part 10 of the Education Act 2002, all independent schools in the English education system are required to register with DCFS (currently the Department for Children Schools and Families, formerly the Department for Education and Skills) before the school begins to operate and admit pupils (DfES 2005, 1). In accordance an independent school is defined as 'any school which provides full-time education for five or more pupils of compulsory school age or one or more such pupils with a statement of special educational needs or who is in public care and is not a school maintained by a Local Education Authority or a non-maintained special school' (DfES 2005, 4). Conversely, voluntary aided schools with a religious character are funded up to 90% by Local Education Authorities, with outstanding costs being covered by (a) relevant religious organisation/s. Throughout this chapter the terms 'faith-schools' and 'Muslim schools' will refer to both independent schools which promote a distinct religious character, and also to schools which are state-funded and voluntarily-aided by a religious body (Jackson 2003, 90). In light of the above definitions the terms 'voluntary aided' and 'state funded' will be used interchangeably to refer to schools with a denominational religious character which receive state funding. As both School A and School B were located in England rather than Wales the chapter will consistently refer to Muslim schools in the 'English context' when drawing on the implications of research findings.

2. The rationale behind Muslim schools: a theological understanding of Islam

The fundamental point which gives focus to the rationale behind Muslim schools is the principle that there is no separation of public and private spheres in the Islamic context (Hussain 2004; Halstead 2004), rather Islam is considered a 'way of life' (Hussain 2004, 322). According to Islam children are born innocent and can only become sinful when deviating from this path (Hussain 2004, 379). Therefore Islamic education represents a requirement for Muslims owing to the belief that in order not to deviate from the true path, divine guidance is needed for all three aspects of a human's life: mind, body and soul (Hussain 2004, 319). In addition to the *fitra* (innocence) of the newborn child, at puberty the child has to take a covenant (*mithaq*) to recognise God as their absolute Lord (Hussain 2004, 379). Islamic education is therefore imperative for the fulfilment of this trust (Hanson 2001, 26).

Further insights into the rationale behind Muslim schools in England and Wales are revealed when considering Islamic concepts of knowledge. Al-Ghazali classified two types of knowledge, firstly 'knowledge acquired though human reason', and secondly 'transmitted knowledge' (Dangor 2005, 520). The latter is obtained from divine revelation and is accepted by Muslim scholars as the primary source of knowledge in Islam (Dangor 2005, 520). Therefore within the context of Islam there are two types of knowledge and no distinction between the sacred and the secular (Dangor 2005, 520). Part of the rationale behind Muslim schools derives from the argument that there is a dichotomy between Western and Islamic epistemologies (Dangor 2005, 521-522). According to Dangor, in the west education has largely become pupil centred in terms of the objectives of education being centred around individual utilitarian gain. He argues that although the common declared objective of the Western worldview is to produce a good individual, the utilitarian character (of the Western worldview) focuses on career opportunities in relation to the marketplace (Dangor 2005, 521). Therefore education in Western countries is concerned with pupil centred outcomes rather than moral and spiritual development whereas Islamic education is about being aware of God rather than serving material needs (Dangor 2005, 522). Although a dichotomous analysis may be problematic, the issues raised in Dangor's discussion can be seen to inform the rationale behind Muslim schools. Whether or not the English education system represents a distinct 'Western' epistemology in reality becomes irrelevant if Muslim communities (and indeed scholars such as Dangor) believe that the Islamic way of life is distinct from that which is fostered in schools without a religious (Islamic) character. A theological perspective then reveals that Islam is not simply a 'religious sphere' that Muslims engage in as part of a wider context of social life but rather represents and encompasses all aspects of life including the spiritual and the social.

3. Introducing School A: origins of the school

School A had been an independent Muslim primary school for between ten and twelve years before making the transition into the state sector for the beginning of the academic year 2004/2005, and at the time of the research was in it's fourth academic year as a voluntary aided school. School A had started out with eight children from three families in a small room in a Mosque, before growing steadily and moving location several times. Growth was slow and gradual over a period of five to six years as word of the school spread between parents and prospective families. After growing to around 120 pupils the school's intake stabilised mainly due to limitations on space, before moving buildings to accommodate the children more effectively. Moving to a larger school building allowed the school to grow again from around 120 to approximately 240 pupils, School A's largest intake as an independent Muslim primary school. On entering the state system as a voluntary aided school the intake dramatically grew in size again over a three year period to around 420 pupils, with 60 new pupils joining each year as a two form entry school which subsequently grew from the bottom up. Following the move into the state sector the school were able to have a new school premises built as School A's third and current home.

4. Nasira's background and role in School A

As a trained teacher who had worked in the state sector over several years before moving on to teacher training, Nasira had extensive experience of the state education system prior to joining School A, her first Muslim school. The school itself had initiated the process of applying for voluntary aided status and had called upon Nasira to offer guidance in light of her expertise in the state sector. The rationale behind inviting Nasira to assist in the application was for the school to draw on her experiences as a means of 'bridging the gap' on the journey towards completing the application process for voluntary aided status, and developing a rapport based on trust with the Local Education Authority given Nasira's knowledge of the system. Nasira joined School A with a view to staying for six months and stayed for five years quickly becoming head teacher spending two years leading up to the transition and three years following the successful application for voluntary aided status.

Nasira's personal background also formed part of the rationale for her involvement with Muslim schools starting with School A. The experience of seeing the school through the transition into the state sector along with her personal experiences gave her insights into the rationale behind Muslim schools. Reflecting on her own experiences growing up as a Muslim, Nasira explained:

> *If you look back a generation or 2, if you look at my generation and my children's generation, for us, we learnt about our faith but, you practiced in the home, and you practiced when you went to the Mosque in the evening or supplementary school. You lived a sort of a twin role. You were children in a school, and you behaved in a particular way; you went home and you behaved in a different way.*

Reflecting on her own particular background, Nasira felt that the approach demonstrated above fit the context of the time and had positive implications because children did learn about their faith. However, current times allow Muslim schools not just to teach Muslim children *about* their faith, but allow children to *practise* their faith in an educational context without compromising either their faith or their education. This capacity to practise faith in the current educational climate further informs the rationale behind Muslim schools. Speaking on behalf of her generation Nasira explained:

> *Unless you're able to practise things, unless you're able to do it and you're doing it all the time then it becomes almost second-hand and further back ... So coming back into it, what we want to do is to be able to take our children a circle back to where they live it. Living something teaches you much more than you ever learn about, you also understand the application, but its not about knowing about faith its about practicing faith in everything that you do all day.*

Nasira's personal background then along with her experiences prior to and during the process of School A's transition to voluntary aided status gives a rational for her own personal convictions surrounding Muslim schools in England which she maintains can be applied as a rationale for the broader group of Muslim schools in the current educational context.

5. Background of intake at School A

Initially the intake at School A was predominantly of South Asian descent but this changed over time. Nasira explained that the intake of the school changed over a period of time following the transition to voluntary aided status in terms of both ethnic background and characteristics of families. Although starting out as a predominantly South Asian setting, the number of Somali pupils at School A grew steadily over a period of two to three years with around two thirds of the intake being of Somali descent at the time Nasira moved to take up the role of head teacher at School B. Reflecting on trends in Somali families at School A, Nasira stated that there is an enthusiasm for their children to have an Islamic education which is demonstrated by the 'huge distances' that Somali families would travel to get to the school. In addition to large numbers of pupils from South Asian and Somali communities, there were approximately 24 languages spoken among children at School A as either first or second languages.

In addition to changes in terms of ethnic composition, the characteristics of families at the school also changed over time, although more directly in relation to the school acquiring voluntary aided status than the increase in ethnic diversity. Nasira explained that, when in the independent sector, both the faith based nature of the school along with its often delicate financial situation resulted in a dependency on two particular characteristics in parents at the school. Initially, they need to be either committed to the faith, or able to pay fees, or both if parents are to attain an Islamic education for their children, and the school is to attain the financial targets required to continue functioning. Although some parents would be on income support they would still demonstrate the extent to which they valued an Islamic education for their children by choosing to send their children to School A. Reflecting on the limited resources at School A in its early days in the independent sector, Nasira stated:

> *I used to say they used to pay money to send children to my prison, because that's what I used to compare it to because of the lack of resources and the tiny rooms, and the conditions, but they valued something they got there that they couldn't get anywhere else.*

On entering the state sector however, those characteristics among parents changed. Initially waiting lists increased dramatically, peaking at around 1000 at one point. The new increase in parental interest is necessary for the sustainability of a school in the state sector, as Nasira explained that a school needs to be at least one form entry, admitting one new class of around 30 per year, and with a total intake of around 200-210. Whereas in the independent sector it is possible to have a smaller intake, to be sustainable in the state sector it is necessary to have an intake of at least 200-210 children. Retaining a larger intake of pupils becomes a cyclical process as one of the immediately obvious effects of the removal of tuition fees was that the financial commitment of parents to providing Islamic education for their children was no longer necessary; therefore anybody could apply. The primary implication of this was that many families who previously could not afford to pay tuition fees now could have access to the school. A secondary implication was that opening up the school so that anybody could apply resulted in interest in families who may not have considered Islamic education for their children had it required economic investment and commitment. The implication the above was that some parents didn't have the same enthusiasm for their faith as families who invested economically in School A whilst it was in the independent sector.

Another effect of entering the state sector and amassing lengthy waiting lists was that the admissions criteria had to be changed. Whereas previously in the independent sector intake was based primarily on parental enthusiasm and willingness to financially commit, numerous filters come into effect in refining prospective families on joining the voluntary aided sector. In Nasira's experience the admissions criteria typically comes to prioritise siblings and locality with those living closest to the school taking priority. Nasira also explains a further dimension in which the school intake changes:

> *The children and school tend to change because you get in many more children with special needs, not only special needs but also with statemented children, because if you have a statemented child, no matter where you lived, you could live 3 counties away, and if you wanted your special needs child to attend a particular school, they have first priority and choice, and you have to offer. And in a sense parents with children who have some sort of a need, right up to the statemented level often choose to send their children to a Muslim school because they feel that "my child will be understood," they'll be in an environment where they'll be cared for, that they will, "they'll understand, my Muslim brothers and sisters will understand that child". And what they don't recognise is that Muslim schools often aren't kitted out, and don't have the experience, and don't have the systems to cope with children with severe special needs, but they still would like them to be there. Over a period of time a school's experiences grow, their ability to handle children with special needs will improve, and that will happen, but in the beginning there is a huge influx for which Muslim aren't quite ready to deal [with].*

The complex systems in place in the voluntary aided sector along with School A's obligations as part of the state sector had a dramatic effect on the nature of the intake at the school immediately following the transition from independent to voluntary aided status. The dramatic change in the characteristics of school intake experienced by Nasira at School A imply that characteristics of school intake may be one of the central defining strands which distinguishes necessary differences between Muslim schools in independent and voluntary aided contexts. Of schools making the transition from independent to voluntary aided, their infrastructure towards admissions is fundamentally and necessarily changed as a direct result of entering the state sector.

6. Positioning Muslim schools in the independent sector: an empirical context

Reflecting on the overall process of entering the state sector Nasira explains that the process is fairly uniform. Initially a sense of need is established usually by either the community, the trustees running the school or parents, and this usually arises in relation to an inability to sustain the school without a change of status.

Other ways of maintaining the school other than parental fee are then explored and the necessary enquiries are made. The sense of need was seen as a central and necessary prerequisite for making the transition in both School A and School B.

The specific position of Muslim schools in the independent sector was also a central factor in School A's decision to apply for voluntary aided status. Nasira explained that in relation to the wider context of independent schooling, Muslim schools typically take the form of small community schools. Small numbers of Muslim families become dissatisfied with the educational environment available to them and pursue something different which takes the form of opening a school of their own. Initially borne of the perception of *need*, such schools can grow to a limited size. However, there are boundaries within the independent sector. Nasira's narrative depicts a Muslim community with very limited economic resources in the UK, and therefore the financial requirements of maintaining a school typically come only from parental fees or small donations. For example, School A was associated with a local Mosque which did make financial contributions. However, limited resources in the community as a whole meant that contributions were small which left fees and donations as the central source of income. In Nasira's experience, rather than having a stable base to build on, those Muslim schools that do persist in this context remain open despite limiting circumstances:

> *They run from problem to problem, they sort of remain open despite circumstances rather than because they have the money to go on. At some stage they reach a position where they've got enough children to think: "this could actually be a viable option" in the state, you've reached a little core, but you never had the resources, you have huge staff turnover, you can't retain any staff, you can't pay decent salaries, your resources are very poor, your buildings start to cave in etc. So you either have to look for sources of money, or close.*

According to Nasira's narrative then there is a conviction that Muslim schools within the independent sector can only grow to a limited size owing to financial limitations. As such, using the term 'independent school' when referring to fee paying Muslim schools grossly distorts the reality of their specific position within the independent sector.

7. Changing nature of School A's resources over time

In discussing the histories of both School A and School B Nasira held the recurring conviction that Muslim schools, owing to factors outlined above, face a finite existence in the independent sector which can lead to an urgency resulting in applying for voluntary aided status. The extent to which independent Muslim schools have access to resources is a recurring explanatory factor in the rationale for both School A and School B's transition into the state sector. Nasira's account of School A's movement from initially a room in a Mosque to finally a purpose built school illustrates the ways in which the school's access to resources changed over time and the ways in which the ethos of the school was affected.

The first location for School A with its eight pupils was a small room used as a funeral parlour for the mosque. As a result, when funerals were taking place children would be encouraged to keep quiet and spatial restrictions also took their toll. The benefits of moving to the second building were that children had dedicated space to themselves for most of the week sharing with the community for Friday prayer. The school was open for four full days with a half day on Friday finishing at lunchtime allowing the community to use the same space for prayer. In the evenings the building was shared with the madrassa, with large numbers of pupils from School A attending supplementary classes after school.

The moving of School A to allow more space and resources for the children was beneficial in several ways. Nasira explained that in addition to the increased space, access to more resources was also hugely beneficial. She stated that:

> ...having resources, first-hand learning, touching, feeling, moving, you actually understand what you are doing for the first time rather than seeing the words on the board and just sort of copying them down in your book. That makes a difference. Teachers, the fact that for the first time in their lives they're having trained teachers, teachers who understand children and understand the process of teaching and how children learn, makes a big difference in the ethos, but the Islamic side of it has sort of carried on throughout and that has been reinforced with everything that's gone on around them.

The successful application for voluntary aided status increased access to resources at School A to a further degree on entering the state sector, with the ultimate result of establishing a purpose built building for the school (School A's location at the time of writing). Nasira explained that the Islamic ethos of the school 'took a battering' on first adjusting to having resources on moving out of the mosque and to the school's second location, however by and the large it had remained constant:

> Going through some of those major changes puts extra stress and pressure on a lot of factors but in the end things change. Fluctuations are much greater when change first happens and then they settle back down to some sort of norm. Then you have some other change, and once again you'll get huge fluctuations and it'll settle down to some sort of normal change.

The specific nature of provision at School A will be discussed in detail in the following subsections so as to give a picture of the objectives and environment of the school over time.

8. Specific vales at School A

During the life histories there was an emphasis on the Islamic ethos at School A having remained constant for the most part throughout the transition to voluntary aided status. On describing the specific values and practices that she felt characterised the school throughout its history, Nasira outlined a strong emphasis on prayer, children practicing their faith rather than simply learning about it, and developing the *adab* (general appropriate behaviour in the Islamic context) of the children. Nasira offers the well oiled argument that for Muslims in the state sector praying at the appropriate times is difficult owing to the lack of provision and understanding within a non-Muslim context. Even if there is a level of provision,

Muslim children will still have to step away from the wider group to pray in a small area allocated to them. A central part of the rationale for any Muslim school, as is demonstrated at School A, is the provision for children and staff to carry out appropriate practices, namely prayer, at appropriate times without the need to fracture the wider group. As prayer times change throughout the year, the delivery of the curriculum changes in accordance with a restructuring of the school day:

> The prayer times change, if the prayer times change the whole curriculum changes, so instead of having this thing, this lesson in the afternoon we have it in the morning, if you need to pray later; it just sort of fluctuates through the day as you need to do it, you've got your joint prayer.

Provision extends to assemblies of which the focus is on the *dua*s (prayers of supplication) and the *sura*s (chapters in the Qur'an) that the children are learning. Nasira illustrates the lived Islamic ethos in the school as an applied way of life. The children live their religion throughout the day reciting/remembering the specific *dua*s at appropriate times:

> The children do things during the day, when you enter the bathroom there's a particular dua, when you start to eat there's a dua, when you finish eating there's a dua, when you walk into a room there's a dua, when you leave the room there's another dua, so all the time you are thanking your creator for making you what he's made you and doing the things that you do. And therefore one: they learn them; two: they say them, so they become second nature, when you meet an adult there's a certain greeting, when you meet another child there's a certain greeting, when you sneeze there's a particular dua etc, so the ability to know them and to practice them and to do them all the time so they become second nature, I think is what the ethos was. Joint prayer in the afternoon and then, actually, understanding the adab and their application, the jurisprudence and its application, the rulings and what they mean in life. So not just hearing about the stories but knowing what those stories mean and what implication there is for us in our daily life.

In terms of the specific values that School A aimed to instil in its pupils, there was an emphasis on respect in several contexts which was inseparably interrelated to one of the core objectives of the school. Initially children were encouraged to have respect for themselves which meant knowing who they were as young Muslims, why God had created them and what He wants of them: respect for others as the process of socialising with family, peers, elders and the community in which the children live; and responsibility for the wider environment as God's work.

Trying to break down the interrelated elements of the school's ethos in the life history interviews proved difficult owing to a philosophy at the core of Islam which had been a recurring theme in informing the rationale for the focus of the research, and which sits as the core rationale behind Muslim schools in the English context: *Islam as a way of life*. In response to attempts to pick out elements of life at School A which would come together as the ethos of the school as a whole, Nasira stated: 'The advantage is in a Muslim school you don't need to see it in layers like that, Islam pervades everything we do.'

However, reflecting on her experiences within the state sector gave Nasira a point of reference which highlighted the specific characteristics of ethos at School A which were not present in state schools she had worked in breaking down the specific elements of School A's ethos informing the school's objectives. Shortcomings of specific importance for Nasira were that Muslim children in non-faith schools do not experience the teaching of the Qur'an and Sunnah (ways and laws of the Prophet) nor did they learn the *adab*, two factors which she felt to be of key importance at School A. Drawing on Nasira's narrative, the content of lessons and indeed elements of everyday school life were drawn back to the God as Creator. In drawing contrast to education in the non-faith state sector Nasira refers to a recent science lesson at School B stating:

> *We were looking at sight that Allah Subhana Wa Tala gives a special layer of rods and cones at the back [of the eye] because he needed us to be able to function in the day and the night.*

Such an Islamicisation of the curriculum and its delivery is obviously not possible in a non-faith state school to the extent that prospective Muslim parents would like. The Islamic ethos at School A facilitates the open teaching of the Qur'an and *surah*s, the open teaching of the language of Arabic to give children direct access to books and resources in both the short and the long term, and also the understanding of the *adab*. The teaching of the Qur'an and *surah*s and Arabic took the form of explicit lessons, whereas the *adab* and lived experience of the Islamic environment was communicated by teachers acting as role models demonstrating appropriate behaviour to the children. Nasira summarised: 'So in anything where they are learning science, where they're learning English, whatever they're doing, they do it in that way; they're allowed to behave and live as a Muslim should.' The process of Islamicisation at School A is consistent with the 'Islamisation project' as described by Niehaus in Muslim schools in the UK and the Netherlands in this volume.

9. Ethos of the school over time

Having established the key central elements of ethos at School A, in light if the above account of the fundamental change in infrastructure concerning admissions and therefore intake following the transition to voluntary aided status, it is important to consider how entering the state sector may have affected ethos at School A over time. Nasira's narrative of the transition illustrates that changes inevitably happened (at least in the case of School A) and the explanatory reasons were complex. The ethos at School A had always been based on a 'loving, caring, family environment' and although changes took place, Nasira's conviction was that they were not always due to entering the state sector. The move to a purpose built school building had some effect as the two previous locations of the school lacked outdoor play-space. Having access to a playground for the first time in 12 years was considered a significant development as children could now develop and grow both physically in terms of exercise and physical education (PE), and socially with outdoor playtimes to break up the day. Nasira explained the feeling of significance of the new school building and the resources it brought:

> *Children need all kinds of things, not just education in terms of the knowledge base that you feed them, they need to grow physically, they need to have a place to run, they need to socialise, they need to do all those things. Those are things that the couldn't have when we were in the independent sector, so the biggest change for us was actually the building itself, to have space, to have space inside the classrooms, to have space outdoors, to get to see the sunlight, to know whether it was day or night, once you got into the building you couldn't even tell what the weather was like outside, in our old building, that made a huge difference.*

Although a great benefit, the children's initial readjustment to having access to space gave rise to a difficult period in terms of the ethos of the school. Nasira's narrative depicts a period of change which was difficult as the children settled into a 'different ethos' directly related to the new access to space and resources rather than entering the state sector. Moving children 'out from a tight space where all they can do is literally sit, and if you got up you stepped on the child next door to you, because in a room this size you would have 30 children sitting, all facing the board', to a purpose built school would have implications for ethos in any school. Although of course access to the new resources was facilitated to a great degree and, considering the financial limitations of independent Muslim schools in the narrative above, would not have been possible at all without making the transition to voluntary aided status.

10. Voluntary aided status in action: the national curriculum

For any school in the English state sector the complete incorporation of the national curriculum is necessary. At School A, Nasira explains that a 'slimmed down version' of the national curriculum was already covered in the school prior to making the transition to voluntary aided status. According to Nasira English, mathematics, history and geography were delivered to a high standard whilst in the independent sector and were taught relatively easily as knowledge-based subjects. Science was a little more difficult in terms of practical limitations: 'we taught science rather than learnt science if you understand the difference, you know, the children didn't have any resources so they didn't get to *do* science and to handle things and to learn from things, they were taught knowledge, scientific knowledge.' Subjects which required more practical application and resources were difficult to cover, and as result subjects such as PE, design and technology (DT) and art suffered as the curriculum was more teacher centred rather than child centred. Nasira felt that a key benefit of entering the state sector was the wider base of the curriculum which was seen as 'broad and balanced.' The approach at School A following the transition to accommodate certain extra subjects directly related to the school's Islamic ethos was to have a longer school day than they previously had. This allowed for all subjects, including Islamic studies and Arabic, to be covered in the school day, which began at 8:15am and finished at 3:30pm every week day with a shorter lunch break than traditionally typical in the state sector.

Approaches to Islamic elements of the curriculum also changed over time. Initially peripatetic teachers specialising in Qur'an and Arabic would give lessons at the school however after a while efforts were made to break that mould. Teachers at the school were given the responsibility to teach Arabic through lessons, but also through everyday repetition and use of the language in school life: 'so as you're passing things and you're touching things or you're holding things you're using the Arabic word, because language is learnt by repetition and the more you repeat it throughout the day the better it is.' Teachers were wary to begin with but their confidence grew with time. However there was an anxiety because, as the language of the Qur'an, the word of God delivered to the Prophet Mohammed (s.a.w.), parents wanted to ensure that teachers were using and teaching the correct *tajweed* (intonation of the voice during recitation.) The words, meanings and interpretation of the Qur'an are of obvious significance, and so there is a particular emphasis on children learning and subsequently using the correct *tajweed* because they will be the words children will be using when reciting the Qur'an. Consequently Qur'an lessons were kept separate from the rest of the curriculum and were eventually taught by peripatetic teachers whereas Islamic studies was taught by class teachers and by peripatetic teachers, with every teacher having enough subject knowledge and personal experience to deliver the curriculum.

11. Voluntary aided status in action: Islamicising the curriculum

A key theme in the narrative of School A (and indeed School B) was an Islamicising of curriculum subjects not inherently related to the Islamic ethos of the school i.e. national curriculum subjects which are present in all state schools regardless of whether the school has a religious character. Although above there are discussions concerning a possible dichotomy of 'Western' and Islamic philosophies as a possible rationale behind Muslim schools, Nasira's account describes an easy union between Islamic ethos and national curriculum subjects. Her conviction was that there were no issues in terms of bringing the two together owing to an inherent flexibility in the requirements of the national curriculum:

> It doesn't say how things need to be taught, it says what children need to learn. Some of it is skill based, some of it is knowledge based. The skill based is dead easy, the knowledge base, even then you can teach from an Islamic perspective. You can say some people believe in the theory of evolution, and they believe that this happened, etc, so you teach it as a perspective. But of course we know that Allah Subhana Wa Tala tells us through the Qur'an that this happened, this happened, and that happened.

Nasira felt that reaffirming the Islamic perspective when teaching such elements of the curriculum removed any complications in delivering the national curriculum in the classroom. The above could give the misleading impression that Islamicising the curriculum simply refers to clarifying when science and Islam clash. In the case of teaching evolution referred to above, this is certainly possible and even probable, however in many cases science can be entirely incorporated into and Islamic perspective without any clashing. Nasira explains:

A Qualitative Narrative of the Transition from Independent to Voluntary Aided Status 107

> Being able to refer back to the Qur'an, if you know the Qur'an ... 1400 years ago Allah Subhana Wa Tala told us through the Qur'an that in the sea there are 2 seas running, there's a salty sea and a non-salty sea, sweet water and salty water, and these 2 seas never mix. And now scientists have discovered that it's to do with the density of the water and the heat etc, etc, and you can refer back ... so they're recognising that the Qur'an is a source of information and knowledge not just duas and surahs that you learn through repetition.

Islamicising the curriculum then refers to grounding elements of science etc in the Islamic perspective thus allowing the easy union in Nasira's account. This approach results in the children learning about their faith in a constant process, rather than leaving it at the door when learning elements of science. Nasira account illustrates that, consistent with the conviction that Islam is a lived way of life, the experience of learning in School A was filled with an overlap of interrelated factors, but with each giving some point of reflection on Islam. In describing the nature of the Qur'an and the ways in which learning about it can fulfil the requirements of the national curriculum, Nasira explained:

> So we're going to learn surah naba [The Tidings, Qur'an 078] because of this that and the other. There's the historical context, or there's the scientific context or, you know there's something you're looking at geography, you're looking at an area, you're looking at mountainous regions and you say the people of the mountain etc, etc, and this is what happened. Or if you're looking at, they looked at Egypt for instance and you were looking at the arid conditions and the river Nile and it bringing, and you sort of look at what that tells you and where it is etc. So although they don't sit and read, it's not like the Bible, a set of stories, its sort of a cross linked ... Mish-mash (laughs,) but a lovely mish-mash!

According to Nasira's account then, Islamicising the curriculum can dissolve a perceived gap between Islamic ethos and elements of the national curriculum which results in a union in the classroom.

12. Learning practices by example

The Islamic ethos at School A was not exclusively delivered through the explicit Islamicising of the curriculum described above. According to Nasira's account, children were also led by example by Muslim staff members in the educational context, as well as other peers in external contexts. Referring to children learning about the Qur'an and it's delivery to the Prophet Mohammed (s.a.w.) Nasira explains:

> They learn in everyday life because their parents are doing it, they're told at the Mosque, they're told at the school, and when you teach the Qur'an you don't need to go from 1 to 30, its not like a book with chapters in that sort of sense because they were delivered at different times and the compilation is different to the order of delivery and you try and tie it into what you are doing.

The above description of the many contexts in which children at School A may have learned about the Qur'an by being led by example demonstrates that Islamic ethos is not confined within the school. Ethos at School A can be seen to not only be characterised by values promoted within the school, for example by Islamicising the curriculum, but also by elder Muslim peers in the children's wider social networks. As children are led by example outside of the school they consequently contribute to the ethos themselves by bringing experience of Islamic values in from outside. Nasira's narrative then describes a two way process where School A's ethos can be seen to exist and be influenced both inside and outside of the school.

Whilst it is perceivable that taking on influences and learning by example in the ways described above may be common with older children in the school, Nasira explains that younger children need to be taught more explicitly. She explains that in her experience all young children need to be taught explicitly how to behave in the school setting, for example being told not to push and wait turns when standing in lines etc. However within the context of an Islamic ethos children can be given a rationale for why they should behave a certain way which will be reiterated to them by elder peers in wider social networks as they become older. Nasira explained that the above represents a process where young children are initially taught explicitly, however over time the explicit support is withdrawn as behaviours 'become second nature'.

13. Language in everyday school life and appointing Non-Muslim staff

Within the context of the school the use of the Arabic language is one of the more identifiable ways in which the staff led children to learn about their faith by example. The use of Arabic phrases such as *masha'Allah* (loosely 'well done,' refers to having acted appropriately in the Islamic context) and *insh'Allah* (God willing) represented a constant characteristic of the ethos at School A which had been present since the school's inception. Another characteristic which developed later on following the school's transition to voluntary aided status was the appointment of non-Muslim staff. The concept of leading children by example initially seems to come into conflict if a proportion of the staff is non-Muslim. If, for example, non-Muslims are appointed as members of teaching staff then it could be argued that potentially whole cohorts of children will miss out on being led by example in the classroom for a year. As demonstrated in the above quotes Nasira insists that being led by example is one of the key ways in which, particularly older Muslim children learn about their faith in the school and outside, and was therefore a key element of School A's Islamic ethos. According to Nasira's account, non-Muslim staff members were encouraged to use Arabic phrases as a means of leading children by example. In referring to non-Muslim staff members' use Arabic as a means to do so, Nasira explained:

> They learnt those phrases beautifully! And they used those phrases all the time. We had [non-Muslim teacher's name], we had [non-Muslim teacher's name], we had, lots of others. They came in on teaching practice, and they learnt those phrases and they used those phrases appropriately, they taught the children those phrases. And

> they didn't find that difficult and they didn't find that contradictory to anything they wanted to do anyway ... And the children take to it, and the teachers take to it, and it is, it becomes normal, it becomes habitual.

Language played another important role in the ethos at both School A and School B. In referring to teachers children would call them 'miss', 'sir' or *ustad* (literally teacher or master) as a means of establishing a more formal relationship than that which Nasira had witnessed at some Muslim schools in her general experience. She explained that there is a trend in some Muslim schools for children to refer to teachers as *auntie* and *uncle* as a means of reiterating a respect typical in wider social networks outside of the school which are prominent particularly in South-Asian communities. The rationale behind the use of these terms to refer to teachers is rooted in the conviction that it implies to the child that the teachers, as guardians, must be treated with the same level respect that they would show their own parents. Nasira's conviction was that this approach leads to too much of a family environment, and as a result children fall into the trap of bringing home behaviour into the school, rather than recognising that teachers hold a more formal role and occupy a different kind of status in the classroom than parents do in the home. Nasira concluded:

> *I actually like a slightly more formal environment in school setting, where we discourage actively the saying of auntie and uncle, and we say miss or sir or ustad, whichever language they use because that it's a teacher, because teacher has a particular place.*

In School A and School B then, language played an important role in both refreshing the Islamic ethos of the schools through the use of Arabic, and also establishing a particular kind of relationship between teachers and children which Nasira felt was something to be actively established within the context of a given Muslim school owing to existing trends. The use of Arabic in everyday life was employed to some degree by non-Muslim staff members, offering them an opportunity to lead children by example in their everyday experience of Islamic ethos. Language was equally significant in the purely educational context as trends seen as typical to Muslim schools with an intake from predominantly South-Asian families were actively avoided. All of the above subsection: the discussion of the use of Arabic, the use of Arabic among non-Muslim staff and examples of the importance of language not only in contributing to the Islamic ethos, but also purely to the educational dimension to ethos demonstrates the complex interrelationships between elements of ethos in a given school. The rationale behind Muslim schools consistently refers to an integrated educational environment where Islam is a lived way of life and is based on the conviction that children should not have to leave their faith at home when going to school. However, the discussion above indicates that language, as a mechanism, seemingly contributed to two distinct strands of ethos: the Islamic and the educational.

14. Final experiences at School A

After three years as a voluntary aided school processes and systems began to stabilise. Nasira explains that the 'expectations of children were quite clear and the children had understood how to react to the changes that happened in their lives: the widening of the curriculum, the showing of some independence, the use of the space, the long day, they were adapting to many of those things.' On reflecting on her final experiences at School A, Nasira explained that although certain systems had stabilised, staff turnover remained relatively high. She explains:

> *There was a continued staff turnover, that's to do with having young female staff, and in the Muslim sector its actually quite difficult because one: you get teachers who are there with you for about a year, 18 months before they marry, so they've completed their education, they're with you for a year, 18 months before they marry, and our marriages are slightly different to the host community's marriages.*

Nasira's narrative indicates that pregnancy typically followed marriage and subsequently female teachers would periodically leave the education system for four to five years, or until their own children are attending school. The result of this is a constant turnover of staff which was outside the school's control. Nasira concluded: 'you learn to live with change and you build your systems and procedures around change.' Nasira's wider experiences of the education system in general gave her insights into how the school was perceived by education authorities. She stated:

> *The local authority found that very hard. In the majority of state schools, not in big cities but elsewhere, what tends to happen is you built a stable staff over a period, and you have staff that have been there for 20 years. I remember in lots of the schools I've worked, you've got people, that's a lifetime and beyond. It's not like that in Muslim schools and Muslim schools constantly change over staff. Authorities find that difficult but gradually they'll begin to accept that things, the way you set up your systems has to be different.*

In addition to rapid staff turnover, Nasira felt that leadership issues were also a cause for concern among Muslim schools and would continue to have implications in the foreseeable future:

> *When the leadership changed [at School A], because, there are very few Muslim trained head teachers around and therefore you're likely to look lower. People with less experience than you would traditionally have in a head teacher, lower qualifications than you would normally have in a head teacher, but unless you make that change the schools aren't going to able to grow. Unless people like National College of School Leadership, the TDA, the DCSF do something about it and they recognise that you've got to think ahead to capacity building, that'll continue to be a problem in the next 5, 10 years for Muslim schools.*

15. Conclusion: what does the term 'Muslim school' really refer to?

Nasira's narrative of School A's transition from independent to voluntary aided status gives important insights into interrelationships between elements of the school's ethos and the processes by which these interrelationships were fundamentally affected on acquiring voluntary aided status. Completing the transition into the state sector resulted in a snowball effect which fundamentally altered the infrastructure of School A. Acquiring voluntary aided status required a change in admissions policies which had a dramatic impact on intake. Although the removal of fees will have opened the school up to those Muslim parents who desperately wanted an Islamic education for their children but could not afford to pay for it in the independent sector, it also inevitably opened the school up to parents who would not have considered an Islamic education for their children outside of free provision. The change in admissions policies also resulted in space and place becoming deciding factors in who attended the school with the majority intake quickly transforming to represent local families rather than committed parents travelling from varied destinations. Siblings also take priority following the shift, and where economic limitations previously meant that only the financially committed could secure places for all of their children, whole families of local children can now attend. The new economic dimension also resulted in a massive change in access to resources, the size of the school building and ultimately an increase in intake. State regulations also resulted in the appointment of trained teaching staff which will have inevitably replaced staff members who did not hold teaching qualifications; in addition to qualified Muslim teaching staff, this subsequently resulted in the appointment of School A's first non-Muslim teachers.

Although the school's infrastructure was fundamentally changed, Nasira's narrative indicates that there were several factors which remained constant throughout the process. The high turnover of female staff, the Islamicisation of the curriculum and the use of language as a means of establishing teacher-pupil status were not fundamentally affected by the transition to voluntary aided status in the same way the school's infrastructure was through changes in admissions and resources. The concept of leading children by example remains a central priority following the appointment of non-Muslim teachers through encouraging integration and the use of Arabic phrases when interacting with children in the classroom and everyday school life. Ultimately the ethos at School A becomes a union between the Islamic and the educational, as resources open up opportunities to teach more practical subjects such as art, design and technology, physical education and science to a greater degree. Nasira maintains that that the school's ethos has not changed following the transition, although she acknowledges that significant structural changes have occurred.

The eventful nature of School A's narrative raises questions as to the nature of Muslim schools in the English context. In contrast to Nasira's conviction above, it is concluded that such changes in infrastructure as those documented in the narrative of School A *must* have implications for ethos; and indeed each of those elements of infrastructure could in turn directly refer to elements of the school's ethos. The changes documented in this chapter can be seen to demonstrate interrelated strands of ethos changing in direct relation to a), taking the initiative to pursue voluntary aided status, and b), successfully going through the process of acquiring that status. Although based on an in-depth micro analysis the above demonstrates the changes that have occurred in one Muslim school entering the state sector. When taking into consideration the small numbers of voluntary aided Muslim schools in England and Wales, (12 at the time of writing, Association of Muslim Schools UK) if just one Muslim school can experience so many changes and transform to such an extent then how can we know what the Muslim school in the English context refers to?

If these changes are necessarily related to the transition then there may be implications for the faith schools debate in the English context in that the concept of the Muslim school used in the debate is ambivalent. It may refer to a homogenised concept of a 'Muslim school' which is not qualitatively informed effectively enough to accommodate real-life narratives of Islamic education such as those documented in the case of School A. As such when using the term 'Muslim school' we run the risk of referring to a homogenised conception blind to the realities of Islamic education in the English context; a false reality rather than a qualitatively informed social phenomenon. In short, if we do not know what the phenomenon of the Muslim school in the English context is then how can we have a useful and informed debate about justifying/criticising state funding for them?

In conclusion then the fundamental structural changes which necessarily and inevitably occurred during School A's transition into the state sector imply that any independent 'Muslim school' awarded voluntary aided status may well be unrecognisable following the transition. Thus when engaging with debates surrounding state funding for 'Muslim schools' in the English context we may be at risk of referring to a qualitatively uninformed false concept of the 'Muslim school.' The solution unquestionably lies in making a conscious effort to inform the debate further by carrying out more in-depth qualitative research into Muslim schools so that we know the phenomenon which we are discussing.

References

Breen, D. (2009) Religious Diversity, Inter-Ethnic Relations and the Catholic School: Introducing the Responsive Approach to Single-Faith Schooling, *British Journal of Religious Education*, 31(2), 103-115.

Dangor, S. (2005) Islamisation of Disciplines: Towards an Indigenous Education System. *Educational Philosophy and Theory*, 37(4), 519-531.

Department for Education and Skills (DfES) (2005) *Registration of Independent Schools: A Guide for Proprietors on the Statutory Requirements for Registration* (Independent and Education Boarding Team).

Halstead, J.M. (2004) An Islamic Concept of Education. *Comparative Education*, 40(4), 517-529.

Hussain, A. (2004) Islamic Education: Why Is There a Need for It? *Journal of Beliefs and Values*, 25(3), 317-323.

Jackson, R. (2008) Teaching about Religions in the Public Sphere: European Policy Initiatives and the Interpretive Approach *Numen*, 55, 151-182.

Jackson, R. (2003) Should the State Fund Faith Based Schools? *British Journal of Religious Education*, 25(2), 89-102.

Inga Niehaus

Emancipation or Disengagement? Islamic Schools in Britain and the Netherlands

1. Introduction

The existence of private Islamic schools in European countries has caused intense public and political controversies in the past few years. Critics argue that the schools make little effort towards promoting integration, that they are exclusive, and lag behind modern educational standards, and that they sometimes even promote Islamic fundamentalist ideologies (see McEoin, 2009). These accusations often overlook the diversity among Islamic schools and the internal developments and discourses within them. Far from being an entity, Islamic schools in European countries differ considerably in size, structure, management, academic results, and religious as well as pedagogical outlook.

Islamic schools in Europe are a rather recent phenomenon: most of them were established in the last twenty years. The motivations behind the establishment of Islamic schools were manifold: Muslim educators and parents intended to provide high quality education for children in an Islamic environment and to affirm and strengthen the Islamic identity of children. Furthermore, they wanted to ensure that Muslim pupils were protected from what they regard as un-Islamic or secular influences within society, and that Muslim girls in particular are taught in single-sex schools during puberty.

Some of the Islamic schools were set up by local Muslim communities and others by particular Muslim organisations like the Turkish Mili Görüs, the South Asian Tablighi Jamaat or the Deoband-movement.

The status and organisation of Islamic schools in European countries vary considerably. They depend on the structure of the education system, the legal and political settings, the relationship between church and state, and on the integration policies, as well as the mobilisation and self-organisation of Muslim minorities.[1] The political structure of a particular country seems to be far more important in the process of institutionalisation than the way in which Muslims mobilise for their demands (Rath et al. 2001, 287).

Most Islamic schools are independent faith schools that offer primary and some also secondary education, like most of the independent Church schools in these countries. These schools follow the national curriculum and offer special Islamic

---

1 Fetzer and Soper (2005, 147), see the church-state relationship as the decisive factor which determines the institutionalisation of Islam: "In each country Muslims inherited a web of church-state interactions based on constitutional principles, legal practice, historical precedent, and foundational conceptions of the appropriate relationship between church and state. This combination of factors eventually determined how each state accommodated Muslims on the issues of religion in public schools, state aid to private Islamic schools, and, in part, mosque building."

Instruction.² Some Islamic independent schools in Great Britain are modelled after those in South Asia that provide religious training for young Muslims who want to become a *Hafiz* or *Alim*. They are usually called *Darul Uloom* or *madrasa*. In recent years a number of these institutions have started to offer national curriculum subjects as well (Mandaville 2007, 238).

In many countries, Islamic schools are still an exception. Germany, for example, has only one government funded Islamic primary school in Berlin-Kreuzberg that was established in 1989 and primarily serves the local Turkish community. Belgium has one state funded Islamic school in Brussels with strong links to Saudi Arabia, and Austria has five schools that serve different ethnic communities. Britain has the largest number of independent Islamic schools with 127, followed by 47 in the Netherlands.

This article will investigate the institutionalisation, functioning and self-understanding of Islamic schools in Britain and the Netherlands in a comparative perspective.³ It intends to offer a critical assessment of the question whether Islamic schools promote processes of identity formation within a democratic society or whether they rather lead to disengagement from the wider society.

It explores the religious discourses within Islamic schools with a special focus on the idea of 'Islamising the curriculum' and on the requirements to teach the national 'secular' curriculum. Furthermore, the religious and pedagogical self-understanding of these institutions is related to their engagement with the wider society in terms of the promotion of democratic citizenship and social cohesion.

2. Islamic schools and educating Muslim children in England and the Netherlands

Presently there are about 500.000 Muslim children receiving education in British schools – between five and six percent of the total school population. Most are from Pakistani, Bangladeshi and Indian background (Open Society Institute 2005, 109 et seq.). The majority of Muslim children attend public community schools (ca. 75%) or Church schools. Only about one percent of Muslim children are educated in independent or state-maintained Muslim schools (Parker-Jenkins 2005, 41). A number of Muslim independent schools applied in recent years for state funding,

---

2 The article focuses on the accredited Islamic schools, which teach in the national language and which offer the national school leaving certificates. There are a number of independent Islamic schools in various European countries which have been established to serve certain ethnic groups and which teach for example in Arabic or Turkish and offer foreign academic certificates.

3 The article is based on the preliminary results of an empirical study of selected Islamic schools in Britain and the Netherlands which was carried out in 2007 and 2008. Methodologically, the project is divided into two phases. In the first phase interviews with stakeholders in both countries were carried out and in the second phase qualitative questionnaires were distributed to pupils aged 15 to 17, asking about their religious beliefs and practices, as well as their attitude towards people of other faiths and their view on the society they are living in.

but as of yet only 11 schools have become so called voluntary aided schools.[4] There seem to be structural, legal and political obstacles to including a large number of Muslim schools in the state sector, aggravated by a public debate which is critical of state support for faith schools (see Jackson 2003b; de Jong & Snik 2002).[5] The majority of schools are still independent, and differ considerably in educational philosophy and religious affiliation.

As in England, the majority of Muslim children in the Netherlands are educated in non-Muslim schools. They are predominantly from Turkish and Moroccan backgrounds.[6] There are 45 Muslim primary schools and two secondary schools that are based in Rotterdam and Amsterdam.[7] About 10.000 Muslim learners attend Islamic schools, which cater for approximately one percent of all primary students in the Netherlands.[8] In contrast to the British situation, all of the Dutch Muslim schools (so called 'bijzondere scholen') are government funded.[9]

In Britain and the Netherlands, the establishment of Islamic schools was favoured by education laws and an educational system which had supported denominational schools – especially Christian – for decades (Parker-Jenkins 2005, 35).[10] Furthermore, a decentralised education system in both countries made it easier for Muslim parents to organise at the local level and to approach the authorities. At times though, the local differences led to circumstances where the establishment of Islamic schools was supported by the relevant municipality in one city but prevented by another (Rath et al. 2001, 264).

Private Islamic schools have to meet certain academic standards that are checked in compulsory national tests and regular inspections, but the schools choose independently in what way and with what educational methods and materials to achieve these goals.[11] In both England[12] and the Netherlands, Muslim

---

4   The process to gain voluntary aided status is extensive and most of the Islamic schools face hindrances. Often political power relations, in particular Local Authorities, determine whether an application for state funding is rejected or approved (see Odone 2008 and Rath et al. 2001, 241 et seq.).
5   The legal provisions for establishing Muslim schools have changed by law since 2003, making it impossible to apply for 'provisional registration' to open a school and then develop the resources and expertise to get full registration. See The Education (Independent Schools Standards) (England) Regulations (2003) Statutory Instrument No. 1910.
6   41 percent of Islamic school students are of Moroccan origin, 40 percent of Turkish origin and the rest from Surinam, Tunisia as well as from Iraq, Iran, Afghanistan, Sudan, Somalia, Eritrea (Inspectie van het Onderwijs 2003).
7   See the website of the Islamic Schools Board Organisation (ISBO). The first Muslim primary school was established in Rotterdam in 1988.
8   90 percent of pupils attending Islamic schools are socio-economically disadvantaged. Around 40 percent of them are of Moroccan and 37 percent of Turkish origin. Most schools are dominated by either of the two ethnic groups (see Driessen & Merry 2006, 204).
9   According to the Dutch Constitution, the state has to support non-religious and denominational schools equally (Article 23).
10 Rath et al. (2001, 263), concluded that, in the process of founding Islamic institutions in the Netherlands, it was more likely that Muslim claims were supported by the authorities in cases where the claims were based on "equal treatment" rather than "specific group rights".
11 In Britain, only the voluntary aided schools are required to follow the national curriculum. The independent faith schools can determine own curriculum.

schools emphasise the education of children according to the values, norms and traditions of Islam as interpreted by the governing bodies. This is achieved by offering special Islamic Instruction, by praying together, by introducing special dress codes and by observing the Islamic calendar. Islamic schools in both countries are highly heterogeneous in terms of internal regulations, educational approaches and Islamic practices. Orthodox schools often impose strict dress codes even on teachers who are non-Muslim, they insist on complete gender separation, follow a certain school of thought within Islam and do not allow the teaching of music and the drawing of humans and animals as prescribed by the national curriculum. Liberal schools, on the other hand, are more accommodating in terms of teaching the core curriculum including music and figurative arts. Children practice their religion according to the respective traditions of their parents, in some schools the wearing of the headscarf is not compulsory and co-education is pursued.[13]

A considerable difference between the British and the Dutch situation is that, in Britain, the majority of staff members at Islamic schools are Muslim while in the Netherlands up to three quarters of the staff members are non-Muslim. This often leads to conflicts between non-Muslim teachers and the Muslim governing body that have to be resolved by the principal (Driessen & Valkenberg 2000, 23). Because the British Islamic schools are much more homogeneous with the majority of teachers being Muslim, it is easier for them to create and preserve an exclusive Islamic environment compared with their Dutch counterparts.

Empirical data from England and the Netherlands show that the academic results of pupils in Islamic schools are equal to the results of pupils at public schools with a similar socio-ethnic composition but on many levels stay below the average performance results.[14]

The public and political debates around Muslim schools elaborate on a number of arguments against their establishment: it is argued that Muslim schools are divisive and exclusive, isolating Muslim children from the wider society. In the Dutch case it was feared that the formation of social groups around separate languages and nationalities could lead to insufficient knowledge of the Dutch language and therefore diminish the social and economical opportunities of learners (Shadid & Konigsfeld 1992, 108). Furthermore, the criticism is levelled that the focus on the religious ethos and instruction in the schools could lead to indoctrination, and makes it impossible for the child to choose independently whether to lead a religious life or not. Finally, doubts have been raised over whether Muslim schools can provide democratic citizenship education that includes tolerance and respect for other faith groups that could only be learnt in a multi-cultural and multi-ethnic classroom setting. (Open Society Institute 2005, 129 et seq.). Criticism even came from within the Muslim communities. The Muslim academic and activist

---

12 The schools that were included in the study are all based in England.
13 In an early study Shadid and van Koningsveld (1992) distinguish in the Dutch context between conservative schools and liberal schools. Most of them were founded by local ethnic groups which were in a few cases affiliated with particular Islamic organisations.
14 See Geert Driessen and Pim Valkenberg (2000) who included half of the Islamic schools in the Netherlands in an empirical study, and the British Ofsted Inspection Reports for Islamic schools which can be viewed at their website (www.ofsted.gov.uk).

Tariq Ramadan, for example, warned that Islamic schools could lead to a situation where" *'artificially Islamic' closed spaces are created in the West that are almost completely cut off from the surrounding society*" (see Ramadan 2004, 131).

On the other hand, academics, policy makers and Muslim representatives bring up arguments for the establishment of these educational institutions: Muslim schools have to have the same rights to exist and get government support as the thousands of other faith-based schools in England and the Netherlands. Furthermore, Muslim schools provide a religious environment where the faith can be practised and observed without compromises and obstacles unlike in many public schools where there are often no special provisions for Muslim children. It is argued that Islamic schools nurture and develop an Islamic identity which helps Muslim children to be assertive and confident when they engage with the wider society and contribute to the integration process. Michael Merry comes to the conclusion that "*Islamic schools do ameliorate the effects of social exclusion and reinforce cultural and religious identities in ways that public schools can not*" (see Merry 2007, 164). In the independent Muslim schools, which do not have to comply with the national curriculum, the secular subjects can be taught from an Islamic perspective and single-sex education can be provided (Parker-Jenkins 2005, 40). From a gender perspective, it is argued that single sex schools keep those Muslim girls in further education who come from conservative families who would have taken them out of public schools at a certain age (Odone 2008, 25et seq.) In recent years another aspect has become very important: the protection of Muslim children against discrimination and Islamophobic attacks which frequently occur in state schools, and which are an expression of the deteriorating public opinion of Muslims and Islam (Open Society Institute 2005, 131 et seq., AMSSUK 2004, 30 et seq.). It is furthermore argued that Islamic schools make Muslim children better citizens by 'providing a moral compass, and instilling a new sense of morality into society' (Parker-Jenkins 2005, 40). The latter argument applies to all confessional schools. Robert Jackson states, regarding the function of confessional schools within a democratic society: '*The key issue in relation to citizenship in culturally diverse societies is whether separate schooling for religious minorities strengthens or erodes social cohesion*' (Jackson 2003a, 16).

3. Islamic schools, the national curriculum and the "Islamisation project"

While independent Islamic schools in Britain do not have to follow the national curriculum, those which are integrated into the state sector (voluntary aided) and all of the government funded schools in the Netherlands are obliged to teach it. Even though they are not compelled to, a large number of the independent Islamic schools in Britain teach the National Curriculum due to the fact that they have to use the already existing textbooks and materials. The reason for this is that schools and school boards lack the financial resources to produce their own teaching materials. Furthermore, these schools have to take part in national exams which are based on the government approved curriculum. Nevertheless, there are considerable variations in how the National Curriculum is applied, and in most subject areas it allows flexibilities in terms of leaving out aspects that are regarded as 'un-Islamic' by some Muslim educators. The more conservative schools for example do not allow the teaching of music, dance and figurative arts that are part of the national curriculum. Liberal schools, on the other hand, are more accommodating in terms of teaching the core curriculum including music and arts.

There are many examples of how the National Curriculum is adapted to the Islamic context of the school. In one Islamic high school in England, the teachers try individually to incorporate the Islamic or Muslim perspective into the so-called secular subjects. An English teacher stated that she does it in two ways: either she chooses poems or literature which were written by a Muslim author or, if she has to do the prescribed texts like Shakespeare's 'Romeo and Juliet', the role and behaviour of the figures in the literature will be discussed from an Islamic perspective and related to the learners' experience of living in a Western society as Muslims.[15] In a biology lesson for example, the teacher talked about the embryonic development of a foetus in the womb. Each picture of the presentation depicting the different stages of growth was underlined with verses from the Qur'an describing the foetal development.[16] In art lessons the learners are taught to do mosaics, design carpets and calligraphy, and in music they are introduced to the singing of Islamic songs without instruments *(nasheeds)*.

For the teachers at this school, islamising their lessons primarily means following the National Curriculum and 'adding on' the Islamic or Muslim references, or looking for Islamic alternatives to certain subject topics. According to the principal, the "*Islamisation of the curriculum*" plays no role for the curriculum development in his school and he promotes a holistic understanding of knowledge: "*We do not need to Islamisise the sciences since all knowledge comes from Allah*". In his viewpoint, knowledge consists of a cognitive domain and an affective domain. The affective side, or the so-called 'hidden curriculum', is strengthened through school prayers, religious studies and character development. In the principal's opinion, the learners are doing well academically and they are also confident in their Islamic identity without the Islamisation of the curriculum.[17]

Eight primary schools in the Netherlands, which have formed one governing body, show an even more liberal approach to the application of the standard curriculum than the British school that was mentioned. They teach the national curriculum without any alterations. Even in arts most of the schools allow figurative drawing, which was introduced against the wishes of a number of conservative parents and school board members. According to a board member it is more important in lessons to make a link between the specific theme and Islam or Muslims, especially in subjects like history, than to Islamise the curriculum as such.[18]

Many Islamic schools feel uncomfortable with teaching sex education, particularly at an early age, and with the theory of evolution. When schools are obliged to teach these topics, it is often done from an Islamic perspective. The evolution theory, for example, is being introduced but with the reference that is regarded to

---

15 Interview with an English teacher of an Islamic high school, 24 May 2007.
16 Observation of a biology class in an Islamic high school, 9 July 2008
17 Interview with the principal of an Islamic high school, 7 July 2008.
18 Interview with a director of an Islamic primary school board, 10 March 2008.

be Islamically incorrect. In this way, distance is created towards those aspects of the National Curriculum which are viewed critically by Muslim educators. In sex education, the teacher would explain the Islamic rules and regulations regarding marriage and relationships between the genders.

In most cases the respective national curricula are flexible enough to allow Islamic schools to make changes and adaptations in the subject syllabi so that it suits the Islamic ethos of the school. Whether or not and in which way schools embark on 'Islamising' the curriculum is largely dependant on the attitude of the school board and the principal, and on the competences of the teachers. Most schools – particularly in Britain – do make reference in all subjects to the Qur'an, Islamic culture and history. If possible, Muslim authors and examples of Islamic countries are dealt with in the lessons in order to reflect the cultural and religious background of the children.

The Islamic content and religious practices are perceived by most students as positive aspects of attending a confessional school. As the results of an empirical study in a British Islamic school[19] show, students regard the Islamic environment and the fact that they can practice their religion freely at school and learn more about their religion as particularly positive. The school is often seen as an extension of the home environment where religion plays an important, often all-en-compassing role. For many students, the school is regarded as a place where they feel protected and accepted, where 'sameness' is emphasised and promoted.[20]

4. Religious instruction and the creation of an "Islamic ethos"

The subject Islamic Studies has an important function within Muslim schools in forming a religious identity. Islamic Studies primarily include the transmission of basic knowledge about the practices and history of the faith. In most cases, it avoids elaborating on different schools of thought within Islamic theology and law. To give an example, the Religious Instruction syllabus of an Islamic high school in Britain is developed by the Religious teachers of the school and is based primarily on the *Qur'an* and the *Sunnah* as text sources. Because of the different Islamic and cultural backgrounds of the pupils, the school avoids teaching according to particular law schools. The emphasis lies on the 'basic Islamic knowledge' and on stressing the commonalities and not the differences of religious practices. The teaching material for Islamic Studies is drawn from various sources, like Muslim organisations and research institutes in England, the United States and even South Africa, where Islamic schools exist and develop in a Muslim minority context.[21]

---

19 Qualitative questionnaires were handed out to 59 pupils (15-17 years) in a British Islamic high school, asking them about their religious attitudes, and their opinions of the school they attend and of the society in which they live.
20 For a more detailed analysis of the students questionnaires, see Niehaus forthcoming.
21 The organisations which produce educational material used by the school for the Islamic Studies syllabus are from the Islamic Foundation in England, IQRA in the United States and the Islamic Studies syllabus developed in South Africa by the International Board of Educational Research and Resources (IBERR). Those curricula follow a classical, rather conservative approach and do not include comparative religion or learning about different movements and school of thoughts within Islam.

One high school which took part in the research, introduced recently published, modern textbooks for Islamic Studies that are designed for Muslim children in the West. Here, the pupils are introduced to topics that support a plural and tolerant approach towards Islam, other religions and culturally diverse societies. Sections deal, among others, with inner-Muslim differences (Shia versus Sunni Islam), Muslim political participation and resistance against unjust governments, as well as the rights and responsibilities of Muslims living in non-Muslim countries. These textbooks are used by the Islamic Studies teachers to prepare the pupils in grade 9-11 for the national school leaving exams (GCSE) in Religious Education. Islamic schools can focus on Islamic Studies within the Religious Education GCSE curriculum, but they need to include comparative religion.[22] The Religious Education Curriculum therefore changed the content and orientation of the Islamic Studies syllabus in Islamic schools, making it more compatible with national and local guidelines.

In the Netherlands the umbrella body for Islamic schools, ISBO (*Islamitische Scholen Besturen Organisatie*), was recently part of an initiative to improve the subject Islamic Studies, which is usually taught in one to two periods per week. The organisation has produced a new curriculum for Islamic Instruction that integrates modern teaching methods, has an interactive and dialogical approach, and which was introduced in the schools in 2007. The implementation of the new curriculum goes hand in hand with the new legal requirements of Islamic Studies teachers to have teacher diplomas. Many of the Islamic Studies teachers are unqualified and received religious education only in their countries of origin. The new guidelines intend to streamline Islamic Studies and bring them up to the same didactical and pedagogical standards as the secular subjects.

Religious instruction in many Islamic schools seems to be oriented on the experiences of the children who live in a multicultural society and the subject includes aspects of citizenship education. To give one example: in one lesson at an Islamic high school in England the pupils were taught that one of the principles of Islam, giving charity, has to be applied to all human beings and learners were encouraged to assist not only people in their faith community but also needy non-Muslim compatriots.[23]

Furthermore, the development of a distinct Islamic ethos or identity is also carried out in some cases with the aim of promoting democratic citizenship. A school board which runs eight Islamic primary schools in the Netherlands is presently working on an identity policy entitled "becoming what you are".[24] The aim is to identify core values within Islam which are universal and which can be binding for all the schools. These guidelines embrace values like "justice" but also social skills like "co-operation". In this way, a school board member hopes, the pupils are able to link with non-Muslims who share the same values. An identity policy is not only important for pupils and teachers as orientation, it also initiates

---

22 Interview with an Islamic Studies teacher at an Islamic high school, 16 March 2009.
23 Participatory observation of a Religious Instruction class at an Islamic high school, 24 May 2007.
24 The quote makes reference to the Islamic belief of *fitra* which means that every child is born with the innate nature of being conscious of God. The child is therefore regarded as "pure" and "without sin".

internal debates about the Islamic ethos and values which should be transmitted. Often, the schools are faced with teachers and parents who differ fundamentally regarding their religious, ideological and pedagogical outlook. The democratic process of defining an identity policy includes all stakeholders and initiates discourses which lead to the definition of common values that determine the position of Islamic schools and Islamic education within Dutch society.[25]

5. Islamic schools, democratic citizenship and social cohesion

Particularly after 9/11 and the terror attacks in Europe in recent years, Islamic schools, especially in England and the Netherlands, have become the focus of public and political debate, and they are viewed critically in terms of democratic citizenship education and integration efforts (Shadid 2006, 18; Ter Avest et al. 2006, 205; Odone 2008).[26] This is aggravated by the fact that certain schools in England and the Netherlands are financially supported or inspired by national and international Islamic organisations and movements who are accused of promoting anti-democratic attitudes.[27] In the Netherlands policy makers and the Education Authorities have recently been mostly concerned about the low academic results and the bad management of these schools, which is also reflected in negative media reporting.[28] These concerns strengthen those critics in the public and political arena who argue that Muslim schools isolate Muslim children from the wider society.

In the light of an increasingly diverse, multicultural society and the public and political 'integration debates', the Netherlands and Britain introduced the new statutory requirement to actively promote democratic citizenship and social cohesion in schools.[29]

---

25 Interview with the director of an Islamic primary school board, 10 March 2008.
26 The 'unease' with Islam and Muslim institutions began much earlier in the Netherlands. Already in the late 1980s and early 1990s the political debates on Islam changed and became more hostile in the light of international incidents (e.g. the Rushdie affair, Gulf War) (Rath et al. 2001, 36 et seq.).
27 In the Netherlands the National Security Service (NSS) investigated certain Islamic schools with regard to their teaching materials in order to find out whether they were inciting hatred or complying with democratic values (Shadid 2006, 18). In its 2002 report, the NSS stated that the majority of Islamic schools comply with legal requirements and democratic values. Nevertheless, twenty percent of the schools were either financially supported by Al-Waqf al-Islami – an organisation that is regarded as fundamentalist – or had school board members who were affiliated to radical Islamic organisations (Driessen & Merry 2006, 212).
28 The Dutch Ministry of Education voiced its concern regarding the quality of education at Islamic schools after recent investigations found out that half of the Islamic schools are "weak" or "very weak" regarding their academic results. Furthermore, about 86 percent of the school boards who run Islamic schools are investigated for financial irregularities and fraud (Ministerie van Onderwijs, Cultuur en Wetenshap: "Problem in het islamitisch onderwijs is ernst", Persbericht, 13.11.08 (available online: http://www.minocw.nl/actueel/persberichten/12144/Problemen-in-het-islamitisch-onderwijs-ernstig.html, accessed: February 16, 2009).
29 A new Bill brought before parliament by the Dutch Secretary of Education in 2006 makes it compulsory for schools in the Netherlands to teach democratic citizenship education. In Britain, the citizenship curriculum was introduced in the schools in 2002 and in 2007

Many Islamic schools have responded to these state requirements and the public discourses by starting to engage actively in social cohesion programmes and by promoting democratic citizenship – especially those schools which receive state funds. The need to open up to society is also reflected in the self-understanding of educators in Islamic schools. The principal of an Islamic high school, which recently gained voluntary aided status, explained that he wishes to bring up children as good citizens, to promote good behaviour and a good relationship with other human beings, and to enable Muslim children to be productive members of the community.[30] This attitude is also reflected in the mission statement of the school: 'Our core values will enable all students to live in harmony with their fellow citizens and contribute positively to the social, political and well-being of their country.' According to the principal, the emphasis lies on 'creating a citizen who is confident in his or her ability to communicate with the wider society'.[31] To give practice to this approach the school engages in a variety of exchange programmes with non-Muslim schools and introduced a community outreach programme where pupils visit social institutions like old-age homes. The school has also started with so-called "extended services" to the community. There is a plan to open the sports and recreational facilities to community groups and to offer adult education and religious studies classes (*madrasa*). In order to facilitate inclusion and integration, the school takes part in a "citizenship and social cohesion" programme which is compulsory for all state funded schools. The school has recently appointed a teacher as social cohesion co-ordinator who initiated a long-term exchange programme with a school in the same city, which includes a group of pupils and teachers who meet regularly.

The openness to society is also reflected in the students' responses. The majority of students indicate that they have positive relationships with personal friends and neighbours which are characterised by mutual respect, tolerance and support.[32] On the other hand there are also experiences of conflict and confrontations which arise from feeling discriminated against, being treated disrespectfully and even being exposed to racist or anti-Islamic attitudes and attacks. The attitude of students towards society and the government is equally ambivalent. For many, the city or even the country they are living in are seen as positive examples of multi-cultural and multi-faith environments which they can identify with and feel a part of. On the other hand, equal treatment and anti-discriminatory legislation is perceived as statutory but students experience a lack of application in practice, and they question the ability of the government to protect their rights as Muslims.

---

maintained schools were legally required to actively promote social cohesion (Education and Inspection Act 2006).

30 Interview with the principal of an Islamic high school, 18 May 2007.
31 Ibid.
32 In accordance with the REDCo results (see Jozsa in this volume) the majority of Muslim students in this sample stated that they have non-Muslim friends and viewed discussing religious, social and political issues with people of other or no faiths as a positive experience. This is an indication that faith schools in general, and Islamic schools in particular, do not lead to or promote social exclusion *per se* by creating segregated spaces which are cut off from the rest of society.

In the Dutch case, the issue of Islamic schools and social cohesion is debated in a different way: here the focus lies on keeping up with required academic and pedagogical standards in order to promote socio-economic integration. An Islamic high school in Amsterdam, for example, is regarded as one of the worst performing high schools in the Netherlands. The Education Inspectorate issued the school with an ultimatum to improve academic results. If they fail to progress, the government will stop the funding and the school may have to close. Being a fairly new school, it seems that the school board who started it lacked the expertise and skills to manage a school. Furthermore, the school attracted academically weak and problematic pupils from public schools. The parents hoped that their children would perform better at an exclusively Muslim school. The reason for the underperformance of Muslim children is often insufficient Dutch language skills – a problem most Muslim schools in the Netherlands are struggling with. The Muslim children who attend Islamic schools are mostly from the second or third generation of Turkish or Moroccan immigrants and Dutch is hardly spoken at home. The acquisition of language skills is therefore the priority of most of the educators at Islamic schools. The other concern is the insufficient qualification of Muslim teachers in particular, many of whom were educated in their countries of origin and struggle to adjust to the teaching methods and curriculum of the Dutch education system.

In many Islamic schools in the Netherlands a shift occurred from focusing on identity formation to improving academic standards and quality of education.[33]

In the Dutch case, the question of social cohesion is therefore not primarily a question of religious identity and democratic citizenship but rather a question of socio-economic status. Islamic schools in this context are generally referred to as 'black schools' and the majority of learners come from marginalized families.[34] Policy makers and educators at Muslim schools see this situation as a threat to social cohesion that could lead to further segregation.

To promote social cohesion and prevent the 'ghettoisation' of Islamic schools a small number of Islamic schools in the Netherlands have become part of a so-called 'broad school'. This means they share a building with one or more other confessional or non-confessional schools and engage together in extra-curricular activities. Sharing one space, though, is no guarantee for social integration as the principal of an Islamic school in a small city experienced. The school started over a year ago within a "broad school", but educators observed that the pupils of the two primary schools that were combined did not interact during break times in the school grounds. According to the principal, the pupils had to be *"taught how to play together"*. Furthermore, on the level of teachers and parents, initiating exchange and cooperation between the schools started slowly and with some

---

33 According to the acting director of ISBO, the generation who started Islamic schools in the Netherlands twenty years ago was primarily interested in creating a 'safe haven' for Muslim children where their Islamic identity could develop. This has changed over the years and today educators and parents regard the improvement of academic standard as the most important prerogative (interview with the interim director of ISBO, 10 March 2008, Utrecht).

34 For a discussion on the development of and distinction between so called black and white schools in the Netherlands see Vedder (2006).

reservations.[35] Broad schools, nevertheless, offer new opportunities for teachers, parents and pupils to enter into constructive dialogue with those who are not part of their religious, cultural or ethnic community.

One argument against faith schools in general and Islamic schools in particular is their exclusivity in terms of admission policies. In theory all confessional schools are open to pupils from other faith communities. In practice, however preference is given to those pupils from the same faith and most Islamic schools have been unable to admit non-Muslim students. The British Community Cohesion Review Team published a report in 2001 where it recommended that it should be made compulsory for faith schools to take in 25 percent of pupils from another or no religious background (Home Office 2001, 34). This policy recommendation was met with criticism from Islamic schools and the Association of Muslim Schools. In the British case, many Islamic schools are in high demand and have long waiting lists of Muslim children whose parents want to send them there. In a situation where not even the requests from Muslim families can be met, it seems impossible in the light of the schools admission policies to open the doors to non-Muslim learners. In the Netherlands Islamic schools are in many cases not oversubscribed but here the negative image and low academic results are seen as obstacles to attracting non-Muslim learners. According to the manager of a large Islamic school board in the Netherlands, the ideal situation would be to have up to 20 percent of non-Muslim pupils in the schools. In this way the schools could become more inclusive but at the same time preserve their specific religious identity.[36]

6. Conclusions

The establishment and curriculum of Islamic schools in Britain and the Netherlands are informed by the pedagogical and religious orientation of Muslim educators as well as the socio-political structure and they include a multitude of different facets. The founders of Islamic schools used the legal frameworks and constitution to operate within the already existing structure which in many cases had supported confessional schools for a long time. However, other factors played a role in the institutionalisation of Islamic education as well, like the relationship between church and state or education and religion in a respective country. In the 'post-pillarised' Netherlands, which is defending its secularisation, the establishment of a new 'pillar' in the form of private Islamic schools is viewed with public and political scepticism and criticism.[37] In Britain the government seeks stronger control over Islamic schools by incorporating them into the publicly funded sector.

Muslim actors are primarily focussed on the national education system and on the role that religion is supposed to play within it. Furthermore, the existing legal and political structures determine the ways in which Muslims strive to implement Islamic education for their children. While in Britain and the Netherlands the establishment and improvement of Islamic schools is the main area of engagement

---

35 Interview with an Islamic school principal, 11 February 2009, Netherlands.
36 Interview with the manager of a school board, 11 February 2009, Netherlands.
37 For a summary of the current debates on the role of religion in education and the position of Islamic schools see Ter Avest et al. (2007).

between Muslim educational organisations and the authorities, in Germany Muslim organisations are primarily focused on the introduction of Islamic Instruction in public schools. Islamic private schools are therefore only one expression of the desire to institutionalise Islamic education in Europe.

The way in which Muslim schools are able to create an Islamic ethos and promote Islamic values and norms is primarily dependent on the educational policies of the specific country, as well as on the ideological and religious orientation of the governing body. Dutch Islamic schools often find it difficult to uphold an Islamic ethos due to the fact that a high percentage of teachers are non-Muslim. On the other side, these schools seem to equip their pupils better to engage with the wider society since inter-faith dialogue happens on a daily basis between Muslim pupils and non-Muslim teachers. However, Dutch Islamic schools are also ethnically divided, with pupils of these schools coming either from predominantly Turkish or predominantly Moroccan backgrounds. Even when they share the same religion, they are strongly oriented towards the cultural identity of their ethnic origin. British Islamic schools, on the other hand, are more homogeneous with most of the children being either of Pakistani, Bangladeshi or Indian background. Culturally and religiously the South Asian heritage is important for the syllabi of the subjects which are taught, including Islamic Studies.

With regards to the concept of Islamising the curriculum, the schools in this study do not regard it as a priority of their activities. Instead of Islamising the entire syllabi and teaching materials, it seems to be important for educators in all disciplines to use Islamic references and examples in the context of secular subjects. The emphasis of the schools is clearly to provide Muslim children with a sound academic education which enables them to cope with the requirements of a professional life or to proceed to further and higher education. This indicates that there has been a shift in discourses within Muslim educational organisations and institutions. While the Islamisation project did influence a number of educators and parents in the late 1980s and early 1990s, the focus has changed to providing excellent academic results within or oriented on the mainstream education system. Integration into society and the labour market seems to be the priority for Islamic schools, at least for those who actively promote social cohesion. The Islamic environment of the school is no longer seen as a means of protecting children's religious identity against the un-Islamic influences of the mainstream society, but rather as a tool to prepare them for their role as active citizens.

In terms of creating a distinct Islamic identity, the research shows that the Islamic schools are diverse in their religious approaches, which is evident in the particular rules and regulations that pupils and teachers have to follow, as well as in the educational goals the schools are pursuing. The curriculum at these schools does not differ much from that at public schools. In this sense the schools are more 'schools for Muslims' than 'Muslim schools', since the focus is clearly on offering a sound 'secular' education within an Islamic environment. The ways in which the Islamic code of conduct and ethos shape the consciousness and identity of the pupils is something which needs to be explored further. What becomes clear from the students' responses is that they feel predominantly positive about the multicultural society they are living in, regarding it as a site of learning about and from each other by establishing positive relationships with fellow citizens. However, at the same time, they also refer to negative experiences of victimisation and discrimination. The ambivalence is visible: on the one hand students regard their school and community as a 'safe haven' where religion can be lived and practised without compromises and where they are protected from discrimination and stigmatisation. On the other hand they express their wish to be active citizens of a plural society and to develop their multiple identities.

Putting the public and political criticism of Islamic schools aside, the establishment a faith school in the countries under question is an exercise of a constitutional right and an expression of parental choice. The establishment of Islamic schools in both countries is a fairly new process compared to the long tradition of Christian schools and they have not had the opportunity to develop at their own pace with the necessary support and resources provided by the respective governments and education authorities. The case studies show that Islamic schools are sites of ongoing discourses where religious traditions and practices are debated, reviewed and changed to respond to the local or national context and to the educational requirements of the specific society. The school boards, which consist of members from different ethnic background and Islamic traditions, are required to develop a vision of the school and determine the religious ethos the school intends to pursue. In doing so, they need to overcome differences related to their cultural and religious background. These processes are important in promoting emancipation and integration into the society by developing a localised understanding of the 'Islamic way of life' that they want to live and pass on to Muslim children. Often, the debates that take place within Islamic schools permeate into the wider Muslim society and initiate new discourses.

It is worth considering the alternatives to institutionalised Islamic schools: Muslim children whose parents desire an Islamic education for them would entirely rely on the Qur'an-schools (*madrasas*) where children are taught in the afternoons or weekends by religious scholars or Imams who are seldom qualified teachers and who are often unfamiliar with the multicultural setting in which the children grow up. The effect could most likely be that these Muslim children experience the dichotomy of secular education in the public school versus Islamic Instruction at the *madrasa,* with both representing different values and norms and using different teaching methods. Furthermore, Qur'an-schools function without inspections and independent evaluations, leaving it entirely up to the religious authority what is being taught. The Islamic schools and Islamic educational institutions in the Netherlands and Britain have started to develop syllabi for Islamic Studies that are based on the experience of Muslim children in plural and multicultural societies. Therefore, Islamic Studies within Islamic schools adapts to the context that Muslim children are living in and the subject does have the potential, and is often used, to promote democratic citizenship.

Nevertheless, some Islamic schools, willingly or unwillingly, are still in a situation where there is hardly any exchange with the community or other schools around them.[38] The perceived stigma of isolation can be overcome by engaging in exchange programmes with non-denominational or other faith-schools in their

---

38 A recent study shows that British faith schools generally have done very little to engage in community cohesion as required by the government guidelines (Runnymede Trust 2008).

areas, by being part of a 'broad school' as in the Dutch case, or by becoming 'community centres' as in the British examples of 'extended services'. Some Islamic schools have already established community-outreach programmes and actively promote social cohesion.

The question of whether Islamic schools promote social cohesion or, rather, lead to segregation is, particularly in the Dutch case, not primarily a question of religious identity but rather a question of socio-economic status. The poor academic achievements of students and their limited chances in the labour market pose a threat to social cohesion and need to be addressed by policy-makers and the government in order to avoid socio-economic segregation. Accordingly, the public debates on Islamic schools have shifted from being critical of ethnic and religious segregation to being concerned about the quality of education offered by Islamic schools.[39]

In Britain there is a trend towards the incorporation of Islamic schools into the state sector by granting voluntary aided status.[40] In this way the government can exercise greater control over the curriculum and performance of these schools. Bringing Islamic schools into the mainstream also means that they are obliged to meet the statutory requirement to implement social cohesion programmes which could lead to a stronger local integration of Islamic schools. For Islamic schools, gaining voluntary aided status leads to the improvement of resources and makes the school more accessible for economically disadvantaged pupils whose parents would otherwise not be able to pay high school fees.

In conclusion, one has to bear in mind that only a very small percentage of Muslim children attend Islamic schools in both countries and the majority is still educated in public schools. The question is, therefore, in which way the situation at public and other private schools could be adjusted and improved to accommodate the special needs of Muslim children.[41] Many of those schools do not have a vision of integration and dealing with diversity in a multicultural context.[42] Islamic schools, on the other hand, seem to be under particular political and public pressure to prove their integration efforts.

---

39 For an account of the public debates on Islamic schools in the 1990 see Rath et al. (2001: 75 et seq.).
40 The government indicated that it will in future support the establishment of maintained faith schools, whether they are newly founded or replace already existing independent schools (Department for Children, Schools and Families 2007).
41 As Jozsa's quantitative analysis of Muslim students' responses in this volume show, the majority of pupils who attend public schools in European countries agree more than other groups with the statement that religious dietary regulations should be taken into account by schools and that students should be allowed to wear more visible religious symbols at school.
42 According to the Dutch Education Inspectorate, one quarter of schools in the Netherlands have no vision for integration (Inspectie von het Onderwijs 2005, 36). See also recommendations for special provisions for Muslim children at public schools (Open Society 2005, 174, and Department for Education and Skills 2007).

References

Department of Children, Schools and Families (2007) *Faith in the System. The role of schools with a religious character in English education and society,* available at: http://www.teachernet.gov.uk/publications.

Department for Education and Skills (2007) *Diversity and Citizenship. Curriculum Review,* available at: http://publications.teachernet.gov.uk/eOrderingDownload/ DfES_ Diversity_&_Citizenship.pdf, accessed: April 15, 2009.

De Jong, J. & Snik, G. (2002) Why should states fund denominational schools?, *Journal of Philosophy of Education,* 36(4), 573-587.

Driessen, G. & Merry, M. S. (2006) Islamic schools in the Netherlands: expansion or marginalization?, *Interchange,* 37(3), 201-223.

Driessen, G. & Valkenberg, P. (2000) Islamic schools in the Netherlands: compromising between identity and quality, *British Journal of Religious Education,* 23(1), 15-26.

Fetzer, J.S. & Soper, C.J. (2005) *Muslims and the state in Britain, France and Germany* (New York, Cambridge University Press).

Hewer, C. (2001) Schools for Muslims, *Oxford Review of Education,* 27(4), 515-527.

Home Office (2001) *Community Cohesion: A report of the Independent Review Team, chaired by Ted Cantle,* available online: http://www.communities.gov.uk/ documents/communities/ pdf/independentreviewteam.pdf, accessed: January 20, 2009).

Islamic Relief (2003) *Citizenship and the Muslim perspective. Teachers sharing ideas* (London, Islamic Relief).

Inspectie van het Onderwijs (Education Inspectorate) (2003) *Islamitische scholen nader onderzocht* (Utrecht, Inspectie van het Onderwijs).

Inspectie van het Onderwijs (Education Inspectorate) (2005) *The state of education in the Netherlands 2004/2005* (Utrecht, Inspectie van het Onderwijs).

Jackson, R. (2003a) Citizenship, religious and cultural diversity and education, in: Jackson, R. (Ed.) *International perspectives on citizenship, education and religious diversity* (London, New York, RoutledgeFalmer), 1-28.

Jackson, R. (2003b) Should the state fund faith-based schools? A review of the arguments, *British Journal of Religious Education,* 25(2), 89-102.

MacEoin, D. (2009) *Music, chess and other sins: Segregation, Integration, and Muslim schools in Britain* (London, Institute for the Study of Civil Society).

Mandaville, P. (2007) Islamic education in Britain: Approaches to religious knowledge in a pluralistic society, in: Hefner, R. W. & Zaman, M. Q. (Eds.) *Schooling Islam* (Princeton & Oxford, Princeton University Press), 224-241.

Merry, M S. (2007) *Culture, identity and Islamic schooling. A philosophical approach* (New York, Palgrave&Macmillan).

Niehaus, I. (forthcoming) Islamic schools in Europe: Religious identity formation and democratic citizenship, in: Reetz, D. (Ed.) *Living Islam in Euope. Muslim traditions in European contexts* (Leiden, Brill).

Nielsen, J.S. (1999) *Towards a European Islam* (New York, Palgrave).

Open Society Institute (2005) *Muslims and Education. Muslims in the UK: Policies for engaged citizens,* available online: http://www.eumap.org/topics/minority/ reports/britishmuslims, accessed: August 19, 2009.

Open Society Institute (2007) *Muslims in the EU: cities report. The Netherlands. Preliminary research report and literature survey,* available at:

http://www.eumap.org/topics/minority/reports/eumuslims/background_reports/download/netherlands/netherlands.pdf, accessed: August 19, 2009.

Parker-Jenkins, M., Hartas, D. & Irving, B. (2004) *In good faith. Schools, religion and public funding* (Aldershot, Ashgate).

Rath, J., Sunier, T. & Meyer A. (1997) Islam in the Netherlands: the establishment of Islamic institutions in a de-pillarizing society, *Tijdschrift voor Economische en Sociale Geographie*, 88(4), 389-395.

Rath, J., Penninx, R. & Groenendijk, K. (2001) *Western Europe and its Islam* (Leiden, Brill).

Runnymede Trust (2008) *Right to divide? Faith schools and community cohesion.* A Runnymede Trust Report summary by Rob Berkely with research by Savita Vij, available at: http://www.runnymedetrust.org, accessed: February 5. 2008.

Shadid, W. & von Koningsveld, P. (1992) Islamic primary schools, in: Shadid, W. & van Koningsveld, P. (Eds.) *Islam in Dutch society: Current developments and future prospects* (Kampen, Kok Pharos), 107-122.

Shadid, N.A. (2006) Public debates over Islam and the awareness of Muslim identity in the Netherlands, *European Education*, 38(2), 10-22.

Ter Avest, I., Bakker, C. & Bertram-Troost, G. (2006) Religion and Education in the Dutch pillarized and post-pillarized education system, in: R. Jackson, W. Weisse, J.-P. Willaime (Eds.) *Religion and education in Europe: Developments, contexts and debates* (Münster, Waxmann), 203-219

The Association of Muslim Social Scientists UK (2004) *Muslims on education. A position paper* (Richmond, The Association of Muslim Social Scientists UK).

Ramadan, T. (2004) *Western Muslims and the Future of Islam* (Oxford, Oxford University Press).

Vedder, P. (2006) Black and white schools in the Netherlands, *European Education*, 38(2), 36-49.

Dan-Paul Jozsa
Muslim Students Views on Religion and Education
Perspectives from Western European Countries

1. Introduction

The quantitative survey of the REDCo project was based on the outcomes of the qualitative study of the REDCo project, whose general results were published in Knauth et al. (2008), partly taking up its findings and seeking to verify central results on a broader, quantitative basis. Three research questions were central for this study:
- What role does religion have in pupils' life?
- How do pupils view religion in school and the impact of religion in education?
- How do pupils consider the impact of religion in society?

The questionnaire had 127 items, and was distributed to at least 400 students per country. In total 8085 students were pooled.

Neither study had a specific focus on Islam or on Muslim students apart from the fact that, especially in the case of the quantitative study, while trying to get a balanced (even if not representative) sample, efforts were also made to include also students from religious minority groups, which in most countries of the involved also meant the inclusion of students with a Muslim background, given the fact that Muslims are one of the largest religious minorities in most of the countries involved.

In the western European countries involved in the quantitative studies, this lead to samples with considerable percentages of Muslim students: in France (13%), England (12%), Germany (10%), the Netherlands (23%), Norway (8%) and Spain (10%), so that we can get a good picture of the views and attitudes of these Muslim students and compare them to the views of the Christian students and students with no religion who were pooled, and who form the biggest worldview groups in all of the samples. See table 1, where the percentages of students with no specific religious affiliation, the percentages of Christian students, and the percentages of those belonging to other religions are given.[1]

This article focuses on the commonalities between Muslim students, when compared to Christian students and students with no religion in the quantitative samples from England, France, Germany, the Netherlands, Norway and Spain. I will try to sketch the common features of the views Muslim students expressed in

---
1   These classifications follow those of the students themselves, without differentiating, however, between different Christian and Muslim sects on the one hand, and also by classifying those students who claim having a non religious worldview like 'atheist' or 'agnostic' as students with 'no religion' on the other. The group of students with 'other religions' is very heterogeneous, including e.g. Jews, Hindus, Sikhs, Heathens, Pagans, Satanists, 'own religion', and in most countries it is very small, so that we will not refer to it anymore in the course of this analysis.

these contexts. In a second step I will also comment on these findings against on the background of the standardised qualitative studies run within the REDCo project.

Table 1: Religious affiliation in the sample of the quantitative study (percentages)

	no religion	Christian	Muslim	other
England	59	19	12	10
France	47	36	13	4
Germany	41	47	10	2
The Netherlands	36	38	24	2
Norway	50	38	8	4
Spain	45	44	10	1

When presenting the quantitative results and speaking about 'differences' between Muslim students and Christian students or students with no religion, I mean statistically significant differences ($p<0.05$) using the Man and Whitney test ('U-test') and the Kruskal-Wallis test ('H-test')[2]. In order to explore differences between the answers to different items we used the Wilcox test. In presenting the findings we will not mention the respective tests used, but these should be obvious from the relationships and connections presented.

This article is based on the samples taken in England, France, Germany, the Netherlands, Norway and Spain, from a total of 6717 students. I will not comment here on the samples, since this was done extensively in Valk et al. (2009). The samples are not statistically representative but aim to be 'purposive' or 'judgmental' samples. I will refer to specificities of the samples in the course of the analysis when needed.

For the statistical tests I used SPSS 17. The samples used are the same as those used in Valk et al. (2009) except for Germany, where I used a more comprehensive sample, including students from almost all West-German federal states[3], while the article published in Valk et al. (2009) aimed to be a comparison between two federal states, Hamburg and North-Rhine Westphalia (see also Jozsa and Knauth in this book). When I give the frequencies of answers I will always give the 'valid percent' numbers.

2. Personal views and experiences with religion

In our samples, Muslim students tend to attribute a higher importance to religion than Christian students and students with no religion, when asked about how important religion is to them. In all contexts, over 60% of the Muslim students who were questioned stated that religion is 'very important' to them, while only very small minorities of Muslim students, between 0% and 6% consider religion as 'absolutely not important', with the others placing the importance of religion for

---

2   We choose to use non parametric tests because the variables generally do not follow a normal distribution (tested with the Kolmogorow-Smirnov-Test).
3   See Köhrs (2009) for a comprehensive description of the German sample used.

them between these two extremes, (see table 2, where the percentages of students belonging to the different worldview groups – students with no religion (*no rel.*), Christian students (*Chr.*) and Muslim students (*Mu.*) – who consider religion 'very important' and 'absolutely not important' are given).

When asked about their opinion with respect to the existence of God or of 'some sort of spirit or life force' Muslim students are more inclined to answer that 'there is a God' than Christian students, who again are more inclined towards this statement than students with 'no religion'. In all samples over 90% of the Muslim students think that 'there is God' and below 2% that there is no 'God, spirit or life force', see table 3, where the percentages of students who adhere to these statements are given for the different groups.

Table 2: Importance of religion (percentages)

How important is religion to you?	Very important			Absolutely not important		
	no rel.	Chr.	Mu.	no rel.	Chr.	Mu.
England	3	37	82	31	3	0.0
France	3	18	68	43	8	4
Germany	7	18	67	27	5	0.3
The Netherlands	7	28	82	44	2	1
Norway	3	12	63	42	12	6
Spain	7	18	68	28	3	2

Table 3: Which of these statements comes closer to your position? (percentages)

Which of these statements comes closest to your position?	There is God			There is some sort of spirit or life force			I don't really think there is any sort of God, spirit or life force		
	no rel.	Chr.	Mu.	no rel.	Chr.	Mu.	no rel.	Chr.	Mu.
England	11	75	98	45	19	2	44	6	0.0
France	8	49	97	33	33	2	60	18	1
Germany	25	56	93	43	37	5	32	7	2
The Netherlands	15	82	99	37	14	1	48	5	0.0
Norway	13	45	96	26	33	2	61	22	2
Spain	27	63	98	36	30	2	37	7	0.0

Muslim students, in all of the contexts studied, generally tended to be engaged in 'activities' related to religion more often than Christian students and students with no religion: they state that they think more often about religion, 'about the meaning of life', pray more often, attend more often 'religious events', read 'sacred texts' for themselves or look at the internet for religious topics (see table 4 where the percentages of students who state being involved in the respective activities at least once a week are given for the different groups).

There are only three exceptions to this general trend in the samples with regard to 'attending religious events'. In the French and the Dutch sample the Christian students tend to attend 'religious events' more often than Muslim students do, while the difference between these two groups is not significant in the Norwegian sample with regard to the same item. The frequencies of involvement in these activities as given in table 4 might not exemplify these exceptions with regard to France and Norway very well, since it gives only the cumulative percentages of students involved in attending 'religious events' at least about once a week, while the U-test used to compare the differences between the groups includes all frequencies. To exemplify the findings of the U-test for this item, it might help to take into consideration, that the percentages of students who state never attending 'religious events' are for students with no religion, Christian and Muslim students respectively: in the French sample 64%, 24% and 45%, the Dutch sample 77%, 13%, 19%, the Norwegian sample 57%, 24%, 27%.

The students were asked about the importance of family, school, friends, and faith community, books, media and Internet as sources of information about religion. Table 5 gives the total percentages of the students who consider these sources of information as important or very important and the total means for the respective countries. Table 6 gives the percentages of the students who consider these sources of information as important or very important for the different groups.

Table 4: Involvement in activities related to religion (percentages)

	Think about religion at least about every week			Read sacred texts for themselves at least about every week			Look at the internet for religious topics at least about every week		
	no rel.	Chr.	Mu.	no rel.	Chr.	Mu.	no rel.	Chr.	Mu.
England	37	85	100	3	40	88	2	6	44
France	13	55	87	1	10	38	1	3	13
Germany	29	57	86	5	12	50	4	5	22
The Netherlands	28	79	95	9	53	72	5	9	52
Norway	29	57	84	2	10	56	2	3	22
Spain	22	60	89	4	7	31	5	7	15
	Pray at least about every week			Attend religious events at least about every week			Think about the meaning of life at least about every week		
	no rel.	Chr.	Mu.	no rel.	Chr.	Mu.	no rel.	Chr.	Mu.
England	10	62	90	4	44	64	34	40	75
France	3	34	57	1	24	26	39	59	75
Germany	16	50	63	10	31	49	43	51	70
The Netherlands	14	77	89	6	57	41	32	56	79
Norway	3	28	61	6	22	32	32	43	64
Spain	17	49	68	11	22	44	50	58	78

Table 5: Sources for getting information about religion (means of estimates, scale from 1 – strongly agree to 5 – strongly disagree and percentages of those for whom the respective sources are important or very important)

	family		school		friends		Faith community		books		media		internet	
	mean	%	mean	%	mean	%	mean	%	mean	%	mean	%	mean	%
England	2.19	63	2.19	70	2.76	44	2.51	56	2.52	53	2.97	32	2.79	40
France	2.12	69	2.94	37	3.14	32	2.38	61	2.51	55	3.08	33	3.40	25
Germany	2.19	64	2.69	48	2.89	41	2.98	39	3.10	33	2.91	39	3.16	33
Netherlands	2.11	68	2.72	45	2.66	49	2.47	59	2.71	48	3.08	32	2.61	49
Norway	2.93	38	2.77	44	3.37	27	3.23	28	3.37	22	3.17	30	3.37	25
Spain	1.87	73	2.78	42	2.79	45	2.94	38	3.02	34	3.08	34	3.20	32

Table 6: Sources for getting information about religion (percentages of those for whom the respective sources are important or very important)

	Family			School			Friends		
	no rel.	Chr.	Mu.	no rel.	Chr.	Mu.	no rel.	Chr.	Mu.
England	51	66	92	67	76	80	36	41	74
France	53	80	95	34	44	28	22	12	50
Germany	54	67	97	40	53	57	39	37	71
Netherlands	48	71	92	29	44	69	33	51	69
Norway	26	38	97	35	49	58	21	27	51
Spain	61	81	99	33	49	55	39	48	54

	Faith community			Books			Media			Internet		
	no rel.	Chr.	Mu.	no rel.	Chr.	Mu.	no rel.	Chr.	Mu.	no rel.	Chr.	Mu.
England	44	70	84	43	54	90	32	25	42	38	25	60
France	48	71	79	51	52	77	36	32	25	26	23	33
Germany	20	50	73	23	35	70	38	39	44	34	30	47
Netherlands	23	71	90	31	42	81	30	33	30	47	44	60
Norway	17	33	70	16	21	68	24	33	51	20	22	54
Spain	22	46	77	25	33	75	31	33	49	28	34	43

A general trend, in line with the higher importance the Muslim students in our samples tend to give to religion, is that sources of information which are mentioned generally tend to be of more importance for them than for the Christian students and students with no religion. There are, however, some interesting exceptions from this trend.

With regard to the importance of the media as a source of information about religion, the differences between Muslim students on the one hand and Christian students and those with no religion on the other are not significant in the English and the Dutch sample, and in the French sample the importance that Muslim students accord to the media as a source of information about religion is even significantly lower than for the Christian students, as well as for the students with no religion.

In the French sample, the difference between the importance of the faith community for Muslim and Christian students is not significant. The same is true for the differences between Muslim students and those with no religion with regards to school and the internet, while the school is regarded as more important by the Christian students than by the Muslim students and those with no religion. In Norway, the difference between Christian and Muslim students in the levels of importance they attached to school as a source of information about religion is not significant, while in Spain the differences between these two groups are not significant with regards to friends and the internet as sources of information about religion.

Another general trend is that the family appears to be the most important source of information for the students in general. This is also true for the Muslim students: no other source of information about religion seems to be more important for them. However, the differences between family, faith community and books in the English sample, and those between family and faith community in the Dutch sample, are not significant with regard to the Muslim students. This does not mean that the family is not as important for the Muslim students in the English or the Dutch sample as for those in the other contexts, but rather that, in these samples, these other sources of information are at least as important as the family. This is remarkable, especially with regard to the importance of faith communities, and particularly so, since the same finding also applies for the Christian students in both contexts. Why the faith communities have a comparable importance for the Christian and Muslim students as the family in these two contexts while the faith community has a significantly lower importance in the other contexts is an interesting question, and one that we cannot answer without further research.

Although the family is generally seen in all the samples as the most important source of information, there are two interesting exceptions. For the students in the Norwegian sample, taken as a whole, school is significantly more important than the family, while for the English sample as a whole, the difference between the importance of family and school is not significant. Additionally, if we look at the different worldview groups in the samples, we see that, in these two contexts, the school is in fact the most important source of information about religion for students with no religion, more important than family, while the difference between family and school is not significant for Christian students, although it is for Muslim students, for whom school has a lower importance than the family.

Of the six countries which were researched, it is precisely these two which have nationally approved compulsory non-confessional religious education, at least in state schools (confessional in most of the confessional schools),[4] and most of the pupils included in the sample attended this model following the nationally approved curriculum. The other countries either have no religious education in state schools, as in France[5] (with generally compulsory religious education in confessional schools), optional confessional models of religious education in state schools, as is generally the case in Germany[6] and Spain[7] (with generally com-

---

4 See Jackson and O'Grady (2007) for a description of the situation regarding religious education in England and Skeie (2007) in Norway.
5 See Willaime (2007) for a description of the situation regarding religion in education in France.
6 Of the federal states taken into account in the German sample, only Hamburg has a model of 'religious education for all' that is somehow special. However, for the students in

pulsory religious education in confessional schools in both countries), or a variety of models of religious education, as in the Netherlands, at least if one takes into consideration the realities in schools.[8]

The finding that school has a importance comparable to or higher than the family only for the pupils in the English and the Norwegian sample holds, even if one takes into consideration only those students who currently attend religious education in the other samples, which might be regarded as a sign that the relatively higher importance of school in England and Norway might not be wholly due to the fact that the subject is compulsory.

When we compare the importance of school in different countries, we also find that, for the students in the English sample, the school ranks significantly higher than for the students from the other samples, and this is true for the students in general as well as for the Muslim students, Christian students and students with no religion regarded separately.

With regard to the Muslim students this is especially interesting when we think that most Muslim students in the Spanish and the Dutch samples attend Islamic confessional religious education, yet still the school is a less important source of information about religion for them than it is for the Muslim students in the English sample.

Table 7 gives the percentages of the students who at least agree, i.e. agree or strongly agree, to some propositions regarding the meaning of religion for them. In all samples, Muslim students tend to agree more than their peers that religion helps them 'to cope with difficulties', 'to be a better person' and that religion is important to them because they 'love God'. With only one exception, over 60% of the Muslim students agree to these statements in all contexts.[9] Muslim students also tend to agree more often than their peers that religion determines their 'whole life', that 'religion is important in our history', and less often that 'what they think about religion is open to change' and that they sometimes 'have doubts is there a god or not' or that 'religion is nonsense', which, again, is in line with the higher importance they accord to religion.

Hamburg the school also holds a lower importance than the family as a source of information about religion, see also Jozsa, Knauth & Weisse (2009). For a description of the situation regarding religious education in Germany see Knauth (2007) and Jozsa (2007).

7 See Dietz (2007) for a description of the situation regarding religious education in Spain.
8 In the Netherlands sample, 23% of the students did not attend RE, 39% attended compulsory confessional religious education and 38% compulsory non-confessional religious education. For all of these groups, however, i.e. also for the students attending compulsory non-confessional religious education, school held a lower importance than the family. For a description of the situation regarding religious education in the Netherlands see Ter Avest et al. (2007).
9 In the German sample only 23% of the Muslim students agreed that religion is important to them, 'because they love God'. In all other samples over 80% of the Muslim students agreed to this statement. Why this is so is not possible to say without further research, but maybe the reason is the German wording or the specific meaning of the word 'lieben' (to love) in the German language.

Table 7: Meaning of religion (percentages of those who agree or strongly agree)

	Religion helps me to cope with difficulties			Religion helps me to be a better person			Religion is important to me because I love God		
	no rel.	Chr.	Mu.	no rel.	Chr.	Mu.	no rel.	Chr.	Mu.
England	21	68	86	20	73	94	11	63	92
France	12	44	67	10	41	69	10	41	82
Germany	17	40	69	20	38	84	9	11	23
The Netherlands	13	64	87	12	52	92	17	66	93
Norway	7	26	66	16	42	83	5	24	84
Spain	15	39	69	21	49	86	10	37	86
	Religion determines my whole life			Religion is important in our history			What I think about religion is open to change		
	no rel.	Chr.	Mu.	no rel.	Chr.	Mu.	no rel.	Chr.	Mu.
England	5	31	67	49	68	83	44	36	20
France	4	15	57	78	88	85	39	47	17
Germany	6	13	58	39	57	75	41	46	15
The Netherlands	6	34	78	52	63	85	32	34	6
Norway	5	7	39	46	63	82	27	39	20
Spain	8	14	59	49	64	80	31	37	15
	I respect other people who believe			Sometimes I have doubts is there a god or not			You can be a religious person without belonging to a specific religious community		
	no rel.	Chr.	Mu.	no rel.	Chr.	Mu.	no rel.	Chr.	Mu.
England	67	84	88	59	51	6	70	68	44
France	84	88	87	41	57	13	38	38	21
Germany	83	92	92	43	43	11	48	46	20
The Netherlands	76	94	90	42	38	6	55	48	31
Norway	76	90	91	43	56	27	50	68	46
Spain	79	89	97	47	44	19	60	64	66

The vast majority of students agree that 'they respect other people who believe'. With the exception of the French sample where there are no significant differences between the groups, Christian and Muslim students both agree with this statement more than the students with no religion while, with the exception of the students in the Spanish sample, which shows no significant differences between the groups, the Muslim students agree less often than their peers that one can be a 'religious person without belonging to a particular faith community'.

Generally speaking, the Muslim students in our samples talk significantly more often about religion to others, be this 'family', 'friends', 'classmates', 'teachers' or 'religious leaders', than Christian students do, and they, in turn, talk more often to others than students with 'no religion' do, which again is in line with the importance accorded to religion in these three groups respectively.

There are, however, some exceptions to this general trend: in Norway and France there are no significant differences between the groups with regard to the frequency of talking to teachers about religion; in Norway the differences between the Christian and Muslim students are not significant with regard to the frequency of talking to classmates, in England with regard to the frequency of talking to teachers, and in Spain and France with regard to the frequency of talking to religious leaders.

Table 8: Talking about religion (percentages of those who talk at least about every week with the respective groups)

	family			friends			classmates			teachers			Rel. leaders		
	no rel.	Chr.	Mu.	no rel.	Chr.	Mu.	no rel.	Chr.	Mu.	no rel.	Chr.	Mu.	no rel.	Chr.	Mu.
England	11	51	88	16	46	64	37	41	60	42	55	59	9	31	62
France	9	31	42	6	11	48	5	10	20	11	15	16	3	24	26
Germany	13	28	72	11	18	50	16	23	31	32	43	23	6	19	37
Netherlands	18	58	84	12	34	69	20	31	69	24	34	62	9	37	54
Norway	13	18	73	13	13	58	18	36	33	36	36	35	19	15	41
Spain	19	33	85	12	17	40	15	21	32	23	34	11	7	18	19

With regard to religious diversity in school and in families, the samples of the different countries are quite varied. Table 9 gives the percentages of those who approved and denied some statements in this regard for the different groups.

In all samples the majority of the students stated that they have classmates of a different religion than themselves. In total: 77% in the English sample, 62% in the French, 80% in the German, 60% in the Dutch, 71% in the Norwegian and 56% in the Spanish sample).

Only a minority of the students stated that they had family members of a different religion to themselves, but the figures are not negligible, and they might exemplify the level of religious heterogeneity and its integration into social life in Western Europe. In total 32% of the students in the English sample stated that they had family members of a different religion, 29% in the French, 30% in the German, 21% in the Dutch, 23% in the Norwegian and 18% in the Spanish sample. The differences between the groups are not significant in the sub-samples, with the exception of the Spanish sample, where the Muslim students tended to have family members of a different religion significantly more often than their peers.

The shares of students who state having friends of a different religion are comparable to those having classmates of a different religion: 75% in the English sample, 76% in the French, 79% in the German, 46% in the Dutch, 72% in the Norwegian and 70% in the Spanish sample.

The vast majority of the students in all samples, over 80%, think that they do not have totally different views about religion than their parents. This finding is in line with the finding that family is regarded by most of the students as the most important source of information about religion.

Generally only a minority of the students, around 30% in almost all samples, think that most of their students would have the same view about religion as themselves, which again can be regarded as an indicator of religious heterogeneity and its acceptance in their life world. About half of the students in all of the contexts studied tend to have friends with the same views about religion: at least every second student in all of the samples stated that most of their friends have the same views about religion as themselves.

Table 9: Religious diversity in the life world of the students (percentages)

	I have family members who belong to different religions						I have friends who belong to different religions						I have students in my class who belong to different religions					
	no rel.		Chr.		Mu.		no rel.		Chr.		Mu.		no rel.		Chr.		Mu.	
	yes	no	yes	no	yes	no	yes	no	yes	no	yes	no	yes	no	yes	no	yes	no
England	32	51	33	65	25	61	68	19	81	11	88	12	69	14	81	9	96	4
France	30	59	29	66	21	75	70	17	80	15	89	9	55	16	59	22	88	7
Germany	32	52	29	60	25	64	76	14	79	16	93	5	82	9	75	22	91	7
Netherlands	26	65	18	78	19	81	50	34	36	58	48	47	73	13	55	39	46	52
Norway	27	60	16	74	19	77	70	16	69	22	89	11	69	12	68	19	91	9
Spain	18	74	15	75	32	65	65	13	72	20	88	8	50	33	55	27	83	12

	My parents have totally different views about religion from me						Most of my friends have the same views about religion as me						Most of the students in my class have the same views about religion as me					
	no rel.		Chr.		Mu.		no rel.		Chr.		Mu.		no rel.		Chr.		Mu.	
	yes	no	yes	no	yes	no	yes	no	yes	no	yes	no	yes	no	yes	no	yes	no
England	15	61	13	84	6	82	47	23	51	31	62	24	22	35	31	37	42	32
France	18	72	16	80	13	83	50	35	52	35	67	23	23	31	29	44	37	38
Germany	19	62	15	75	10	76	54	21	60	22	75	16	31	31	39	29	36	42
Netherlands	15	77	9	90	8	92	52	26	65	29	86	12	35	32	52	27	81	17
Norway	17	67	13	81	20	80	52	28	67	24	56	39	33	36	48	32	28	63
Spain	28	82	17	89	11	99	54	22	55	24	68	20	32	28	35	32	42	34

	At school I go around with young people who have different religious backgrounds						After school I go around with young people who have different religious backgrounds					
	no rel.		Chr.		Mu.		no rel.		Chr.		Mu.	
	yes	no	yes	no	yes	no	yes	no	yes	no	yes	no
England	45	30	63	22	86	12	34	39	45	39	70	28
France	67	14	72	15	90	7	51	27	62	24	73	23
Germany	79	12	74	21	84	12	54	30	55	33	61	30
Netherlands	65	23	45	47	36	60	48	39	40	51	44	51
Norway	55	26	55	26	87	13	39	40	41	40	81	19
Spain	62	20	64	24	89	6	57	26	60	27	77	19

	At school I prefer to go around with young people who have the same religious background as me						In my spare time I prefer to go around with young people who have the same religious background as me					
	no rel.		Chr.		Mu.		no rel.		Chr.		Mu.	
	yes	no	yes	no	yes	no	yes	no	yes	no	yes	No
England	26	74	23	77	29	71	26	74	21	79	36	64
France	8	90	6	92	9	87	5	95	5	95	7	93
Germany	19	81	19	81	32	68	20	80	19	81	41	59
Netherlands	16	84	40	60	59	41	15	85	37	63	61	39
Norway	27	73	27	73	25	76	32	68	29	72	28	72
Spain	27	73	29	72	34	66	30	70	34	66	38	62

In all contexts, the majority of the students pooled also stated that they socialised with students of different religions as themselves at school. However, in most of the contexts studied, this religious heterogeneity decreases in the students spare time, although only a minority, around 20-30%, stated that they prefer to socialise with people of the same religion as themselves.

Generally, in all contexts, the Muslim students more often have classmates and friends of a different religion than the Christian students do and they stated more often that they socialise in school and after school with young people from different religious backgrounds, with the only exception being the Dutch sample, where the majority of the Muslim students pooled attended a confessional Islamic schools attended mostly only by Muslim students. However, with the sole exception of the Norwegian sample, Muslim students more often tend to have friends with the same views about religion than Christian students and students with no religion.

Table 10 gives the percentages of those who at least agreed, i.e. agreed or strongly agreed, and of those who at least disagreed, i.e. disagreed or strongly disagreed, to statements regarding their interest in the religion of their friends or best friend. in all samples, the Muslim students tend to be more interested in what their best friend thinks about religion. With regard to the interest in what their wider group of friends think about religion, there is no such clear tendency.

Table 10: Interest in what friends think about religion (percentages)

	I like to know what my best friend thinks about religion						It doesn't bother me what my friends think about religion					
	no religion		Christian		Muslim		no religion		Christian		Muslim	
	agree	disagree	agree	disagree	agree	disagree	agree	disagree	agree	disagree	agree	disagree
England	31	26	55	15	80	6	72	8	53	24	58	20
France	39	27	44	22	51	16	73	18	66	15	56	15
Germany	31	31	45	20	71	8	42	28	30	49	22	56
Netherlands	29	48	56	20	75	11	71	16	43	33	37	32
Norway	30	30	41	19	59	9	61	15	65	12	50	9
Spain	32	29	38	23	65	8	50	23	39	19	31	39

3. Religion in school

The attendance of religious education by students in general, and by Muslim students in particular, depends strongly on the sample and on the religious education models offered in the specific context, see table 11, where the percentages of students who stated that they attend religious education classes at the time of the questioning are given for the different groups, as well as the means of the years of attendance during their school life.

Table 11: Attendance of religious education (percentages of those who do attend RE and means of the respective years for which the students have studied RE during their school life)

	RE this year or not?			How many years have you studied RE?		
	no rel.	Chr.	Mu.	no rel.	Chr.	Mu.
England	98	100	96	7.59	8.27	8.00
France	2	22	11	0.17	0.83	0.08
Germany	74	84	44	6.51	7.60	3.72
Netherlands	73	80	95	3.95	6.76	4.79
Norway	97	99	94	8.11	8.14	7.24
Spain	47	72	23	7.12	9.19	2.71

In the English and the Norwegian sample, almost all students stated that they attend religious education, which should not be a surprise since religious education was compulsory in all the schools included in these samples.

In the Dutch sample, almost all Muslim students attended religious education, along with a vast majority of the Christian students and the students with no religion. The Muslim students in the sample mostly attended schools with compulsory religious education models (50% from a confessional Islamic school with a compulsory Islamic religious education model, 44% from Christian schools, where religious education is compulsory too and from the legal status also confessional, but in fact more or less 'confessional' regarding the content of the teaching, depending on the school). The reason why only 75% of the students with no religion and 80% of the Christian students attended religious education in the Dutch sample is that a considerable number of these students attended schools where no religious education was offered, or where the subject dealing with religion was called 'History of culture and Christianity' or 'Worldview', and was apparently not always regarded by the students as 'religious education' (see also Bertram-Troost et al. 2009).

In the German and the Spanish contexts, where religious education is generally confessional[10] and optional, in state schools at least, Muslim students generally attend religious education less often than Christian students do and even less often than the students who state not having a religion do, most of whom had a Christian family background. This is, on the one hand, a general effect of confessional religious education models, which tend to systematically 'discriminate' religious minorities due to the difficulty of offering confessional religious education for all religious groups in all schools, 'forcing' the religious minorities either to attend one of the available religious education classes offered or to opt out of religious education. Apart from that, religious education for Muslim students only started to be introduced in these two contexts some years ago, and a complete satisfaction of the actual demand is far from being reached, even in those schools with a large share of Muslim students.

---

10 In Germany this is true for all federal stated included in the sample with the exception of Hamburg, see the remarks made in this respect above and Knauth (2007).

Table 12 gives the percentages of students who at least agree to some statements concerning their experiences with religion in education. The majority of students in all samples at least agree that they 'get knowledge about different religions' at school, and 'learn to have respect for everyone, whatever their religion', and 'have opportunities to discuss religious issues from different perspectives' and that learning about different religions at school helps them 'to live together', with large majorities of students at least agreeing that they 'get knowledge about different religions' at school: 92% agree in total in the English sample, 69% in the French, 76% in the German, 73% in the Dutch, 90% in the Norwegian and 56% in the Spanish sample. Differences between some of the countries are quite considerable: the students generally most often agree that they get knowledge about different religions in the English and the Norwegian sample, i.e. in those contexts where the religious education is non-confessional, significantly more than in all other contexts, while the students in the Spanish sample tend to agree less than those in all other samples. On the other side, it is the students in the German sample, taken as a whole, that agree less than those in all other samples that at school they learn respect for everyone, whatever their religion, while on the other side the students in the English and the French sample agree with this statement more than those in all other samples.

Table 12: Experiences with religion in education (percentages of those who at least agree to the statements)

	At school, I get knowledge about different religions			At school, I learn to have respect for everyone, whatever their religion			At school, I have opportunities to discuss issues from different perspectives			I find topics about religions interesting at school			I find religions as topic important at school		
	no rel.	Chr.	Mu.	no rel.	Chr.	Mu.	no rel.	Chr.	Mu.	no rel.	Chr.	Mu.	no rel.	Chr.	Mu.
England	90	95	92	89	93	90	77	87	80	36	68	76	39	70	70
France	63	76	70	91	88	92	53	49	64	38	55	78	22	40	52
Germany	72	83	62	69	73	78	54	62	57	29	42	65	33	54	65
Netherlands	71	68	84	74	74	90	54	54	75	22	39	77	26	55	71
Norway	88	93	80	74	85	84	61	64	68	27	35	65	28	44	74
Spain	50	61	51	76	84	92	51	51	54	29	35	46	23	46	52
	Learning about different religions at school helps us to live together			Learning about religions at school helps me to make choices between right and wrong			Learning about religions at school helps me to understand current events			Learning about religions at school helps me to learn about myself					
	no rel.	Chr.	Mu.	no rel.	Chr.	Mu.	no rel.	Chr.	Mu.	no rel.	Chr.	Mu.			
England	46	74	69	24	49	57	52	71	64	18	46	50			
France	64	76	81	13	31	41	55	63	51	7	20	38			
Germany	45	60	71	19	26	45	40	49	58	15	26	49			
Netherlands	39	66	80	12	34	53	31	38	63	10	19	45			
Norway	44	61	78	22	31	49	36	44	56	13	20	44			
Spain	55	67	91	25	47	74	28	41	69	22	39	61			

In all samples, the Christian and Muslim students alike tend to find topics about religion in school more important and more interesting, and they tend to agree more than the students with no religion that learning about religions at school helps them 'to live together', 'to make choices between right and wrong' and to learn about themselves. With the exception of the English and the Spanish sample, where the difference between Christian and Muslim students are not significant, the Muslim students find topics about religion even more interesting and more important than their Christian peers. With the exception of the English sample, where the differences between Christian and Muslim students are again not significant, Muslim students agree even more than their Christian peers that learning about religions at school helps them 'to live together', 'to make choices between right and wrong' and to learn about themselves.

With the exception of the English sample, the majority of students disagree that 'learning about religions leads to conflicts in the classroom'. With regard to the Muslim students the same is true for all samples apart from the German one, of whom only 39% disagree with the statement (see table 13, where the percentages of those who at least agree respectively disagree to some statement concerning religion and conflict in school are given for the different groups.) In some contexts, Muslim students seem to perceive the conflict potential of learning about religions in school more intensively than their peers: this is the case for the Muslim students in the German, the Spanish and the French sample, where the Muslim students tend to agree more often than their peers that learning about religions leads to conflicts in the classroom.

In all of the samples the majority of the students with no religion disagree that they have problems showing their 'views about religion openly in school'. With the exception of the French sample this is also true for the Muslim students. However, in some samples Muslim and Christian students alike tend to have more problems showing their views about religion openly in school: this is the case for France and Norway. In other samples there are no significant differences between the three groups in this respect: this is the case for England and Spain. In the German sample the Muslim students tend to have more problems showing their views openly in school than Christian students and students with no religion alike while in the Dutch sample, the Christian students tend to have the most problems showing their views about religion openly in school.

Table 13: Religion and conflicts in school (percentages of those who at least agree and of those who at least disagree to the statements)

	Learning about religions leads to conflicts in the classroom						I have problems showing my views about religion openly in school						A student who shows his/her beliefs openly in school, risks being mocked					
	no rel.		Chr.		Mu.		no rel.		Chr.		Mu.		no rel.		Chr.		Mu.	
	agr.	dis.	agr.	dis.	agr.	dis.	agr.	dis.	agr.	dis.	agr.	dis.	agr.	dis.	agr.	dis.	agr.	d.s.
England	26	46	24	50	20	54	14	62	28	50	26	64	38	38	38	39	32	46
France	14	65	15	68	25	53	5	50	28	43	23	38	21	63	27	51	16	54
Germany	16	58	11	67	27	39	9	68	9	69	15	73	24	46	24	48	20	54
Netherlands	6	70	8	76	3	84	9	77	23	49	12	73	11	57	16	60	11	82
Norway	16	60	18	55	18	55	8	65	22	54	20	57	25	53	33	33	16	57
Spain	15	55	13	62	34	51	15	53	16	52	19	61	19	54	20	52	20	62

The majority of students in all samples at the least agree that learning about religion helps them to 'understand others and live together with them', 'to better understand current events', and 'to develop their own point of view and to learn about their 'own religion', see also table 14. With the exception of the students in the Dutch sample, the majority also agrees that learning about different religions helps them to understand the history of their 'own country and Europe' and, with the exception of the students in the French and the Dutch sample, the majority also agrees that learning about religion helps them to develop moral values.

Table 14: Impact of learning about different religions (percentages of those who at least agree to the statements)

To what extent do you agree, that learning about different religions helps:	To understand others and live peacefully with them			To understand the history of my country and of Europe			To gain a better understanding of current events		
	no rel.	Chr.	Mu.	no rel.	Chr.	Mu.	no rel.	Chr.	Mu
England	66	76	88	52	59	62	59	72	76
France	50	59	80	80	85	69	60	65	62
Germany	49	63	80	50	62	80	47	55	72
Netherlands	55	79	89	40	49	58	48	53	69
Norway	64	79	97	60	71	86	74	86	88
Spain	56	67	86	61	67	77	47	49	72

	To develop my own point of view			To develop moral values			To learn about my own religion		
	no rel.	Chr.	Mu.	no rel.	Chr.	Mu.	no rel.	Chr.	Mu.
England	70	83	86	58	69	84	42	79	84
France	60	74	73	26	49	44	36	75	77
Germany	50	63	72	34	53	67	51	77	81
Netherlands	42	67	74	23	54	69	25	72	82
Norway	55	64	83	47	61	74	40	75	91
Spain	53	60	80	47	61	78	55	76	92

Generally speaking, there is a tendency in all samples for Muslim students to consider the impact of learning about religions to be greater than their peers do. However, if we look more closely there are exceptions with regard to some of the issues mentioned in the samples. Interestingly enough, with the exception of the English sample where the differences between the Muslim and the Christian students are not significant, Muslim students in all samples tend to agree more than Christian students and students with no religion alike that learning about different religions helps them to 'understand others and live peacefully with them' as well as to learn about their 'own religion'.

With regard to the visibility or the consideration of religion in general school life there are some differences between Christians, Muslims and students with no religion in all of the contexts studied (see table 15 where the percentage of students who at least agree to some statements in this respect are given for the different groups).

The Muslim students in all samples tend to agree more than both Christian students and students with no religion that religious dietary laws should be taken into account in school, that students should be able to wear 'more visible religious symbols', that they can be absent from school 'for religious festivals', that students should be excused 'from taking some classes for religious reasons' and also, with the exception of France, where the difference between Christian and Muslim students is not significant in this respect, that the school should provide 'facilities for pupils to pray in school'. On the other hand the differences between the level of agreement of Christian and Muslim students with regard to wearing discreet religious symbols are not significant in any of the samples.

Table 15: Religion in school (percentages of those who at least agree)

	Students should be able to wear religious symbols at school: discreet ones			Students should be able to wear religious symbols at school: more visible ones			Students can be absent from school when it is their religious festivals			Students should be excused from taking some classes for religious reasons		
	no rel.	Chr.	Mu.	no rel.	Chr.	Mu.	no rel.	Chr.	Mu.	no rel.	Chr.	Mu.
England	81	88	87	45	60	94	47	73	96	27	31	80
France	79	79	80	13	15	35	40	55	87	11	18	36
Germany	64	81	76	31	32	76	51	59	90	23	22	51
Netherlands	88	88	78	64	48	94	54	67	90	21	28	52
Norway	77	90	86	61	73	86	61	66	83	28	26	40
Spain	52	64	57	37	35	66	55	59	94	31	25	60

	At school meals, religious food requirements should be taken into account			Schools should provide facilities for pupils to pray in school			Voluntary religious services could be a part of school life		
	no rel.	Chr.	Mu.	no rel.	Chr.	Mu.	no rel.	Chr.	Mu.
England	55	63	92	28	47	88	18	59	72
France	58	60	84	6	18	27	23	33	30
Germany	51	55	92	16	29	58	25	41	42
Netherlands	31	40	79	31	56	84	25	46	69
Norway	55	62	86	17	18	55	9	18	34
Spain	50	57	94	11	13	42	11	21	35

Table 16 gives the percentages of students who agree or disagree with statements concerning the inclusion of religion in education. With the exception of the French sample, the majority of the students generally disagree that religion should not have any place in school life. The same is true for the Muslim and the Christian students in all samples with the exception of the French one, and even the shares of students with no religion who disagree are quite high.

In the French sample 44% of the students agree that they do not need the subject of religious education because other school subjects cover all they need to know about religion. The shares of students who agree to this statement in the other samples are much lower: 30% for the Spanish sample and 26% for the Norwegian, around 15% for the rest. In all samples the Christian as well as the Muslim students agree less than the students with no religion that the subject of religious education would not be needed and the need for such a subject seems to be felt by the majority of the Christian and the Muslim students, with the exception of France and Spain, where only 43% of the Muslim students disagree to the respective statement.

Table 16: Models of including religion in education (percentages of those who at least agree respectively disagree)

	There should be no place for religion in school life						There is no need for the subject of religious education. All we need to know about religion is covered by other school subjects						Religious education should be optional					
	no rel.		Chr.		Mu.		no rel.		Chr.		Mu.		no rel.		Chr.		Mu.	
	agr.	dis.	agr.	dis.	agr.	dis.	agr.	dis.	agr.	dis.	agr.	dis.	agr.	dis.	agr.	dis.	agr.	dis.
England	13	61	4	89	8	84	24	48	5	75	6	82	70	18	40	35	44	28
France	37	22	20	43	15	48	55	14	35	31	27	40	87	5	83	7	61	16
Germany	20	52	8	74	9	78	26	45	10	72	10	69	76	11	58	23	70	14
Netherlands	11	66	3	84	5	91	32	34	9	69	10	69	64	22	41	42	66	22
Norway	33	41	21	54	10	69	33	38	22	50	12	53	62	20	50	29	51	21
Spain	21	47	7	69	6	72	44	25	18	50	22	43	88	5	78	10	88	6

	Religious education should be taught to students together, whatever differences there might be in their religious or denominational background						Religious education should be taught sometimes together and sometimes in groups according to which religions students belong to						Pupils should study religious education separately in groups according to which religion they belong					
	no rel.		Chr.		Mu.		no rel.		Chr.		Mu.		no rel.		Chr.		Mu.	
	agr.	dis.	agr.	dis.	agr.	dis.	agr.	dis.	agr.	dis.	agr.	dis.	agr.	dis.	agr.	dis.	agr.	dis.
England	68	10	84	4	86	2	18	48	15	51	24	48	15	66	6	73	14	74
France	11	64	25	46	24	45	12	23	19	25	11	34	25	58	27	59	21	68
Germany																		
Area states	23	47	21	52	25	44	24	35	32	32	29	39	58	20	58	18	75	15
Berlin	44	31	50	28	33	42	22	44	30	37	33	49	29	45	31	51	67	30
Hamburg	64	12	81	7	79	6	15	56	17	59	20	53	10	73	8	81	13	71
Netherlands	61	19	71	8	74	5	12	57	23	49	32	47	10	70	26	53	37	35
Norway	50	18	60	15	62	11	25	40	34	32	40	26	25	48	27	48	27	39
Spain	23	48	25	47	28	43	36	25	43	20	46	19	54	24	61	20	74	15

In the contexts with models of religious education where students are taught together, whatever differences there might be in their religious or denominational background, this model of religious education is approved by the majority of the students surveyed – in England 75%, the Netherlands 68%, in Norway 56%, and in Hamburg 72% prefer this model –, while in contexts with a confessional model of religious education, where students are separated in religious education according to their religious background, as is generally the case in Germany or in Spain, this model is favoured by the majority of students – in the relevant states in Germany 59% of the students favour such a segregated model of religious education, and in Spain 59% do.

The reason that a confessional model of religious education is approved in these contexts often seems to be the fear of the conflicts that the students think might arise in a joint religious education model. In these contexts Muslim students tend to approve a model where the students are separated in religious education according to their religious background even more than Christian students do, which is in line with their stronger perception of the conflict potential of learning about religions in school in these contexts, which has been mentioned already.

Generally, the majority of students are in favour of getting 'objective knowledge about different religions' as well as learning 'to understand what religions teach', learning to 'communicate about religious issues', and also learning 'the importance of religion for dealing with problems in society'. Only small minorities in all contexts consider that students should be guided towards religious belief in religious education, regardless of whether the religious education model is confessional of not. However, in all of the contexts, Muslim students stress this aspect of religious education more than the others.

Table 17: "What should students learn in school?" (percentages of those who at least agree)

	Get an objective knowledge about different religions			Learn to understand what religions teach			Be able to talk and communicate about religious issues			Learn the importance of religion for dealing with problems in society			Be guided towards religious beliefs		
	no rel.	Chr.	Mu.	no rel.	Chr.	Mu.	no rel.	Chr.	Mu.	no rel.	Chr.	Mu.	no rel.	Chr.	Mu.
England	64	73	78	59	84	90	65	83	88	59	80	84	12	34	60
France	56	71	70	45	65	76	57	68	80	56	65	48	4	12	20
Germany	68	86	84	41	64	81	52	70	84	52	72	82	16	28	48
Netherlands	48	66	83	60	79	90	56	73	88	44	61	70	7	21	32
Norway	47	59	84	59	76	87	47	58	82	41	63	68	7	15	30
Spain	55	64	82	48	65	82	49	64	78	34	49	74	18	33	46

An astonishing example might be the fact that in the English sample, although a non-confessional model or religious education is in place here, 60% of the Muslim students, but only 34% of the Christian students and 12% of the students with no religion think that in religious education students should be guided towards religious belief.

4. Impact of religion in society in the views of students

Table 18 gives the shares of students who agree or disagree with different statements concerning attitudes towards religion for the different groups.

In total, between 10% and 30% of the students, depending on the sample, agree that 'without religion the world would be a better place'. If we look at the different 'worldview' groups, then we see that there are significant differences between them in all samples. In all samples Muslim students disagree with this statement more than Christian students, who again disagree more than students with no religion. The share of students who disagree that the world would be better without religion remains below 50% in all samples in the group of students with no religion, while the vast majority of the Muslim students, about 60% to 90% depending on the sample, disagree with the statement, mirroring their more positive attitude towards religion in general.

With regard to the statement 'religion is a source of aggressiveness' the situation is quite similar: Muslim students disagree with the statement more than Christian students, who disagree more than the students with no religion. This is true of all samples, with the exception of the Norwegian one, where the difference between Christian and Muslim students is not significant.

Table 18: Attitudes towards religion (percentages of those who at least agree respectively disagree)

	Without religion the world would be a better place						Religion is a source of aggressiveness					
	no rel.		Chr.		Mu.		no rel.		Chr.		Mu.	
	agr.	dis.	agr.	dis.	agr.	dis.	agr.	dis.	agr.	dis.	agr.	dis.
England	34	29	10	72	6	84	25	39	5	76	12	88
France	36	25	24	49	6	73	27	37	19	51	7	80
Germany	20	46	9	67	5	87	27	38	18	52	9	72
Netherlands	25	45	3	84	4	93	13	62	4	34	3	92
Norway	41	25	23	44	13	67	32	28	21	39	14	40
Spain	25	33	7	65	9	80	18	48	6	76	3	85
	Religious people are less tolerant towards others						Religion belongs to private life					
	no rel.		Chr.		Mu.		no rel.		Chr.		Mu.	
	agr.	dis.	agr.	dis.	agr.	dis.	agr.	dis.	agr.	dis.	agr.	dis.
England	25	30	11	53	4	50	35	23	18	61	10	66
France	20	47	17	57	14	60	55	17	49	24	49	27
Germany	23	31	14	35	18	47	56	15	47	20	44	33
Netherlands	13	53	4	70	8	68	53	21	38	30	35	41
Norway	22	27	17	30	15	36	45	18	48	14	45	28
Spain	24	34	13	51	22	49	28	32	27	37	41	30

In total only a minority of the students, between 7% and 20%, agree that 'religious people are less tolerant' and that 'religion is a source of aggressiveness'; however, the share of students who neither agrees nor disagrees with these statements is substantial in the samples, between 30% and 50% in total, so that in most samples the total share of students who disagree to the statement remains below 50%, with the exception of France and the Netherlands. The differences between the worldview groups are not that 'systematic' and accentuated as is the case for the statement 'without religion the world would be a better place'. With the exception of the Dutch sample the differences between Christian and Muslim students regarding their attitude to the statement 'religious people are less tolerant' are not significant. There is a tendency, however, for students with no religion to agree more often than Christian and Muslim students alike that religious people are less tolerant, with the exceptions of Norway, where there are no significant differences between the three groups, and Spain, where the difference between Muslim students and students with no religion is not significant.

When it comes to the question of whether or not religion belongs to private life, the differences between the national samples become quite interesting. The majority of the students in total agree with the statement in France (52%), and in Germany (51%), almost the majority in Norway (46%) and the Netherlands (43%), and just a minority in Spain (30%) and in England (28%). With regard to the specificity of the Muslim students there is no clear general tendency in the samples: in the Norwegian sample, for example there is no significant difference between Muslim students, Christian students and students with no religion in this respect, while in the German sample, on the other hand, Muslim students tend to agree less often to the statement than Christian students, who in turn also agree less often than the students with no religion; in the Spanish sample we found that the Muslim students tend to agree the most, with no significant differences, however, between them and the students with no religion.

Table 19 gives the shares of students who at least agree respectively disagree to different statements regarding religion as a topic of discussion.

In all contexts the majority of the students, independent of their worldview, consider that talking about religion would not be embarrassing. With the exception of the Norwegian sample where the differences between the groups are not significant, Muslim students disagree more often than their peers that the topic would be embarrassing.

Speaking generally, the students in all contexts tend to consider talking about religion to be more boring than embarrassing. This does not hold in all contexts for all the groups, and for the Christian and Muslim students alike there are exceptions, however it is true in all contexts for the students with no religion: for them, talking about religion is more boring than embarrassing, which might be exemplified by the shares of those who at least agree with the statements respectively: with the sole exception of the Spanish sample the shares of students with no religion who agree that talking about religion would be embarrassing are below 10%, while the shares of those who consider the subject boring are around 40% in all contexts. In all samples, however, Muslim students consider talking to be less boring than their peers do, a finding which is again in line with their greater interest in religion in general.

Table 19: Religion as a topic of discussions (percentages of those who at least agree respectively disagree)

	In my view, talking about religion is embarrassing						For me talking about religious topics is boring						To me, talking about religion is interesting because people have different views					
	no rel.		Chr.		Mu.		no rel.		Chr.		Mu.		no rel.		Chr.		Mu.	
	agr.	dis.	agr.	dis.	agr.	dis.	agr.	dis.	agr.	dis.	agr.	dis.	agr.	dis.	agr.	dis.	agr.	dis.
England	7	68	8	76	2	90	40	34	10	68	8	80	48	25	82	5	84	8
France	10	68	16	61	8	77	47	28	26	47	8	75	59	16	67	11	79	2
Germany	7	72	4	81	2	92	37	32	18	52	4	83	48	23	66	10	86	2
Netherlands	4	85	5	77	2	93	39	33	14	56	6	85	33	41	59	17	86	4
Norway	2	75	7	71	11	71	44	26	32	37	16	55	38	32	51	22	70	2
Spain	13	57	5	73	5	88	43	24	22	37	11	75	46	20	61	11	91	2

	Talking about religion helps to shape my own views						Talking about religion helps us to understand others					
	no rel.		Chr.		Mu.		no rel.		Chr.		Mu.	
	agr.	dis.	agr.	dis.	agr.	dis.	agr.	dis.	agr.	dis.	agr.	dis.
England	39	34	66	9	80	6	49	23	71	4	82	8
France	43	28	61	19	66	7	53	20	65	12	68	10
Germany	32	35	48	20	68	12	39	26	51	13	70	10
Netherlands	22	57	57	20	67	11	30	38	52	16	75	8
Norway	24	48	33	29	56	11	43	29	62	14	75	25
Spain	33	30	54	14	79	6	34	24	45	15	77	3

	In my view, talking about religion only leads to disagreement						Talking about religion helps me to live peacefully together with people from different religions					
	no rel.		Chr.		Mu.		no rel.		Chr.		Mu.	
	agr.	dis.	agr.	dis.	agr.	dis.	agr.	dis.	agr.	dis.	agr.	dis.
England	40	27	15	51	6	71	24	39	46	2	65	10
France	8	44	15	62	17	67	17	44	33	29	44	23
Germany	22	41	12	58	9	66	20	37	31	23	53	14
Netherlands	21	50	6	76	7	85	21	49	43	16	80	8
Norway	32	27	23	40	14	48	23	39	31	22	58	5
Spain	30	28	19	50	17	57	20	33	32	22	60	8

In all samples, the majority, or almost the majority, think that talking about religion helps them to shape their own views and to understand those of others. However, only minorities, sometimes substantial ones, like in the Netherlands (44%) or England (37%), think that talking about religions would help them to live together with people of different religions. It is only minorities, again, who think that talking about religion only leads to disagreement.

With respect to the impact of talking about religion, Muslim and Christian students tend, in all contexts, to be contexts more positive about its effects than the students with no religion: they agree more often in all contexts that religion helps them to shape their own views, to understand others and to live peacefully together with people from different religions, and agree less often that talking about religion only leads to disagreement. In all samples there is a tendency for Muslim students to be even more positive about the impact of talking about religion than the

Christian students are, but there are some exceptions: in the English sample the differences between these two groups are not significant with respect to shaping their own views and understanding others, while in the French sample the difference is not significant with respect to the statement that 'talking about religion only leads to disagreement'.

Asked about their views concerning the possibilities of living together, the vast majority of the students in all contexts, over 70%, irrespective of their worldview, disagree with the statement 'I don't like people from other religions and do not want to live together with them'. However, the majority, or almost the majority, depending on the context, think that 'disagreement on religious issues leads to conflicts', while, again, the majority in all contexts, irrespective of worldview, think that 'respecting the religion of others helps to cope with differences' (see table 20 where the shares of students who at least agree respectively disagree to the different statements are given for the different groups).

Table 20: Possibilities of living together (percentages of those who at least agree respectively disagree)

How far do you agree?	"Disagreement on religious issues leads to conflicts."						"Respecting the religion of others helps to cope with differences."						"I don't like people from other religions and do not want to live together with them."					
	no rel.		Chr.		Mu.		no rel.		Chr.		Mu.		no rel.		Chr.		Mu.	
	agr.	dis.	agr.	dis.	agr.	dis.	agr.	dis.	agr.	dis.	agr.	dis.	agr.	dis.	agr.	dis.	agr.	dis.
England	69	6	52	13	50	24	54	15	82	1	82	4	10	70	4	86	4	86
France	77	7	72	9	53	22	79	6	84	4	81	2	5	85	2	86	8	82
Germany	46	14	42	15	40	19	58	8	73	5	79	6	7	75	4	84	6	84
Netherlands	54	15	42	25	36	33	71	12	87	1	83	6	5	80	5	80	4	84
Norway	54	12	45	12	43	13	55	10	71	6	70	7	10	70	5	81	7	75
Spain	52	12	48	16	43	23	54	10	65	8	80	9	13	60	10	68	6	79

The students were also asked: "There are people from different religions living in every country. What do you think would help them to live together in peace?" Table 21 gives the shares of those who consider the different possibilities presented to them to be at least quite important respectively 'not important'.

The vast majority, over 70% up to 90%, consider that it helps people to live together, if they 'share common interests', 'know about each other's religion', 'personally know people from different religions' and 'do something together'. The positions regarding the potential of strong state regulations and of relegating religion to the private sphere are quite divided, with considerable shares who consider these strategies to be important, considerable shares who consider them not important and considerable shares who answer: 'can not say'. With regard to the positions concerning all these strategies there are no systematic differences between the groups.

Table 21: "What helps us to live together in peace?" (Percentages of those who think that the respective 'strategies' are at least 'quite important' – very important or quite important – and of those who think that they are not important)

	If people share common interests						If they know about each other's religions						If they personally know people from different religions					
	no rel.		Chr.		Mu.		no rel.		Chr.		Mu.		no rel.		Chr.		Mu.	
	im.	not	im.	not	im.	not	im.	not	im.	not	im.	not	im.	not	im.	not	im.	not
England	83	11	92	6	94	6	81	13	89	10	94	4	75	19	79	20	90	6
France	68	16	74	17	62	16	69	20	82	13	82	10	67	22	75	14	73	15
Germany	73	15	81	12	81	13	72	17	84	11	92	6	66	22	75	17	82	14
Netherlands	74	12	82	11	81	10	76	16	93	5	92	6	76	14	88	7	86	11
Norway	70	16	75	14	76	16	72	16	82	9	91	2	66	20	74	16	82	7
Spain	69	9	76	11	77	12	65	17	75	16	88	8	61	18	78	12	94	5
	If they do something together						If everyone keeps their own religion in private						If the state has strong laws about the role of religion in society					
	no rel.		Chr.		Mu.		no rel.		Chr.		Mu.		no rel.		Chr.		Mu.	
	im.	not	im.	not	im.	not	im.	not	im.	not	im.	not	im.	not	im.	not	im.	not
England	72	20	80	19	94	4	37	45	22	56	18	45	36	37	35	37	47	33
France	82	10	83	9	81	9	52	23	41	28	39	27	33	28	26	31	27	26
Germany	67	20	78	15	82	16	51	29	42	39	46	29	32	37	32	42	32	35
Netherlands	70	19	77	19	84	11	24	56	22	63	31	52	39	33	51	30	42	55
Norway	70	15	83	9	80	11	37	40	28	49	44	46	22	41	24	40	33	32
Spain	62	16	73	19	88	9	31	36	28	45	45	41	34	21	41	28	40	9

5. Summary and conclusions

The analysis presented in this article shows a lot of commonalities between the Muslim students in the sub-samples analysed, as well as a lot of differences between the Muslim students on one side and the Christian students and the students with no religion on the other. Multivariate analysis shows that a lot of the differences found between Muslims students, Christian students, and those with no religion have their basis in the respective importance of religion for the students in these groups. In fact the importance of religion strongly influences the students views with regard to the questions dealt with here and most differences between the three groups become non significant in a multivariate analysis that takes into consideration the importance of religion for the students in all sub-samples.

If we focus on the commonalities concerning Muslim students in the different samples, however, as we did in this article, we can draw the following conclusions:

- **Role of religion in students' life**

Over 90% of the Muslim students pooled stated that believing in God and religion in general is important for them, more than for the Christian students and those with no religion. Over 60% of the Muslim students consider religion to be very important to them and they are more often engaged in activities related to religion, generally talk more often about religion with different people in their life, are more often interested in what their best friend thinks about religion, and consider more often than their peers that religion helps them to cope with difficulties and to be a better person, with 60% to 90% of the Muslim students agreeing to these statements depending on the sample.

Their views about religion seem to be more fixed than those of their peers: only comparatively small minorities of the Muslim students consider that what they think about religion is open to change or state sometimes having doubts about the existence of god. Respect for other people who believe is shared by around 90% of the Muslim students.

Family is generally the most important source of information about religion for the Muslim students, with over 90% consider it to be important for them in this respect. This is followed by faith community, which is considered important by at least 70%, then by books (over 60%), and friends (over 50%.)

The importance of school as a source of information about religion depends on the context, both for Muslim students and for students in general: however, one can say that school is important for the majority of Muslim students in contexts where religious education is available for them, without it, however, reaching the same level of importance as family and faith community or even books. School is most important as a source of information about religion for the Muslim students in the English sample. This is also true for the Christian students and, especially, for the students with no religion, so that we can conclude that the English model of religious education seems be the one that manages best to take into account the different interests that students have when it comes to religion in education and to be accepted by the vast majority of the students irrespective of their worldview background.

At least for the age group pooled, the importance of family as a source of information about religion goes hand in hand with sharing the same views about religion as the parents, which is true for the vast majority of students and for over 80% of the Muslim students.

The religious heterogeneity in the life world of the students strongly depends on the contextual life world of the students, which is also defined also by the neighbourhood and the school attended. The level of religious heterogeneity in the family for the Muslim students is comparable to those of the other groups, about 20% of the Muslim students pooled had family members of a different religion. Generally, the Muslim students more often have classmates and friends of a different religion than the Christian students do, and they more often state that they socialise in school and after school with young people from different religious backgrounds, which is a consequence of belonging to a religious minority. However, where this minority position is broken up in the specific context of the school or the neighbourhood this finding is reversed.

- **Religion in school and the impact of religion in education**

Although the length and the actual attendance of religious education by Muslim students depends, as it does for other groups, on the context and the model of religious education offered, and although the importance of school for the Muslim students remains behind of that of family, faith community and books, Muslim students tend to accept the school as a place of learning about religions, often considering religions to be not only more important, but also more interesting than their peers do, and generally considering that learning about religion in general and in school in particular has a bigger and more positive impact.

The majority of Muslim students agree that they get knowledge about different religions at school, that they learn to have respect for everyone, whatever their religion, and that learning about different religions at school helps them to live together, albeit with some big differences between the samples. Again, the majority of the Muslim students find religions to be an important topic at school, agree that they have opportunities to discuss issues from different perspectives at school, and that learning about religions at school helps them to understand current events.

With the exception of the French sample, the majority of the Muslim students state that they do not have problems showing their views about religion openly in school, although in most of the samples minorities of around 20% state that they do have such problems. Likewise, the majority of the Muslim students consider that learning about religion does not lead to conflicts in the classroom while, with the exception of the Dutch sample, around 20% of the Muslim students do perceive such conflicts.

The vast majority of the Muslim students agree that learning about different religions helps them to understand others and to live peacefully with them, to develop their own point of view, to learn about their own religion and to understand the history of their own country and of Europe, as well as current events and, with the exception of France, also to develop moral values.

In all contexts it is only a minority of below 15% of the Muslim students who consider that there should be no place for religion in school while, with the exception of France, it is always the majority of the Muslim students who consider that religion can have a place in school. The majority of the Muslim students agree that students should be able to wear discreet religious symbols; that students should be excused from school for their religious festivals, and that religious food requirements should be taken into account at school. With the exception of France, the majority of the Muslim students also agree that students should be able to wear more visible religious symbols, with the exception of France and Norway, the majority of Muslim students likewise agree that students should be excused from taking some classes for religious reasons and, with the exception of France and Spain the majority of them think that the school should provide students with opportunities to pray during school time. Again with the exception of France and Spain, the majority of the Muslim students seem to advocate religious education as a subject, or at least do not think that it would not be needed, because all they would need to know about religion would be covered by other school subjects. With the exception of the English sample, the majority of the Muslim students want such a subject to be optional. In all contexts with a model of religious education where students are not separated according to their religion, the vast majority of Muslim students agree with such a model, while in all the contexts studied where students are separated when they learn about religion in school, the majority of the Muslim students agree with such a model.

Independently of the model of learning about religion in school, the vast majority of the Muslim students want to get objective knowledge about different religions at school, and to learn to understand what religions teach and to learn to communicate about religious issues. With the exception of France, the majority of the Muslim students also want to learn the importance of religion for dealing with problems in society while, with the exception of England, the majority of Muslim students do not want to be guided in school towards religious belief, even if they tend to stress this aspect of religious education more in all of the samples.

- **Impact of religion in society in the views of students**

The vast majority of Muslim students disagree that the world would be a better place without religion. With the exception of the Norwegian sample, the majority of the Muslim students disagree that religion would be a source of aggressiveness. With the exception of the English sample, considerable minorities of about 30%-50% of the Muslim students agree that religion belongs to private life, while minorities of about 25%-40% disagree and tend not to consider religion as belonging to private life. Only minorities of Muslim students of under 20% agree that religious people are less tolerant towards others, while considerable shares neither agree nor disagree, even if, in some samples, the majority of Muslim students disagree with the statement.

The vast majority of Muslim students disagree that talking about religion would be embarrassing or boring. Again, the majority of the Muslim students agree that talking about religion is interesting because people have different views and that talking about religion helps them to shape the own views as well as to understand others. With the exception of Norway, the majority of the Muslim students disagree that talking about religion would only lead to disagreement while, with the exception of France, the majority of the Muslim students agree that talking about religion helps them to live peacefully together with people of different religions.

Between 30% and 50% of the Muslim students think that disagreement on religious issues leads to conflict. Only small minorities, below 10%, of Muslim students agree that they do not like people from other religions and do not want to live together with them, while the vast majority, over 75%, disagrees. The vast majority of the Muslim students think that respecting the religion of others would help to cope with differences and that it helps people to live together, if they share common interests, know about each other's religions, personally know people from different religions and do something together.

References

Bertram-Troost, G., Ipgrave, J., Jozsa, D.-P. & Knauth, T. (2008). European Comparison. Dialogue and conflict, in: Knauth, T., Jozsa, D.-P., Bertram-Troost, G. & Ipgrave, J. (Eds.) *Encountering Religious Pluralism in School and Society – A Qualitative Study of Teenage Perspectives in Europe* (Münster, Waxmann), 405-411.

Béraud, C., Massignon, B. & Mathieu, S. (2008) French Students, Religion and School: The Ideal of *Laïcité* at Stake with Religious Diversity, in: Knauth, T.,

Jozsa, D.-P., Bertram-Troost, G. & Ipgrave, J. (Eds.) *Encountering Religious Pluralism in School and Society – A Qualitative Study of Teenage Perspectives in Europe* (Münster, Waxmann), 51-80.
Dietz, G. (2007) Invisibilizing or Ethnicizing Religious Diversity? The Transition of Religious Education Towards Pluralism in Contemporary Spain, in: Jackson, R., Miedema, S., Weisse, W. and Willaime, J.-P. (Eds.) *Religion and Education in Europe: developments, contents and debates* (Münster, Waxmann), 103-123.
Dietz, G., Rosón, J. L. & Ruiz F. G. (2008) Religion and Education in the View of Spanish Youth: the Legacy of Mono-Confessionalism in Times of Religious Pluralisation, in: Knauth, T., Jozsa, D.-P., Bertram-Troost, G. & Ipgrave, J. (Eds.) *Encountering Religious Pluralism in School and Society – A Qualitative Study of Teenage Perspectives in Europe.* (Münster, Waxmann), 21-50.
Europäische Kommission (2008). *Diskriminierung in der Europäischen Union. Wahrnehmungen, Erfahrungen und Haltungen. Eurobarometer Spezial 296*, available at: http://ec.europa.eu/public_opinion/archives/ebs/ebs_296_de.pdf, first accessed: October 15, 2008.
Ipgrave, J. & McKenna, U. (2008) Diverse Experiences and Common Vision: English Students' Perspectives on Religion and Religious Education, in: Knauth, T., Jozsa, D.-P., Bertram-Troost, G. & Ipgrave, J. (Eds.) *Encountering Religious Pluralism in School and Society – A Qualitative Study of Teenage Perspectives in Europe* (Münster, Waxmann), 113-148.
Jackson, R. and O'Grady, K. (2007) Religions and Education in England: Social Plurality, Civil Religion and Religious Education Pedagogy, in: Jackson, R., Miedema, S., Weisse, W. and Willaime, J.-P. (Eds.) *Religion and Education in Europe: Developments, Contexts and Debates* (Münster, Waxmann), 181-202.
Jackson, R., Miedema, S., Weisse, W. & Willlaime, J.-P. (Eds.) (2007) *Religion and Education in Europe: Developments, Contexts and Debates* (Münster, Waxmann).
Jozsa, D.-P. (2007) Islam and Education in Europe, with special reference to Austria, England, France, Germany and the Netherlands, in: Jackson, R., Miedema, S., Weisse, W. and Willaime, J.-P. (Eds.) *Religion and Education in Europe: Developments, Contexts and Debates* (Münster, Waxmann), 67-86.
Jozsa, D.-P. (2008) Religious Education in North-Rhine Westphalia: Views and Experiences of Students, in: Knauth, T., Jozsa, D.-P., Bertram-Troost, G. & Ipgrave, J. (Eds.) *Encountering Religious Pluralism in School and Society, A Qualitative Study of Teenage Perspectives in Europe* (Münster, Waxmann), 173-206.
Jozsa, D.-P. & Friederici, M. (2008) European Comparison: Social Dimension of Religion, in: Knauth, T., Jozsa, D.-P., Bertram-Troost, G. & Ipgrave, J. (Eds.) *Encountering Religious Pluralism in School and Society – A Qualitative Study of Teenage Perspectives in Europe Europe* (Münster, Waxmann), 389-369.
Jozsa, D.-P.. Knauth, T. & Weise, W. (2009) Religion in School – a Comparative Study of Hamburg and North Rhine Westphalia, in: Valk, P., Bertram-Troost, G., Friederici, M. & Beraud, C. (Eds.) *Teenagers' Perspectives on the Role of Religion in their Lives, Schools and Societies – A European Quatitative Study* (Münster, Waxmann) 173-211.
Körs, A. (2009) Jugend und Religion in Deutschland und Europa. Jugendliche Einstellungen zu Religion in Lebenswelt, Schule und Gesellschaft im Vergleich acht europäischer Länder, in Jozsa, D.-P., Knauth, T. & Weisse, W. (2009) *Religionsunterricht, Dialog und Konflikt Analysen im Kontext Europas* (Münster, Waxmann)

Knauth, T. (2007a) Religious Education in Germany: Contribution to Dialogue or Source of Conflict? A Historical and Contextual Analysis of its Development since the 1960s, in: Jackson, R., Miedema, S., Weisse, W., Willaime, J.-P. (Eds.) *Religion and Education in Europe: Developments, Contexts and Debates* (Münster, Waxmann), 243-265.

Knauth, T. (2008) "Better together than apart": Religion in School and Lifeworld of Students in Hamburg, in: Knauth, T., Jozsa, D.-P., Bertram-Troost, G. & Ipgrave, J. (Eds.) *Encountering Religious Pluralism in School and Society – A Qualitative Study of Teenage Perspectives in Europe* (Muenster, Waxmann), 207–245.

Knauth, T., Jozsa, D.-P., Bertram-Troost, G. & Ipgrave, J. (Eds.) (2008) *Encountering Religious Pluralism in School and Society – A Qualitative Study of Teenage Perspectives in Europe* (Münster, Waxmann).

Skeie, G. (2007) Religion and Education in Norway, in: Jackson, R., Miedema, S., Weisse, W. & Willaime, J.-P. (Eds.) *Religion and education in Europe: Developments, contexts and debates* (Münster, Waxmann), 221–242.

Ter Avest, I., Bakker, C., Bertram-Troost, G. D. & Miedema, S. (2007) Religion and Education in the Dutch Pillarized and Post-Pillarized Educational System: Historical Background and Current Debates, in: Jackson, R., Miedema, S., Weisse, W. and Willaime, J.-P. (Eds.) *Religion and Education in Europe. Developments, Contexts and Debates* (Münster, Waxmann), 203-220.

Valk, P., Bertram-Troost, G., Friederici, M. & Beraud, C. (Eds.) (2009) *Teenagers' Perspectives on the Role of Religion in their Lives, Schools and Societies – A European Quatitative Study* (Münster, Waxmann).

Willaime, J.-P. (2007) Teaching Religious Issues in French Public Schools. From Abstentionist *Laïcité* to a Return of Religion to Public Education, in: Jackson, R., Miedema, S., Weisse, W., Willaime, J.-P. (Eds.) *Religion and Education in Europe: Developments, Contexts and Debates* (Münster, Waxmann), 87-102.

List of authors

Dr. Aurora Alvarez Veinguer is Senior Lecturer of Social Anthropology at Universidad de Granada, Spain. E-mail: auroraav@ugr.es.

Dr. Ina ter Avest is Senior Researcher and Lecturer in Religious Education at the Faculty of Psychology and Education, VU University Amsterdam and at the Department of Theology of the Utrecht University, the Netherlands.
E-mail: kh.ter.avest@psy.vu.nl; k.h.teravest@uu.nl.

Damian Breen is an ESRC PhD student in the Warwick Religions and Education Research Unit, University of Warwick.
E-mail: damian.breen82@googlemail.com.

Dr. Gunther Dietz is Research Professor of Intercultural Studies at Universidad Veracruzana, Institute of Educational Research, in Xalapa (Mexico).
E-mail: guntherdietz@gmail.com.

Dr. Dan-Paul Jozsa is Researcher in Religious Studies and Islamic Studies at the Georg-Eckert-Institute for International Textbook Research, Braunschweig. He was Co-Projectleader of the REDCo project at the University of Münster.
E-mail: paul.jozsa@googlemail.com.

Dr. Anna van den Kerchove is researcher, also in charge of training about religious issues and « laïcité », at the Institut Européen en Sciences des Religions (IESR), affiliated at the Ecole Pratique des Hautes Études (EPHE), in Paris.
E-mail: anna.van_den_kerchove@ephe.sorbonne.fr.

Dr. Thorsten Knauth is Professor for Religious Education with focus on inter-religious learning, and Director of the Institute of Protestant Theology at the University of Duisburg-Essen, Germany. He was Director of Research Management and Co-Projectleader of the REDCo project.
E-mail: thorsten.knauth@uni-due.de.

Dr. Jordi Moreras is a Sociologist and Anthropologist, Professor of Sociology at the University Rovira i Virgili, Tarragona, Spain, and member of the Research Group on Social and Organizational Analysis (ASO-URV).
E-mail: jordimoreras@gmail.com.

Dr. Inga Niehaus is research coordinator at the Georg-Eckert-Institute for International Textbook Research, Braunschweig. She was working as a researcher in the collaborative research programme "Muslims in Europe and their societies of origin in Africa and Asia" which was coordinated by the Centre for Modern Oriental Studies in Berlin.

Dr. Marjoke Rietveld-van Wingerden is Assistant Professor in the Department 'Theory and Research in Education' at the VU University Amsterdam.
E-mail : m.rietveld@psy.vu.nl.

Dr. Francisco Javier Rosón Lorente is Researcher at Casa Árabe e Instituto Internacional de Estudios Árabes y del Mundo Musulmán, in Cordoba, Spain.
E-mail: jroson@casaarabe-ieam.es.

Dr. Sol Tarrés Chamorro is Associate Professor in Social and Cultural Anthropology at the University of Huelva (Spain). She is a specialist in Islamic religious studies in Spain. She is currently working on the project "Atlas of Religious Minorities in Andalucía". E-mail: soltarres@gmail.com.

Dr. Wolfram Weisse is Professor of Religious Education at the University of Hamburg, Germany, Director of the interdisciplinary centre "World Religions in Dialogue" and coordinator of REDCo.
E-mail: weisse@erzwiss.uni-hamburg.de.

Dr. Wim Westerman is Assistant Professor in the Department 'Theory and Research in Education' at the VU University Amsterdam,
E-mail: WE.Westerman@psy.vu.nl.